INTERSTATE

D1252944

JULIAN SAYARER has made many journeys by bicycle and as a hitchhiker, writing books and articles that give a passing view of the world's roadsides. In 2009, he broke the 18,000-mile world record for a circumnavigation by bicycle, and went on to write his first book, *Life Cycles*. He now lives in London, where he used to work as a bicycle courier, a story told in the book *Messengers*.

Arcadia Books Ltd
139 Highlever Road
London W10 6PH

www.arcadiabooks.co.uk

First published in Great Britain 2016
Copyright © Julian Sayarer 2016
Map illustrations: Emma Molony

A catalogue record for this book is available from the British Library.

ISBN 978-1-910050-93-4

Typeset in Garamond by MacGuru Ltd
Printed and bound in Great Britain by
TJ International Ltd, Padstow, Cornwall

ARCADIA BOOKS DISTRIBUTORS ARE AS FOLLOWS:

in the UK and elsewhere in Europe:
BookSource
50 Cambuslang Road
Cambuslang
Glasgow G32 8NB

in the USA and Canada:
Dufour Editions
PO Box 7
Chester Springs
PA 19425

in Australia/New Zealand:
NewSouth Books
University of New South Wales
Sydney NSW 2052

INTERSTATE

Hitchhiking through the State of a Nation

JULIAN SAYARER

A

For the immigrants

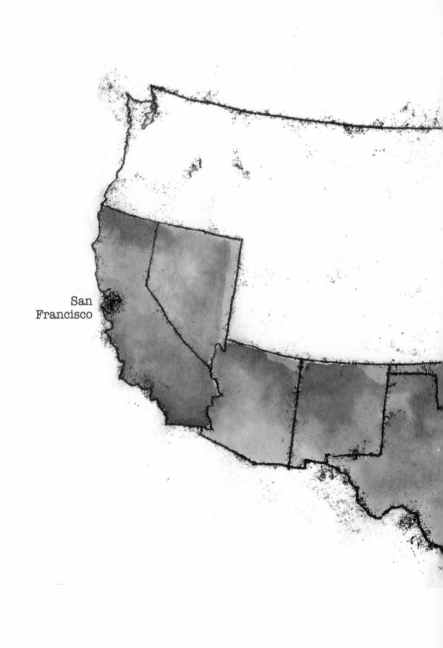

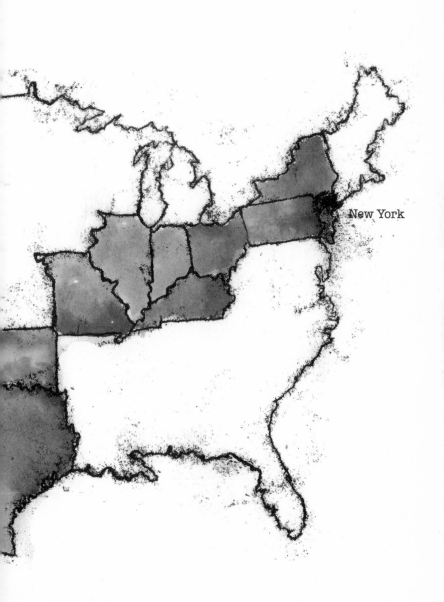

New York

I-78, NJ – November 9

Thundering beasts, monsters everywhere … packs screaming … automobile howls. Apocalypse passed through already, the stage left town. Horns fire, tracers of light cut ribbons through the dark. One more then, another story, the last with that fire under me. Forgive me the remains of my youth … those years when all the time stretching out ahead seems like long enough to right all the wrongs, and with a body so full of life that nothing could ever be insurmountable. Concrete hems me in, high either side in an Interstate grave. I-78.

Down here I am an anomaly, have slipped through gaps: the only thing left that has no place or purpose. Everyone else around is Interstate 78, between junctions 23 and 24: a licence plate, an insurance policy, a verifiable, mobile component in a social-economic landscape. Whereas I'm simply here, still full of all the imprecise cross-purposes that made us human to begin with. In the white floodlight burns the crimson flame of the last creeping ivy, its wick stripped and the final leaves flailing in the wind of the traffic. Horsemen pass, they make their way through the clouds. They canter, horseshoes toll behind stars shut away beyond the sky a blue so cold.

My boots hammer at the hard asphalt, all set rigid so that the only thing that moves in here is sound. It is deafening, is chaos, nothing but a highly regimented panic. A drum pounds out, keeps rhythm on this stationary motion, like a flick-book where each image is at every moment replaced by another all but identical version of itself. One car gives way to the next and between them all they form hydras, rise up Interstate.

I was not supposed to wind up hitchhiking to California, simply found myself doing it when the plans came undone, left me taking that all-American option of drifting aimlessly west when things go wrong, as if better things wait there. Scorched in that hinterland between the coasts, drifting in that ruin, great strips of me fell away and were lost to places and moments where people survive on nothing but miserable nostalgia, refined sugar and a confused sense of loss. De Tocqueville, he had it easy. Out there you find the warnings to the world, and the roadsides – as always – conceal nothing, for all who pass along them are anyway too transitory to warrant deceiving or concealing. Whatever the madness waiting, at least it was a good month in the markets. Bullish, unawares, those things they ticked on over.

In the chill night, the highway breaks to a construction site. I climb in over concrete balustrades, on to the flatbed of the truck that hauled an illuminated sign out here. Bulbs the size of my head point the traffic left, my body glows in the glare. The metal flexes a tocsin underfoot and *boom, boom, boom, boom* echoes from construction vehicles all around. Narrow spines carry conveyor belts, scoops, generators and *Ingersoll Rand Rand Rand*. I trail beneath the metal drum of a steamroller, the leaning arm of a digger, steel teeth of the scoop shining with the light, nibbling at tarmac. I jump down, slide down a bank of sand, collapsing beneath me, sand to the top of my boot. The traffic is back at my side, the trucks slipstreaming one another, throwing great gusts of wind that break against my back. My thumb stays down. It is against the law to hitchhike after dark in America. That has nothing to do with the judiciary either, it is simply against all law of reason or probability to even try. This is the kingdom of fear and those cars they don't stop. Fright has them: by day it's bad enough, at night there's not a chance. These guys all know the facts, the statistics: one in thirty Americans are murderers, nine out of ten of those have beards just like mine. I might have made that up, but that's what statistics are for nowadays, with facts strewn all about and an impression of truth more valuable than any flesh/bone reality you care to name.

Interstate keeps on into New Jersey, heads for Hoboken but all the traffic is being pulled the other way, thrown out of New York then bouncing back in. The roads all point backwards, travelators: the metropolis its own force of gravity, constantly sucking up, in, throwing out, spitting humans like globules of metal-wrapped phlegm. I pick my way through the debris of the reservation: drifts of crisp, dead leaves. I see the naked, plastic dolls with immaculate hair, the books with their pages crimped and ashen, a memory of family outings, of imagination. In the woods beside me I see eyes shine, they turn and then the white tail of a deer races out of sight.

Walking the Interstate at night, and the end of the world has already been and gone. I'm the only one left alive: the only human still standing, the last one on earth. None of them feel a thing. All the rest is traffic and noise, the ceaseless chase, the oblivion to end them all, a progress that never sleeps. Please, let ten thousand years pass before again we talk of progress. I block it all out, only a moment, the most I can manage. Its powers are strong. I bend my will and I stop the noise and still the movement so that I am alone again. The pages of the book flutter up at me, as natural as the flecks of falling snow, they twitch my way. A noise rears up louder than all the others, white lights strike down, the gates are opening, the truck thunders over me, closer than all the rest and the heat of engines warm on my cheek. Pack up the sun, dismantle the moon, the night is torn down and its only remnant some love letter to the world, the pages of the book blowing one to the next.

PART I

NEW YORK CITY

Manhattan – Brooklyn – George Washington Bridge

DOW JONES: 15591.54 (+0204.16)

Meatpacking District, Manhattan,
NYC – November 2

Axels rattled. The delivery fleet pulled out on to Eleventh Avenue, a set of tyres dropped, crushing an empty beer bottle. In the arc of a sickle, the vans followed one another, each full-length driver door wide open to reveal men in their brown postal uniforms. The city sky, dawn, faded a shade of plum, soaking into the red face of the depot with its US flag in the brickwork of the wall. Chassis kept on hammering, kept thudding, booming out as wheels dropped down the cliff face of an iron-braced gutter, just as they had the previous morning. Rubber dragged over crumbling tarmac where the line of post trucks took to the streets and then disappeared one by one. Opposite the depot a tree, its limbs long and trunk thin, was shuttered inside the planks of a scaffold that formed the edge of a building site, soot-blasted branches protruding as if from a set of medieval stocks. An edifice of cars and jeeps, stacked three-high on a tier of girders way up in the air, shone a keen black and reflected the scene of the street like the surface of a dark, metal pond. Sunlight crept in through the hatch of the depot and brushed in silver the steel gullies, hoists and winches, now still, from where Manhattan's parcels had been dispatched.

It was a good time. Sure there'd been some rough years, more than I'd bargained for, but finally I was breaking through, glowing, incandescent. Paid to make movies, and in New York to boot. My head ran amok, caution blown to smithereens. Life rose back up, reconstructed with American Dream. The voice of a hustler whispered in my ear: 'Man! For a while there, I was worried about you, but just look at you now.' All that skies-the-limit hot air had turned out right: never give up, persevere, and eventually, everybody finds the thing they're good at, what they're meant to do. We all figure out how to make it work.

Manhattan was a fine place for that epiphany to strike home, and in bold strides I made my way up Eleventh, heading for the office where it would all get under way. A wave of yellow leaves shot from up the steps of the subway, blown out on a warm air to land around me with the clatter of a subway carriage below. That city, that metropolis, that colossus – how it towered that morning, how far back on its neck a head must roll in order to clap eyes on sky. Trestles hung from rooftops as workers painted hundred-metre high murals of whisky bottles on to towering walls, that landscape big enough to hold all our dreams with still more to spare. We've each been taught how we look on those streets, can picture our lone silhouette strolling avenues with the skyscrapers reduced to nothing but frames for our supreme spectacle. Manhattan offers the grandest insignificance going, some human forest where humans crawl under a canopy in solid glass and brick, each lifting helicopter some tiny homage to you alone.

The advertising confirmed my suspicions and took me in, almost plausible when riding such a high as mine. In New York you find exceptional on every corner. Merit was up in lights, system-works wallpaper, that transcendental ideology that remains the only unifying feature in America's polarised politics. One by one, the billboards made their case. *Have an idea. Make it happen* came the contribution of the Spanish bank. *Let your next project be the one you're remembered for* promised another. An adult college hawked its wares on the side of bus stops, three of its pitches passed me on the streets rolling by: two with the same mother studying in order to earn good and set her daughter up in stage school, a third with a different mother aiming to improve her wages so as to support her daughter, a talented dancer. Work hard and see your children through to stardom: the barometer of good parenting in New York City. Any other time and all this would have seemed oppressive, fanciful, but with that current run of luck, the whole thing was coming across as remarkably well judged.

*

'What do you mean, "it's been cancelled"?'

That was the most talkative anyone had been all day. It was the nearest we would get to an explanation for the six-hour wait in a lobby without a word, the transatlantic flight now without a purpose. All along it had been obvious that no news was bad news, the 'Hollywood No' was waiting for us patiently: the response of those whose time is too precious and important to even bother knocking you back. It was a long, emotionless face that had finally given the confirmation: a messenger-secretary, well versed in breaking illusions. One of us piped up:

'But what do you mean the project's been cancelled? I thought we were making it work.'

'Sorry – cancelled – maybe next year.'

We filed out, and the east wind laughed all down 43rd Street.

Bedford-Stuyvesant, NYC – November 3

SMS: 'Sorry about the project. Really! We'll sort it out back home.'

Back in London nothing waited for me but landlords and other troubles too rough to mention. Even without the problem of having nowhere to live, I'd learned long before that autumn that, when you've nothing in the world to call your own, it's a good bet to spend time in places where you've no business expecting things be any different. Broke and without any prospects in the UK was a continuing disappointment, in the US it became possible to kid myself and those I met into believing this a new start and only the calm before the stardom. From a bookstore on St Mark's I bought a map of the USA, opened it out and jumped into its frontiers, weighing up journeys and destinations as if in my own operations room and plotting by which route I could most effectively take America.

Beyond all the pie in the sky, right then I was also feeling the advantage of the foreigner. To those you meet the place you are from becomes a curiosity, prompting mainly questions that spare the nitty-gritty interrogations that reveal who you are to those who know your culture. In the USA they are more interested in hearing about a football team or Buckingham Palace than your job, mortgage or lack of either. However easy air travel might be, people will be impressed that you have made it across the world, and mostly assume you have proved successful enough to leave the place you came from. They take your appearing in their neck of the woods, moreover, as a very tasteful compliment. Showing up and living in cities across the world, amassing anecdotes and insights as I went, I became rich in the currency of geography even as I remained steadfastly poor in financial terms. Because people generally presume the two journey together, equating travel with prosperity, the misunderstanding had served me well for a while already. Your job becomes less interesting than your British accent, and people remain unaware that certain vowels in that vanishing accent place you from an anonymous and economically depressed region of the Midlands.

That autumn, the Midlands town I'd come from was perhaps to play a part in my life a little longer yet. Long ago the place fixed in me a constant need to escape that I still hadn't quite shaken. Most of my formative years had been spent with a need to get out of where I was, and once you've grown up in parts you never wanted to find yourself, you have to actively figure out the instinct to put down roots. Settling doesn't come naturally. Parents found dead from overdoses, bullying-induced suicide, teenagers who knew what it was to get in a bag of amphetamine and spend a sleepless weekend playing videogames. When the neighbour opposite stabbed his girlfriend to death, the strangest thing was that he'd always seemed an OK guy. I don't mean to further that burgeoning stash of crime and tragedy-infused poverty pornography ... but growing up close to that lot hardwired me with a need to get out. Always twist, never stick. It's not that any one of those catastrophes was so commonplace, but when they happened, it had never seemed quite so tragic as it should.

Those impulses all contributed to me taking a gamble on some half-baked film project in New York. Then, when what should always have seemed inevitable finally happens and it doesn't work out, when even New York City starts reminding you of your problems, you jump again, hotfoot it west. Cities beckoned me with different curiosities: Seattle on its isthmus beside the Pacific, New Orleans down in the Louisiana bayou, Durango in Colorado, perhaps even the man-made oil sprawl of Houston could be worth a visit. For a while I weighed it up, but really, in such a spot as that, in the United States there exists only one time-honoured option. California. San Francisco, and with me still junked up so high on America to find myself believing the plan resembled a sensible course of action. There were a couple of people I knew there, no more than friends of friends really, but if you're going to be a travel writer, the first certainty is that you're going to have to travel: to learn to haul yourself, for no real reason, through life less orderly.

After a day of drifting, however, and whatever the whistling call of the freight trains, leaving New York City right off the bat had started to seem a taller order … an awful lot of middle America separated me from whatever might await on the West Coast. I'd crested the peak of my mood, could feel myself wavering as I looked down at the next inevitable trough. For a while already, I'd been living life as only constant iterations of a month: the future did not exist, was a luxury pulled up after our parents' and before my generation made it out of nursery school. The only way to make social mobility, against all odds, was if you crashed through each precarious wave with a jubilant energy oblivious to the murderous odds and menagerie of potential failures that awaited. Where the excitement of the open road had first sprung, an uneasy sadness was growing fast, leaving me clinging on for something more familiar. Sometimes a city, padded against reality by the tastes of the wealthy, can quickly get to feel so comfortable. Long hours I rotated in the grids of Manhattan, crossed the East River's bridges and watched the city, ever walking between those few appointments that remained to attend to. Even at only a couple of dollars, the subways felt an unnecessary expense, and when you've nothing going in your life and time to kill, walking becomes an invaluable companion. There's no point arriving anywhere too fast.

*

The first tangible component of the journey sat on the next stool of the bar. Attached to its dark green, plastic lining was a handwritten note from one of the crew, by then already flying home to London:

'Really good bit of kit. Not used it for a while ... keep it as long as you need.'

A bivvy bag is somewhere between a tent and a sleeping bag, scarcely a substitute for either, and yet absolutely perfect in its functionality. The thing saves the trouble, weight and space of a tent, but should still see you tolerably warm and dry with minimal effort. Beside me it waited, filled with an uneasy promise of the road ahead, while I considered how many days I could afford to delay a departure. A game of American football flickered on a television suspended from the ceiling in the far corner, the green of the field the only colour in the darkness of the bar. In booths behind me, friends met for evening drinks, their profiles across tabletops and with one old man the only set of eyes directed my way, watching the game over my shoulder.

The barman finished polishing silverware, hung a red cloth on the rail before him. He walked over, pointed to my small, empty glass with the beer froth drying to the sides. I gave a nod, watching as he filled another. In my pockets, I rummaged for remaining bank notes: found three fives and a one. The beer would be five. My barman, an apron round his middle, smiled insincerely as he put down a decorative paper coaster with my new, amber glass on top of it. 'Enjoy it, sir!' He grinned an enthusiasm that stopped at the teeth. I put down the five with a nod. The grin remained, so too a few spots of spilt beer around the base of the glass. He went in hard with expectation, and I fell into line. No energy to resist, one dollar wasn't going to make a difference to my fortunes. I lay down one spare buck, so that his smile relaxed and, for a second, perhaps he meant it. For only an instant, he thawed. My paper bill slipped into his machine, hoovered down his throat as his forced politeness met my forced generosity. From his apron, he pulled a cloth, wiped up the few small spots of beer on the bar.

Behind me, directing some anger at the television in the corner and a commotion in the game of football, the old, grey-haired man began to grumble loudly. In my seat I shuffled, wondering how long he might have sat there alone. My head turned a little his way. He sensed my interest, and rose up:

'Can you believe it?! They changed the rules on tackling quarter-backs! Now you're not even allowed to touch 'em!'

A girl in the next booth turned to him, 'Why did they do that?'

Surprised at the attention, the man gave a start, jolted from his disapproval. A small wrinkled head protruded from his large winter jacket. Quietly he finished an answer, taking his hat from the table in front of him and turning it shyly in his hands.

'To make it easier to score points. People like high-scoring games, so more people watch.' His eyes glazed over, wrinkled fingers went on kneading his hat in his hands as he muttered quietly, 'I don't know what was wrong with the old ways. I didn't mind that it was lower scoring.'

The girl acknowledged his explanation with a frown, and we all turned back to our own lives. From the kitchen, dressed in chefs' whites, a Mexican man appeared and put down more buckets of cutlery for the barman to continue polishing.

Another beer finished and the barman, like clockwork, stepped closer and pointed to my empty glass. I considered it a moment, but one more five-dollar beer was still cheaper than the prospect of finding a room for the night. Again, I nodded. From my pocket, I pulled the two remaining fives and as the barman returned a new beer, I put one note flat on the bar: slid it forwards. The same, big smile came out for me, but faded fast. Again, some drops of beer, and a streak of liquid where the glass had been pushed towards me, shone on the counter. The barman returned to his cutlery with a scowl, left me to the spillage. Sometimes, with a British accent, you can get away with it – they just think we're all cheap in Europe. That's why it was a mistake giving the first dollar, because after that, he knows you know.

He left me longer with an empty glass before motioning my next. From down the bar, another man ordered a beer and I watched as he paid with a twenty and received his change of a ten and five ones, the barman bumping up the opportunity for giving: five crisp possibilities to buy yourself the glow of a good person. One side of tipping is to augment the poverty wages of the USA, the other is the opportunity for regular folk to have a go at philanthropy … a chance to feel momentarily like the rich guy in a relationship.

The barman sauntered my way, poured me a new glass, his shoulders arched at the insult of what he suspected to be another untipped drink. I scratched around my notepad with a pen, distracting from the tension before the looming moment in which he would again get nothing but the price of the beer. We both saved up our lines for the exchange to follow. He put down the beer: the old spillage now dry, a few drops of a new spillage and no wipe of a cloth forthcoming. I put down the five-dollar bill. And that's it.

He recoils, shaking his head in disgust.

'Nuh-uh, I ain't begging you for this.'

I look up at him, 'it looks like you might be', running through my mind, my eyes, but surprised by the man, so shaken by my affront that he drops completely from any previous politeness. He wears a denim shirt, buttoned to the collar: a few pocks pit his left cheek, and his hair is swept to a side parting but falls a little to his forehead as his annoyance makes him spread his arms across the bar, palms down flat, marking out his territory against my bad behaviour. It's not that I begrudge his need to earn a living, it's that he thinks it should come with false nicety, worked a dollar at a time from customers and not from fair pay from his boss. He points his finger at the bar. Spits the words.

'You give me a tip, that's what makes our wages.'

Normally that would have me bent over with guilt, but not this week so American and dog-eat-dog. The first words to come, thank god, fall simple, plain and true: 'It's not my job to pay your wages.'

We look at one another, neither of us so familiar with the confrontation. Our eyes lock.

'I don't care. I don't know how you do it in Europe, but here we tip.'

To be honest, it's not his fault. He genuinely does think I'm filth, showing up and breaking a convention that everybody else round here honours. He thinks me an insolent excuse for a human being every bit as much as I think he's desperately insincere and tipping culture not much more than institutional begging.

'I did tip you. The first drink ...' more than my last five hundred British bartenders had received.

This offends him even more: 'It's a dollar a drink! You've had three!'

The guy's so incredulous at me it at least brings on my own dismay.

'It's a *tip*!' I growl, 'it's supposed to mean something, it's supposed to be a recognition of something more than just' – I escalate – 'pouring a beer and doing the job you are meant to do anyway. If I have to give it you anyway, it's just a tax.'

Heads are turning from the booths and so I go for my pocket, dig around, give the guy the chance to retreat rather than accept the enormous descent from some sort of pride that I feel this single buck will cost him. I find a bill, tattered and stained, but there's no flinch. He wants it, doesn't realise that telling me to stick it up my own ass can make him the victor in all this. Normal service is about to be resumed and he's turning part-amiable even as shelf-stackers, post office workers, library receptionists, secretaries and mechanics – not to mention the Mexican, washing cutlery beyond the kitchen door, probably sending money home to support an entire family – are finishing days without even a thought of tips, still less thinking it their right to demand one.

'And what if I've not go so much money to pay an extra dollar for each drink?'

'Don't come to the bar.'

I give him his grubby currency with a shake of the head and some vain wish that this exchange of bad blood have some productive outcome, however slight.

'There you go. But make sure you tell your boss to pay you properly.'

He takes the dollar, nodding as he walks away.

Williamsburg, NYC

With elegant fingers pressed to polished wood, she slid on to the vacant stool, leaning an elbow into the bar and resting the side of her jaw on a raised shoulder.

'Where did you get your accent?'

Big, blue eyes settled on me, drew a smile. Like some sort of audio passport, a British accent in the USA must be worth at least a hundred miles of Interstate and a half-dozen beds for the night when travelling against its US counterpart.

'Why are you laughing?' She smiled the question back.

'Britain. I got it in Britain, it's just funny, the way in the US people address the accent, like it's something distinct from me.'

Her face winced a little, but she replied gently, 'We just think it sounds nice, that's all!' She gestured discreetly to the barman's back, 'Are you having problems with some of our traditions?'

*

Sylvia bought my next drink, the barman given a tip and a smile that looked partway apology and partway an assurance that she'd taken responsibility for the idiot foreigner. Early on she explained how she had once driven across the country with a group of friends, and with warmth she went on to recall the endless hospitality of the guides from her last family holiday, hiking in Costa Rica. In gratitude for all those moments and more, Sylvia assured me in earnest that it was her pleasure to look after a wanderer passing through.

She led the way to a nearby restaurant, a minimalist establishment with furniture in bare wood and the paintwork part sanded from it. Overhead there dangled exposed cables and wiring, apparently leading neither to nor from anything, but giving some not so subtle nod to the past, the tangible, and the internal organs of a building. A waitress ushered us to a window seat, putting down a carafe of water and two jam jars from which to drink.

'They seated us in the window.' Sylvia gave a mocking roll of the eyes. 'It's a compliment, means they think we're attractive enough to show off as customers.'

Sylvia nodded in response to my open mouth, pointed to some far tables.

'They put ugly people at the back.'

Eating falafel, drinking banana and date smoothies, we learned about one another's lives. Sylvia belonged to an illustrious family of fashion designers and high-end tailors, had recently joined the ranks of the company and now, still in her early twenties, was living a version of her very own sartorial dream. Her hair was in plaits over her shoulders, cheeks a lush and healthy red, and from her ear lobes hung two slender chains with small, golden spoons suspended from them. Having left Europe in the 1920s, the family had been making clothes for Manhattan's highest society ever since. Now renowned, they oversaw wardrobes, recommended cufflinks and measured the inseams and gaits of the richest people in the world: we were talking top of the pile, 1 per cent rich, super-rich rich. The effect of all that proximity to money was that Sylvia and her folks didn't think themselves the least bit wealthy: there wasn't a single oil well in the family, only a couple of homes in downtown Manhattan, just the one holiday villa in the Caribbean. She lived not far away, her own fifteenth-floor apartment on Wythe Avenue, by the waterfront of the East River, the place bought outright by her parents and renovated with no expense spared.

Momentarily, Sylvia broke off from her history, jarred, and her eyes in their thick-rimmed, angular spectacles, shifted focus to me.

'You need a napkin?'

A hardboiled egg had squeezed from the flatbread in my hand, forcing red cabbage juice to run down the back of a finger and on to my wrist. I nodded, picked up my own napkin and dabbed it clean. Sylvia took a bite of her falafel, gave a tiny groan of enjoyment as the sound of suction slurped in my straw.

'These days, Brooklyn's changing so fast. There are places here where before you'd never have gone out after dark, and now they have fashionable bars and art galleries.'

'Gentrification?' I said through a half-mouthful of falafel.

Sylvia nodded, 'Yeah gentrification, but there are gentrifiers and then there are *gentrifiers*. I mean, some people move here, and they have money. *I have money, right*,' she clarified with a hand apologetically on her breast, 'but I like the community around here, the people and the old places and hangouts. Some people move here and they dislike that: they want it to change, they feel threatened by it,' and Sylvia waved a hand at our surroundings, 'they want it all to look like this: upmarket food, diners and gyms. Everyone seems to have a gym membership now!'

I laughed, 'You included?'

She gave a confessional smile, touched the full curve of a hip. 'In New York everyone works late, so then you eat crap food or takeaway, so you put on weight, and then because you put on weight you have to go to the gym to lose weight. And because you are going to the gym after you finish work, you've got no time for going on a date, or for cooking, so you eat takeaway again.' She sighed a smile, 'That's just how it goes here.'

In Sylvia was neither the first bad thought or energy: life had come, she would say so herself, pretty easy and with an abundance of comfort. It was as if she was confused by what all the fuss was about, why anyone wouldn't just get on with savouring it all and being nice to others.

Beyond where we sat, the far side of the glass window, a bin bag had been torn open and left flapping on the breeze. Litter fell from it, cans and glass bottles spilling to the street as lamplight shone on plastic. From out of an alleyway came a figure, reaching forwards as a woman operated the lever of a long handle and mechanical claw. Her face had Chinese features, a plump nose, and her eyes suddenly flickered an alertness to the rubbish, so that she made straight for the bin and its scattered debris. Into a bag upon her back she dropped cans, plastic bottles, containers and glass. Once that was done she put the mechanical arm back to a holster, and with gloved hands reached into the bin itself. One after another they came out: nuggets of petroleum and aluminium-based waste to raise a few dollars at a supermarket-recycling machine. The woman gave a little smile: damn, but she looked almost as happy with that overflowing litter bin as we were with our falafel. Sylvia and I watched. Sylvia swallowed a morsel of food and broke the silence in that same cheer with which she seemed to observe everything.

'It's really good that people go out and recycle.'

I grimaced. Somehow that didn't sound right.

'I don't know.' I gave my mouth a wipe. 'Don't you think it's a bit embarrassing, in New York City, and the richest country in the world, to have people going through bins to earn a bad living?'

Taken aback, Sylvia flinched a little as I went on.

'I mean, couldn't they just have recycling bins, and pay people a wage to sort through them?'

'Nobody forces them to do it.'

That night I spent on Sylvia's sofa, in a home full of her young life's happy memories and hopes for a glittering future. A real warmth she had, a kindness of heart and knowledge of the wider world – no doubting. But lack of money, it had never occurred to her, neither necessity.

It was Nathalie who came through for me in the end, Nathalie knew my old friend Milap, four years since I'd cycled through and he still not ready to leave New York. We all met in a Brooklyn streaked with rain, gathering for beers at the Washington Commons, where she told me a room at her house was going spare for a couple of nights. Her boyfriend was taking time out of the city while they figured out some difficulties their relationship had hit upon. It wasn't much, but it was a bed, and would be available long enough for me to prepare to leave the city.

When she had still been a teenager, Nathalie and her family, without paperwork or much English to speak of, had come from Peru to the hot concrete and neon of Miami. The scholarships of America's Dream had eventually put her into Yale, where she made it her personal business to figure out altering that same Dream so it didn't abandon all those, without her brains, she'd seen left behind. She was living in Brooklyn, working as a campaign organiser and involved with New York's imminent mayoral election. Her task was to coordinate the efforts of community and labour organisations delivering a popular, leftist candidate who had come from nowhere and now looked likely to become the first Democrat to take City Hall in two decades.

That night we were drinking to Nathalie. When I reached the bar, the air was abuzz with talk of her television debut, a stellar performance on national evening news. We all hunkered round someone's phone and watched as, eloquent and politely raging, she wiped the floor with both the panel and host. She had been talking her speciality: Hurricane Sandy and the fact that three-quarters of its victims – the poor ones and those from an ethnic minority – were still holed up in caravans and a poverty even worse than they had known before. The night I arrived in New York City had coincided with the one-year anniversary of the storm's landfall, when it crushed great swaths of outer New York, having already – with less attention – flattened parts of the Caribbean on its approach. That first night, both a taxi driver and hotel clerk had told me the same line, excitedly: 'One year ago today ... three hundred and sixty-five days.'

Milap pointed to the small, glowing screen, 'You seem very calm about it all.'

'I'd been pretty nervous,' Nathalie shrugged, 'but then when they put me in the green room, I thought "so this is happening" and I got on with it.'

In front of the cameras Nathalie had done great, everyone charmed by such uncompromising reason. Nathalie had fire in her, fire and that rare kind of social justice that has been seared by watching decent people keep struggling no matter how hard they tried, but itself manages to scrape through and come good. Sure, she was a little save-the-world, but with her you could tell she meant it: the goal was a firm plan, neither a vague ideal nor only incoherent resentment. She glowed with warmth, smiled so wide and often that the corners of her mouth would push high into her cheeks. Her Peruvian bloodline ran back towards Incas rather than Conquistadors: a nose short and eyes narrow, her hair and irises shining a peerless black. Around our small table there must have been at least a half-dozen of us, but soon the noises of a busy bar retreated, and all sight and sound stilled to leave attention folding inward and everyone but Nathalie fading slowly from view. She talked of the discrimination her grandparents and other indigenous Peruvians had suffered, then spoke of lands wrecked by unregulated mining corporations. She asked my thoughts on New York, taking the keenest of interest in the opinions of someone who knew less than she did, as if those were the ideas outside of her control and so all the more vital to understand. In her there aligned a razor perception of the ills that beset her community, but an energy and an optimism that with enough love and determination, it could all be made good.

Slowly my focus spread back to the rest of the table, where I realised that, quite apart from Nathalie, all around was politics. My god, but it was America again, and when they get it right they get it so right. It was like stumbling into a salon, Paris in the 1780s, and as if to prove the point, up strode a latecomer with a full beard and pirate earring, slinging down a kit bag beside the table as everyone embraced. Glasses of beer rose and fell, chairs scraped as people shifted body language and lifted arms to make their impassioned points. Hands waved at every sentence, carved the air, parting it in readiness for the landing of the next thought, and I wondered to myself whether this furnace of opinion in a bar is where all politics begins, or if it is where it happens instead of ever becoming politics. From off to one side, a voice broke through the clamour. A flat palm hit down hard on the table, landing in a clearing of empty glasses.

'I'm telling you, the Haitian Revolution,' he smiled at the fact he was not being taken seriously enough, 'was the most important event in US history, when Haitian slaves retook the island. That's the only reason we ever even had abolition here, because slave uprisings were becoming more and more common, and more successful. The government knew it was only a matter of time before there was a new republic of free slaves settled all across the South.'

From down the table a voice put in, supportive of the need for more and faster change. She talked of an old black lady in Detroit, shot dead when approaching the home of a white stranger to ask directions but the shooter eventually cleared under stand-your-ground laws. 'You want to live in that country?' The voice demanded rhetorically as my attention fell to her side, where two men held hands and one of them playfully pushed away the face of the other.

'You ignore him. He gets like that: these white, suburban gays who just want to get married like a straight person.' A glance of flirtatious challenge passed nose-to-nose between them. 'They just wanna join the mainstream, don't care that the biggest problem in the gay community is still the rate of HIV among poor black men.'

I listened as all around went the unrestrained politics of those eternal revolutionaries who once made America. Ideas were exchanged without the slightest barrier, no sexuality or race, unfettered by inhibition and cast each time in a strong sense that everyone at that table expected only to be free when all humans everywhere were free. With the same energy and vision, the zeal for a new world that settled the frontiers and prairies under the big sky, they held a council of war on how to rectify the entire human condition. Beers emptied and refilled, the clock hands stroked off hours, and then Milap turned to me with a tone inviting me to confide.

'That's quite a journey you've got in store. Are you planning to go out and find what happened to blue collar America?'

'It's not really like that. I'm just going to head for San Francisco, see what I find along the way.'

Milap gave a slightly more serious look, 'But have you read the Case and Deaton paper, on how fast Americans are dying?'

I shook my head and Milap leant in, like he was sharing secrets of deep importance. 'You should. Mortality in the white working class is increasing rapidly, it's starting to get a lot of attention. Suicide, alcoholism, opioid addiction, people on legal painkillers who then gravitate to illegal stuff.'

'They're dying faster than everybody else?'

Milap shuffled his shoulders from side to side. 'No, not exactly. Blacks still have a higher rate of mortality, but for blacks and Latinos the mortality rates are improving steadily, people are getting healthier. For white working classes, things have been getting steadily worse for the last two decades. It's unique in all the developed world. America's blue collar is basically dying. Some academics are comparing it to the AIDS crisis in the gay community in the eighties.'

I tried to take it in. 'And what do people think it is?'

Milap drank his beer, shook his head with an intake of breath,

'Who's to say? But you can't talk about it accurately without also considering ...'

Raised voices interrupted from a few chairs away, two others continuing the discussion of the Hurricane Sandy clear-up.

'Classic *disaster capitalism*,' shouted a man, getting to his feet to leave, 'No different to Hurricane Katrina. The same corporations sweep down and cream off federal money to provide half-assed reconstruction efforts. Just your typical neoliberalism. Vast amounts of public money goes to the private sector because of the mere perception that paying corporations is efficient.'

Another man, in a leather jacket with a sheepskin collar, pushed back from the table, threw up his arms with a condescending smile.

'Man, *neoliberalism*.' He laughed, 'Such a bogeyman! The one thing you can blame everything on! That and *narratives*. I'm so tired of those two words.'

Milap gave a knowing shake of the head, as if a familiar impasse were about to be reached. Nathalie put down her drink, responded for everyone, prodding a finger into the chest inside its leather jacket.

'Of course you don't need the word "narrative "when you're already on top of them all.' She smiled, somehow not in the least confrontational or aggressive, 'And who needs to think strategy exists when the world works for you already? Why would you bother describing a set of ideas you don't even need to change?' Even the accused man sat with a smile on his face, as if accepting the judgement Nathalie dispensed. 'It must be nice to think there's no structure to society, to just believe that you're only in your rightful place.'

And from that moment, I was falling for her.

We talked until the bar closed: shutters down, half the house lights turned up and the other half off, one remaining member of staff leafing through a magazine at the bar. Nathalie and I drank later than everybody else, walked the five minutes to her house together, bumping drunkenly towards each other every few steps. A cold wind pushed by us, brushing rain from an avenue of trees. Rubbish bins, blown over and rolling an arc back and forward, stroked the concrete like a cymbal as a few figures crept out of bars and into the streetlights. Suddenly animated, Nathalie returned to the subject of the mayoral election next day.

'His name's Bill de Blasio. He came from nowhere, and in the last weeks of the primaries, he just shot up.'

Rummaging in her bag, she handed me a campaign flyer, showing a man with an expression set serious but kind.

'He hit all the right policies: stop and frisk and how being hassled by the cops has such a damaging impact on young black men, taxing the very rich to pay for free universal childcare, keeping New York hospitals public. He's going to win, we just need him to win big to secure a mandate for the policies.'

We arrived at the large metal door to her block, a couple of bicycles chained up outside. Succumbing to tiredness, I only half-listened to her enthusiasm, looking at the image of de Blasio's face in my hand. By and large, I do not like mainstream politicians: I do not trust polished smiles or the distance between the life of the average politician and average voter. As her key turned in the lock, Nathalie fell forward on the door. As if hit by a thought, she gave a short jump on the spot, reached out excitedly to put a hand on my elbow.

'I'm busy tomorrow morning, but I'll be campaigning for him in the afternoon, knocking on doors to get out the vote,' her eyes shone at me. 'You wanna come?'

I do not like mainstream politicians: I do not trust polished smiles. I do not like the notion of my ideals for a better world being represented by someone I know only by their face and slogans. Nathalie looked over at me, smiling, simply smiling from the doorway as her breath lifted visibly on the cold night. I'd never endorse a single one of them, never give out even one of their flyers, never ask people to trust in their promises.

Crown Heights, NYC – November 5

SMS: 'Thank you for joining the de Blasio campaign for a fairer NYC!'

From the shop next door were loud voices, back and forth and making me smile, giving me hope:

'You voted yet?'

'Goin' this afternoon, I think.'

'You make sure you do … We need turnout, he's gonna need a mandate if we're to make any real changes.'

A Mexican man walked from the pavement, stepped into the road and crossed, pointing back at the shopkeeper to finalise his instructions. My coffee cup turned cold in my hands, and a man with a pencil-thin moustache stood outside his shop, calling after his departing friend to reassure him there was nothing to worry about, he'd be voting. Beside the shopkeeper, a large plastic container went filled with brooms and brushes sticking up into the air. The shopkeeper held one in his hand, leaning leisurely on the wooden handle as he scratched the bristles of the head over the pavement, throwing up dust and pushing a line of twigs, leaves and cigarette butts away from his shop front. I looked at his face: skin an olive grey that suggested he was Arab once, before he became American. My heart sang with the words of both men, sang with a *people-still-care* tone.

I spoke up, 'Polls are saying he could win by fifty clear points.'

The man turned to me and, clutching the broom to his side, glared hard. His shirt untucked, loose sleeves rolled up, collar unfastened. His voice boomed:

'Hell, man, it's all about power! World's changed. You can't just look to only your own corner no more.' He pinched his hands together, holding this world in a small parcel of air. 'It's power, man. Hell, China! Just think! It's all changed and it's all power!'

And as he stared intensely into me, I looked at that man selling brooms on a Brooklyn street, tried to separate the heat from the light in his words. He shook his head, returned to sweeping with an air of disappointment that I had nothing more to add.

*

Those streets ran longer than I thought, their numbers up into the thousands, so that by the time I arrived at our meeting place, Nathalie had been waiting for me a while. We had moved far south and some way east of her neighbourhood, where canvassing was not judged a wise use of resources, gentrification having already done the hard work of any Democrat's Get Out The Vote campaign. We were to head out into Crown Heights: Troy, Montgomery, Schenectady, Utica Avenue. I'm sure that by the time you read this, those places will have gone the same way, all storefronts of matching crockery and baby's bibs, but not so very long ago they were calling it safe Democrat territory, nonetheless set within communities described as extremely poor and totally disengaged.

At a community hall doubling as a campaign base we were handed four brown paper wallets, each containing a hundred Crown Heights doors for us to knock. We set out, cold faces pushing into a wind direct from Canada. We split up. I took odd numbers, Nathalie evens as I went about my democratic duty for the Americans, all British and enthused for Bill de … *what was he called again?* The flyer smiled it up at me from my hands: 'de Blasio'. Bill de Blasio. All day long, nobody will want to know about the guy he's up against, and me never so sure I even remembered his name. The feeling of a fraud rose in my chest, as if trying to trick people into something. At the end of each block, I met Nathalie and we swapped stories of the unopened doors, the resignation or apolitical anger waiting behind some of those that did.

'All you're doing is reminding people to vote! It doesn't matter if you're not from here.'

'Maybe. But still, I hope I don't meet anyone who actually cares about this election. They'd see right through me.'

Odds are on my side: the Democrat campaign have already said their main opponent is a low turnout, forecast to be only a quarter of the electorate. In my visits to New York, I have never been to the Guggenheim, never seen MOMA or the Metropolitan, but now that I've tried talking politics with hundreds of Brooklyn doorsteps, I feel I've got as close to authentic as any other experience of the city allows. Slowly, the pages of targets begin to shuffle over: Nathalie and I working steadily through those lists of diehard Democrats who once gave their addresses as regular, committed supporters to be counted on when it mattered most. If these guys are committed, I'm terrified what apathy must look like.

A man faces up to me, comes to the door in a dressing gown. He shouts: 'De Blasio! They're all as bad as each other!' He hands me a newspaper clipping, apparently explaining why he is so indignant. He barks: 'I wrote emails all about this! To de Blasio! To the press! You can see the trails of stuff across the sky!'

My eyes skim the columns and find no mention of de Blasio, the words of newsprint offer no further insight. The man's angry face buckles a little, he pulls his dressing gown around him and his irritation eases as, I suspect, he feels that rare happiness of actually having found an audience without having to leave the comfort of his own home. Under the strip lighting of the hallway, in his eye is a gleam of knowing, as if he is the wise one, who has seen through the lies and found a truth he doesn't mind sharing.

Pounding streets, the varied responses to democracy all go swirling through my head in a cocktail of political confusion. Critics of our political system will often offer the maxim that you get the democracy you deserve, and even if that is not entirely untrue, less acknowledged is that politicians also get the electorate they deserve. Where it is neglected, made cynical and dumbed down, that collective creature may be led to the water of the public good, but will never be made to drink. Play only to the lowest denominators, and eventually voters will never give you cover to do the things that, all too late, we realise must be done in the best interests of everyone. In that man, beneath his dressing gown, twisted a slow rage in lieu of politics. People cannot be made to suffer indefinitely the anxiety of hardship, given commerce instead of culture, gossip instead of information, and yet remain perceptive and rational.

*

He stands proudly in the frame of his doorway, in only a vest and underwear.

'Oh yeah? An election … where I got to go?'

This is good, reaffirming engagement. I check the map: 'Well, sir, looks like your polling station is on Midwood Street, just a block away.'

'A block!?'

The man lets out a groan. De Blasio wants to tax the very wealthy to subsidise childcare, he will keep community hospitals open, is going to build affordable housing and stop the NYPD frisking his son based on the colour of his skin. I sigh, grieving.

'Yes sir, it's a block away.'

*

The light fades early in the afternoon, Brooklyn's streets still far from finished but our part coming to an end. I knock another door, opening to reveal a cheerful, happy face.

'Yes sir, we already did it. Don't you worry, we're voters in here!'

The words strike with a realisation that in the coming America, people might identify not even as Democrat or Republican, but as non-voters or voters: that small and diminishing group who were inculcated with the spirit that they had a right and a duty to help forge the choices of their society. Most, it seems, are content simply to be ruled. They will find their meaning elsewhere, for democrats are dying out, by which I don't mean the Blue Party, but the ones who actually believe in democracy at all. The day's main rule of thumb is that the fewer wrinkles they have, the less they care.

Outside an apartment building a young man smokes down a cigarette. Around his neck are headphones, off his ears so that music spills out. Drums and synthesisers pour into the evening with the music that never stops. I can't help it, I ask him: 'Did you vote?'

'Vote?'

'Yeah, did you vote today?'

'Nope.'

'Why not?'

He shrugs, he scuffs, he angles away. I look at him: the embroidered emblem on his cap is a crisscross of letters standing proud from the fabric of the peak. His tracksuit, black and red, makes him what looks like twice the size of the body emerging from it, but is in proportion with the oversized shoes upon his feet: bright white and large in the dusk. Just as all the vehicles, food portions and packaging is made so much larger than it need be, just like everything else in this country has to be made big in order to be taken seriously, so a young man has doubled his size: his presence on the street bolstered against the calamity that would be not being seen. Our society is twin and incompatible systems: politically we are arranged in terms of democracy, which rests on education and the intelligence of voters. Economically, we are arranged in terms of an employment and consumerism that often rests on neglect of both.

We look at one another: perhaps a similar age, he with no idea that the decisions of his community have all but no bearing on my own life. I wonder if his value system – his perception of who he wants to be, and what he believes in – is all encapsulated in the brand of his tracksuit, his trainers, that embroidered peak of the baseball cap. Or does he want more: is he maybe unsatisfied, but never felt these politics were his to be part of? The thoughts linger in me, Nathalie finishing the opposite block on the end of our last sheet of addresses. Crown Heights is almost through, and so I lean on him, smile gently but nonetheless say: 'People died so that you could vote.'

He shrugs. He scuffs. Like he's been asked to tidy his room.

'Yeah, yeah, I know.'

*

The penultimate door of the night comes not a moment too soon, and behind it waits my favourite: the one that makes the other hundred almost worthwhile. I'd never guessed that such hope could be waiting there, and if not hope then at least a dignified resilience as the ship goes down. First of all and she's furious, she's enraged, is Saratoga incarnate. Flames are licking under the door as I knock and rush straight out:

'Excuse me I'mwiththedeBlasiocampaign! We're just reminding people ...'

The door opens wide. Black lady, silver hair, nostrils flaring with indignation. She opens the door wider still, stands tall in the doorframe. Stares me down. She lets rip.

'All day, the phone calls ... phone calls ... you people calling me. And now this! *This is the worst!* That you would come to my house in the evening ... that you'd disturb me in my own home!'

I look at her, I fidget nervously. Scared is quite a big word but this is different, British people don't get angry like this, at least not on the outside. We keep it all shut away. I look at her face: big teeth pointing out at awkward angles, black spots on her cheeks, a yellow band tied around her head to hold up the grey, wiry hair. She's pretty big, comfortably my size, packing some weight. Club-like arms hang from the broad frame of her body, fists clenched and make no mistake she is irate. She gathers herself, growing taller by the second. The words blow out slow and deathly, one at a time.

'I have been voting since I was twenty-one years old.' She leans over me, 'I have voted at every election. I do not. Need you. Or anyone else. To remind me how important it is to vote.'

She looks at me. She stares cold as I light up in a smile. I could kiss her, buck teeth and all. She's beautiful. She's my hero.

Park Slope, NYC

At the campaign office that morning, a tall, officious young man had broken the news: 'We'll see you at the party tonight, but it's absolutely by invitation only. The place is going to be packed.'

'So my friend can't come?' Nathalie asked with sad loyalty.

'Sorry, they'll be checking tickets.'

At nine that evening, we show up at the venue, a disused barracks with a victory party by then well under way. They wave us in: not even a queue, only a line of NYPD guarding the door, looking mean, as if obliged to watch over an enemy celebrating the end of stop and frisk.

Inside the hall the air is heavy with the smell of ageing power, a crowd thrumming with excitable smiles and a frantic energy. Those assembled consist of two types of people: one looking hardy, down-to-earth, dressed in windproof jackets, knitted hats and scarves well-suited to having spent a day in the cold. They wear regular trainers appropriate for walking, look like ordinary people, engaged with politics because how else can you expect to get the sort of world you would want to live in?

This first cadre stand relaxed, dotted among a greater number who are dressed in suits of grey or black. This, you sense, is their party, their turf and their moment: the night that comes round all too seldom to glorify their vocation and validate the political class within the safety of a hired hall. I don't go in for definitions of attractive, don't believe in ugly or beautiful. Whatever the cliché, to my mind it all comes from within and the idea of 'good looks' is only a nonsense of convention: nothing but skin and cheekbones and a little of that inner poise people don't even realise is all they're seeing when they speak of how attractive a person is or is not.

And yet, despite that, whatever my certainty that physical appearance is only ever a phantom, the sense hits me hard. Something in them it seems so *ugly*. Sure they're often a little overweight, pale, even the black people among them look like they could do with some sunlight and fresh air. These guys aren't so easy on the eye but, more than that, it is the insides that appear to radiate unstoppably out. They look greedy, and yet somehow uneasy: there bubbles an eagerness for power and the respect that comes with it. That mood goes rising up to the cavernous roof above, because a little of that dream has been realised by the result today. I try to shrug off the nasty populism of the street outside, the dangerous, maverick idea that we'd all be better off if these people just left us alone, and yet all about are stereotypes, people reared as if to climb ladders. They've put on bow ties, they've pulled on dark tights and strapped on heels. They are wearing long coats and braces, show cleavage. Men stick out chests, women have shadowed their eyes, the black women have straightened their beautiful, thick hair, burnt it straight between a pair of hot cinders. Only the insincerity on offer is strong enough to distract attention from a spectacle so depressing.

Don't mistake me, this is no disavowal of democracy. I'm not suggesting ignoring elections, voluntarily disempowering yourself … just maybe pass on the victory party. De Blasio has won, won big and is about to ascend to office. He was the right candidate, the one we want in the job: kicks in the right direction and a million times better than the alternative. 'They're all the same' – but if that isn't music to the ears of any politician who only wants power for the sake of their donors and making parents proud. As I see it, you vote for de Blasio, make him win so that the crummy, system-works alternative has to start kicking in the same direction if they are to win an election next time out. Meanwhile you demand more from de Blasio, you shoot down his bullshit, cautiously salute his positive steps, and consistently demand more until, finally, you get something better. That's how politics works. All the rest is just Disney and fairy tales, a sickness of short-termism where people come to believe that systemic change can and should happen within their personal attention span, maybe a year at most, and certainly within their own lifetime. In sinister fashion – whether from gossiping commentators or a hysterical public – politics is reduced to entertainment, sensation, rather than the slow labour by which we finally build things right.

Nearby, I watch as Nathalie slips into the melee. Nathalie is just herself, which is a working strategy in even the most artificial of crowds, those places where being true to who you are is most conspicuous and most endearing. We stand close together as she speaks to others. She dances a little, foot-to-heel-to-toe-to-foot-to-toe. She's got a big smile, gives a half-roll of the eyes and an excited clap of the hands as a familiar face in a waterproof jacket comes close. She's surrounded by people, they're all talking to her. She puts them at ease, has inside her life enough for all of them.

From a stage erected at the front of the hall, I listen to the master of ceremonies grow gradually louder. He grips hard at his lectern, now and then punches at the air, goes on making oaths that stretch from fanciful to promised land and then settle on plain absurd. He clears his throat and a hush falls as people breathe out expectantly. An assortment of campaigners stand behind on a bandstand: dreadlocks, blonde bobs, wrinklies, children and wheelchairs. The hapless things they look exhausted, ready to drop. Some poor bastard on crutches has even been given a placard instead of a chair. I've been in the room the best part of an hour now, with the stage all locked in permanent grins, arms raised above their heads and clapping for a battalion of photographers.

Finally the hush of the crowd opens into the hush of the master of ceremonies, a tall man with a square jaw, leaning slightly down and then – with a raised fist and as if announcing a prize fighter – he booms out the name of the victor. From the photographers comes a volley of light, a flashing cascade, a crash of created images. From the crowd comes a cheer, and yes, this is it – here come the family! The de Blasios! Introducing the de Blasios! Voters don't just want a mayor, not in America. They want a husband, evidence of virility, a father and potential dinner host too. They take the stage, de Blasio and his children: his daughter, his son with a giant, curling Afro.

De Blasio steps up with a smile as bright white as the house lights, gets set to grandstand. The acoustics of echo and electricity seem to crush back down at him. He starts talking, booming. I make out the first words: 'New Yorkers, we've climbed a mountain here today!' He keeps going, but I'm getting only echo and a moving face even as the crowd looks on, enthralled. All I can hear is mountains, more mountains – 'hard to climb' – a journey decades, centuries in the making. 'Lots of paths to take' ... so many paths. We've got to choose one, only one ... 'the path we started on tonight is hard and long and difficult.' de Blasio starts nipping expectations in the bud. 'Some people will have doubts, will turn back.' Is de Blasio talking politics or hiking? This speech has an entire national park in it, an itinerary of outdoor pursuits. The crowd cheers as de Blasio talks about challenges ahead: 'New people will join us, lend a hand, along the path.' Here come some rocks and a flowing river, before another mountain rises up.

In a booth beside the stage, a sound engineer flicks a dial as the words ring out: 'A City!' At last, we've found our way out of the wilds. Cheers lift again, heads tipped back in secular reverie. 'This city, the greatest city ...' Bill pauses, pauses for effect. The anticipation killing me, what's he going to say next? He crashes into the last of the sentence: '... *in the world!*'

De Blasio's been swapping speech notes with the Mayor of London, either that or they've both had their scripts written by the same computer programme. And who'd have known, after a campaign all about a divided city, a tale of two cities, of rich and poor, all the time, de Blasio was actually envisaging a tale of New York – greatest city in the world – and all the scummy places you find elsewhere. He goes on: 'A city where, no matter how big your idea ...' What? What's he about to say? ... 'you can make it a reality.' Round this way and words like that flow more plentiful than even the sodas. The crowd is pulsating, the choir humming and de Blasio takes the opportunity to get back to nature for one more mountain.

Checking out, I drink my beer. I can feel Nathalie next to me, I look round, her nose points out in profile from the frame of pure black hair. The lights of the room reflect white from her eyes as she lifts her head to peer between tall shoulders and get a view of the stage, de Blasio disappearing down inside a sea of arms, a smashing of hands, a rapturous applause.

Rooftop

'Wait a minute,' Nathalie pushes back from the front door of the apartment, turns to me. 'You want to go up to the roof?'

With the creak of a hinge, sky lifting out above, we climb the final step and from up there, across the waters, New York glows so glorious large, shining down as if for us alone. Two bodies pull themselves up on high, some fugitives from the metropolis, passing through the small hatch and on to the top of that building in Brooklyn. Nathalie steps briskly across the rooftop, calling over her shoulder.

'I was a gymnast once,' and nimbly she springs up to her toes, legs slicing like scissors, forwards and fearless to the ledge. I see her silhouette skip, skip over the watertowers and stairwells as it pirouettes and I watch her tiptoe through our shiny city, lit by the three-hundred-metre candelabra of Manhattan.

'Jeez! It's all I did as a teenager in Lima.' She lifts one leg into a clear triangle against the other, which bears her weight and stands perfect straight while city lights cast her body in black. Her arms lift to a point over her head, then fall flat, so that Nathalie spreads with all Manhattan golden and ablaze across her proud shoulders. And I ache, I yearn, and I am suddenly hit by all the joys I've ever known in life, but clueless as to who to thank for them, where to keep them all, and why it is they seem to spill back out from me in the indescribable sadness rising all about. She holds her arms spread, palms down, and then relaxes as I walk over to stand beside her. We look at one another, moonlight shining on her skin: face framed by the strong black line of hair and fringe, head framed by skyscrapers either side. World Trade – Chrysler – Nathalie – Rockefeller – Empire State and then the tops of the Brooklyn Bridge, up on their stilts of brick.

Brain winces, lets out a groan – *we've been here before! You're going to California!* – but from a cavity in my chest beats a brass band, a parade with banners and a will-o'-the-wisp whispering at me: *but what if she's the one?* My head gives a kick, hisses: *shuttup, idiot!*

We sit silent, cross-legged on the edge of the building, looking over across the East River, fairy lights coiled round the creepers of climbing plants behind us. After a while, quietly she asks:

'What did you think about the party?'

'It wasn't really my thing.'

'You don't believe in it, that kind of celebration?'

'I think they're self-important … and I don't like self-importance.'

Nathalie waits a moment, considering, 'It might seem like that, but the whole campaign was sort of built from the Occupy protests, on the streets and at Zuccotti Park.' Her voice accelerates with the confidence of her convictions. 'Nobody was talking about these things before then, and now a guy who believes in them, on some level, just took office. Sure, the system waters down those movements, but it takes on the message.' Nathalie pauses, 'Change happens slowly, and sometimes people expect so much.'

'You think Occupy can happen again,' I ask, 'or is that it, for now?'

She looks far away: a little smile, a little sad. 'It took a lot of energy from a lot of people, and I think people needed to feel that the anger from the financial crisis, bailing out the banks, had done something productive.' She pauses a moment, 'I think it would be tough for it to happen again, for a while. The mood has shifted, and the authorities will be harder on it next time. The City changed Zuccotti Park, after the protests. They made it sound positive, called it 'redevelopment'. It was supposedly innocent, but they dug up the grass and replaced it with concrete, stone. That wasn't a coincidence. It was a lot easier to camp out on grass. Next time it will be colder, harder. Fewer people will be willing to stick it out as long as we had to.'

'You think the guys in that party back there hold the same values, or hold them that strongly?'

Nathalie shakes her head a little, as if I've missed the point, 'You can be only a protester, you can be angry, but then what?'

I notice how articulate she is, as if because at all moments she is only ever saying what she feels, that she spends her entire life feeling those things and waiting for the emotion to be called to expression.

'Sure, some of them aren't so great, but there are people in that room who feel just the same way as you do, they're just willing to dress a certain way, and tolerate a certain type of person, in order to try and get it. What makes that less valuable than protesting from the outside?'

She's right, of course she's right. I nod, a little grudging, change the subject. 'What made you care so much?'

She gives a laugh, reminded for a moment that others don't. 'My life, really. My parents had manufacturing jobs in Peru. Steady, working-class jobs in factories, like most of our neighbourhood. Then the US passed NAFTA, the free trade agreement that let the big US companies into Latin America. That killed manufacturing in Peru. The local businesses couldn't compete with the imports any more.' She looks at me, 'So the factories all closed.'

The image hangs with us over New York, the two of us on the rooftop. 'Eventually you have to leave. Of course you have to leave, when you can't feed your family properly. That's when my parents left, for Miami, and started sending money back. I lived with my grandparents in Lima for a few years, until my parents put together enough to bring us over.'

'Undocumented?' I ask, and Nathalie nods. 'What would you do? You have to leave, with or without papers, because there's no work. You go to bed hungry sometimes. Then are you supposed to emigrate and live without your kids?'

I listen, thinking of the luxury that leaves some in this world with a need only to talk about politics, to discuss it like a game, to make jokes and quips about it, while others inherit lives destined to be determined by it.

'What did your parents do in Miami?'

'My dad worked as a taxi driver, but he couldn't make enough money. My mum went out to work, cleaning jobs, things like that. They still couldn't make enough money. I watched them both work themselves into the ground, just to survive. I remember my dad would get back from a day of driving, and he'd sit at the table with his forehead on his hand.' Nathalie spoke, recalling slowly, 'And as a kid, I remember every evening seeing such a tired hopelessness in his face.'

For a moment I deliberate, consider whether or not I want to go there, towards that conversation, share myself. A bell rings on the opening door of a late night shop far below us.

'That's sort of the same as my father. He worked from the age of six, selling chewing gum and bottles of water to buses of tourists on the west coast of Turkey. Then, when my mother was pregnant with my sister, they moved from Istanbul to London. In the eighties, I think casual racism was acceptable in Britain, and as a Turkish man, my father struggled to find a teaching job. He was out of work a lot.' I get stuck, swallow the ending, 'It was pretty tough.'

A compassionate smile spreads so gentle over her lips, '"Emre" is a Turkish name?'

'After Yunus Emre ... an old poet, sort of like William Blake, but Sufi.'

Nathalie pauses, then speaks with a tenderness that somehow says sad things as if they were happy, as if it is impossible for her to separate the good in an action from whatever hard consequences it might also bring.

'It's strange, to live always with these connections to places that become so far away. I don't think we'll ever be able to understand how much they went through so that we could have better lives.'

Next to one another, our shoulders close, arms stretched out behind us, we watch the city in silence and – motionless on a rooftop – I fall, spiralling down into the chasm that ends them all. Nathalie looks at me, I look at her. We smile an understanding of sorts. It's not only me. She holds my eyes a little longer than she needs to. We sit together, I can feel her close, not her body, nor her clothes, but her warmth meets mine, keeps after it and wraps me in its mist. Blankets, sprites and lights hold us close, ward off the winter, but inside of me I'm dying, I'm dying because I sense we'll never find out, life will never afford us the time or the place to discover what this could amount to. We'll be snatched away in our different directions, and whatever peace I one day find will be tempered by the what-might-have-been of Nathalie. Upon us, all politics breaks down. And suddenly I'm so personal. The body nearest mine is the only thing that matters, and the systems that rule all us billions become just a banal, ugly imposition against this moment. In

Nathalie is a paradox, because it is her love of the world that moves me so, and yet, looking at her, I don't care an iota for the rest of it. Right now I want nothing but to stay on a Brooklyn rooftop forever, even as the rest of the city crumbles into its own footings and we sit here, cross-legged and indifferent to the apocalypse all around: her hands in mine, mine in hers, and by that logic alone, every last thing destined to be fine. Dreams go lifting over time and up on that rooftop arrows rain down on me. You're never so vulnerable to Cupid as when about to set out on a journey, that boy he brings you down for such a simple, throbbing target practice.

'You'll leave tomorrow?' she asks, and I nod, a part of me wishing she'd ask me to stay, knowing that that's not how this one goes. I can't fall for her because she has a boyfriend, and because ordinarily we live an ocean apart. I'm getting too old not to start being more sensible about these things, but a voice comes for me … my brain has long-since walked off, jumped from the building and gone to bed. Only my body and soul are still awake. The voice wells from inside, whispers romance, hypotheticals and just-maybes from the boy who read *The Red and the Black* when he was still too young. Give kids whatever brash, stunning visual tat you can cobble together, give them simulations, give them the most elaborate contortions of depraved pornography, lay on a million songs with their electronic hooks all optimised for effect, but it's Stendhal that'll really alter a life forever, chop off your head and bring economies to standstill, unleash the most reckless of emotions and immunise hearts with a hot blood proofed against that hellish monotony life threatens.

Nathalie lifts, excited by an idea. 'Maybe I'll come meet you in California. We could go hiking in Yosemite. I always wanted to do that.'

'How are things with your boyfriend?'

She smiles a smile that makes me somehow so happy for her, because I suspect it is a smile that ultimately is for him and not for me.

'He's an amazing guy. Guess we're just figuring things out.'

We understand one another, but still my heart flies free. In Nathalie is salvation from the waiting road and its indifference, from all the projects and ambitions that could ever fail to materialise. In her is the repair that makes everything better: the sweet twist of a nervous stomach, the tender ache of longing. Her voice is each happiness, her touch a beauty impossible to believe. Momentarily, I see every mistake made better. Each wasted day of life comes gifted back to me in this instant. My nose tunes to the fantasy, can smell the scent of meadows lined by pine trees with busy apiaries in their shadows. Birds fly over our children, our grandchildren: their photos on a mantelpiece and everything complete at last. I see a young boy pedalling a bicycle, wobbling from side to side but not realising that his mother has removed her steadying hand from beneath the saddle and that he is now riding all alone. I see the torrent of a water cannon, dashed to spray and rainbows against protesters huddled together in the main, concreted square of a hot, foreign city. A line of stretched, angular mouths crane up from a nest as a mother wren flies back down, wings beating, and a grub held in her beak. The enormous metal disc of a freight train, always a freight train, and the wheels roll over a gleaming rail as its engines are released and all comes gliding down to me from the turrets of Manhattan, colliding there upon that rooftop and that moment. Nathalie's face looks into mine so completely unaware that hereafter, from this hour of the most merciless beauty, the New York wind stops. And I am lost to her.

The record screeches to a standstill, a stylus snaps as shouts boom faint from the street below. A man, stumbling, falls with an open beer can from the grocery store and out into the street. The anonymous voice of the storeowner rises upwards. 'Get outta here, you jerk! Shuttup! Just shuttup with your goddamn bellyaching!'

George Washington Bridge –

At last I took the A-train, crossed beneath the East River from Brooklyn to Manhattan. Kept heading north, into gathering dusk we rattled through those subway stops like theatre sets, soot-stained girders that cut the platform into frames of sixteen-millimetre film where the life of each New Yorker freezes in a passing instant. Carrying briefcases, department store bags, life's belongings and the fruits of a day's begging in a paper coffee cup. Dressed in suits, rags, duffle coats and fluorescent orange overalls smeared with oil. A man with a battery of upturned boxes and buckets sat with drumsticks on a small stool and, without reaching my ears aboard that train, I knew he thrashed a rhythm for a city waiting to be left behind. Back inside the tunnel, opposite me I saw a reflection: saw a face with a beard, a bag leaning against the side of a stranger. I know that was the image, the body and costume the other passengers saw as me, but I swear that I was never even there.

At 181st street I got out, walked those few blocks westwards, where the Hudson roared ill-tempered against the traffic and the flooding wind. Bent forward, I made my way diagonally towards the uprights of the George Washington, shredding the air to a hundred tiny gales where the frame of the bridge stood against the twilight, ominous, and the metal of it soaked with the cold of a winter getting under way. A few days earlier, I had looked up from Manhattan at the pencil-sketched outline of that bridge, faint against the clouds. Looking at it then, I felt nervous about what I was going to do when it finally came to crossing for the West, nervous about the prospect of leaving one life in a city, moderately comfortable, and starting another that would be less so. People had been eager to help out, to support with advice of calamity and what would go wrong. I swear, if people felt compelled to tell you everything that *could* possibly go wrong in even the most boring year of a life, you'd start having doubts, too. Even then, though, I knew that come this moment of walking up to the bridge, I wouldn't feel nervous, I'd just be walking. New Jersey getting closer, I remember anew that people mostly take the liberty of advising on disaster only once you break with expectation, commit a small aberration that exposes all the things they never did themselves. That's when they really start dumping on your prospects, giving you a dressing-down … when you're about to do something that reminds them, makes them uncomfortable and illuminates the truth of what their own life has become.

Up the banks I stumble, past thin grass and a dusty earth around the helter-skelter of the walkway. In front of me rests a mattress and dirty bedding tucked under a concrete column. Something is written, scrawled on the concrete just above the bed. Stumbling, hesitant, I venture up. Nobody in sight but, cautious, I want it to stay that way before I break into a stranger's public bedroom. Blankets, grimy sheets, quilts all strewn, I near, I call out: *Hello! Hello!* Is someone under the covers? No. I peer in. The writing's on the wall, above the bed, someone else's heartbreak: valedictory love letters on the concrete upright of major infrastructure, a bedroom breakup played out on the streets of New York. A scrawled marker pen writing sharp angles: *'I love you, forgive me, baby … don't thank about just dow it?'*

Walking on, I climb the long ramp to George Washington Bridge, hear the walkway underfoot and then the old drum of trucks pounding at the metal runway beside me. I can feel it, somewhere in me I feel like I'm taking a big risk here, perhaps not the one you expect either, but each time I leave it gets harder to go back. The bridge flexes more as I near the centre, where the road is held by steel cables rather than supported through concrete and iron. They say this bridge sits a full three metres further from the water in winter, when the steel of its limbs contracts and pulls up from the river. The slack lets back out as the metal warms and expands those few degrees in summer, lowering the road towards the water. Hudson cries out from under me, cries out *Vespucci, Vespucci, Vespucci.* Amerigo Vespucci ... don't doubt that is the most important name that ever was, the Italian who charted these United States and gave the whole continent his name. The maps that came afterwards, they now own this land, title deeds of geography and arrogant abstractions that reduce the earth to human purposes. Maps ... but they are the ultimate annexation: both ugly and beautiful, evil and virtuous, they instrumentalise territory and make it ours to control.

Once more then, a final time. My future becomes open-ended, which makes me somehow comfortable, even where I suppose for others it'd have the opposite effect. There must be Mongolian somewhere in this Turkish blood, a nomad of some description. Plans scare me: the more ordered and established the plans, the more terrifying I find them. Each predetermined obligation feels like a direct threat, a reminder that time is finite, one thing I must do instead of the infinite possibilities I could be picking my way among. More than that though, the thing with plans is that one of them always leads to the next, and then the next. Plans hunt you down in packs, they just keep coming, and next thing you know you're plucking out your first grey hair and a body bruises from the mere bump against a bedpost.

Up on the bridge, regular as ever, the suicide phones stand guard as I march above that river of the blackest ink swarming into letters. I hear that rich voice sing soft: '*Because my love for you, would break my heart in two*' and no more can I understand why I feel like the only one so sorry for this place, nor can I understand the idea of a love that doesn't make you love all the world. Hear me out, at a hush but ... this is not only Nathalie, things far greater are inside me now. I'll tell you of them soon, but not yet, please not yet. Let me imagine a while longer that they are not in fact so real. Let me get on with my task and I will write dynamite, great sticks of dynamite, things written from a place that sounds like it's already dead. I'll go tossing them down into the world, watch them explode in incandescent and ferocious bursts that will go pattering to fall softly back to earth as the most precious of smithereens. What's coming from this road ahead is for the individual, for history was too cruel to them, and this nation is full with nothing but. It is for the collective, for we are stronger as one and the modern world forgets it at its peril. And, most of all, it is for love, for without love then no good shall ever come, and all shall pale to such sorrowful shades. It will be written from a time when humans were the greatest of all creatures, precisely because we were still able to believe in forces and meanings larger than our own lives, back when we were still capable of being heroes.

Inside, rising from the stomach, my body senses the miles up ahead, comprehends the mood to come and premonitions still weeks of road from light of day. The sadness is stoppered deep, those emotions have no form and are fettered by this city, where such feelings cannot be expressed in a landscape so controlled and angular. Below, the Hudson is howling, breaking on the rocks that guard this gaping land of such irrepressible big sky. The curtain lifts on frontiers vast enough for European peasants to lose all their senses and take a full four centuries and counting to re-gather any sanity. Once this is published, you mark my words but they won't be happy. This land of self-censorship, where even the most mild, sensible criticism has to be prefixed with 'I love my country but.' In no time at all there'll be an American fatwa on my ass, they'll turn me away at the border. Never again the bowl of chilli in the Manhattan diner at 2 a.m. Never again the vitality of those wide, sparkling eyes. I only hope that what's coming is worth it. At last, I go stepping off of the one-mile bridge where – so quick – mouth wide open, America swallows me.

PART II

OUTSIDE

NYC – Cincinnati

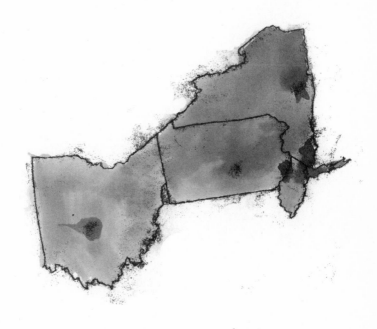

DOW JONES: 15591.54 (+0102.04)

I-78, New Jersey

Throw my bag in the back, lifted over the bucket of a child seat strapped down. Aaron will be my first ride. He has the beard of both a Semite and a black man on his chin, frayed like ends of copper wire and growing to a stop halfway up his cheeks. We pull out on to the highway.

'Where you headed?'

'California.'

'California!?' He looks. 'You going for a girl?'

I laugh, think of Nathalie now behind me in Brooklyn. 'No, not for a girl,' I answer plainly. 'You're from New York?'

'Y'know, my mother was from Jamaica, her mother was Puerto Rican. My father was Argentine Jewish.' He laughs, 'So I guess I'm from New York.' Cars move by, overtake us. 'Manhattan originally, now New Jersey, because we can't afford Manhattan no more.'

He leans back in his seat, arms spread between the rest and the window, fingers just stroking the top of the wheel.

'I like driving, so when I saw you on the Interstate I thought, "I'll see where he's going". My wife'll kill me if I drive you too far. I told her I was going to the shops, but really, I just like a drive at the end of the day.'

The concrete walls of the highway roll by, an eighteen-wheeler drifts up. It seems an odd place to want to spend time, but not one to bemoan right now.

'I'm grateful to you. You're my first ride.'

'Well, you're in good hands.' Aaron looks over. 'I'm a taxi driver.'

'You don't get bored of it, after driving all week?'

'Well, by profession, I'm a teacher. History teacher. Found myself out of work and suddenly I had to hustle.'

There it is, the first time: that word that defines the USA, where surviving is a minor act of conjuring and chicanery, and no safety nets separate someone trained for teaching from a destiny of driving.

'I started driving to pay the bills, just the same as I did when I put myself through college.'

'It's hard to find work?'

'It's always hard to find work, whether you're a teacher or something else. Everything's made in China. We can't compete.' Aaron knocks down on the indicator, overtakes an estate car. 'And of course it's going to be cheaper to make things in a country with no regulation, and where companies can trash the environment and workers have no rights. If America had a fifty-first state that was like that, then they'd make everything there! It's a hypocrisy, right in the heart of our democracy, because we buy into a place that's against what we're supposed to stand for!'

For neither the first nor last time, I find myself thinking how the world could be so full of people like this: who all seem so invested in something different, and yet who are together able to change so little. Outside the car, dusk is coming down, so that I sense slim likelihood of another lift after this one, confirmation that I should have left the city many hours earlier. The brake lights of the jeep ahead flare up, as Aaron turns from me back to the road, wide nostrils the only dark in his face now bathed red.

'Teaching must be a tough job, too. I hear you guys are pretty vilified in the US.'

Aaron rolls his eyes: large eyes, big whites. He points a finger from where it rests on the wheel, out of the windshield. 'It ain't so simple as that. I mean, I voted Republican in the last election. I wasn't voting Obama a second time. And being a teacher, it's different in different places. In New York, if you can find work, it's fine. New York has the highest density of teachers anywhere in the US. Their union,' Aaron smacks a hand with power as he looks over at me, 'it must be a hundred thousand or more, and so they're strong, and so it's OK being a teacher there.'

I listen in, or rather, I half-listen. When you hitchhike you pay your fare in airtime, just the same as when you sleep on somebody's sofa: you're indebted, owe your ears and a polite audience. Sometimes it's a burden, but Aaron's good. We'll meet orators much worse than this.

New Jersey passes: the debris at its roadside no longer exists, everything invisible, only the road and all else lost to the speed from inside the tin. There are no more charred books, no more dolls, only the falling yellow leaves, the road cutting through trees with bark stained by exhaust fumes. I think of Aaron's politics, his being so quick to talk about them. Is it me? Do I bring out the political in him because it interests me? Does everyone have this much politics inside them, waiting to get out? Perhaps it is simply the case that hitchhiking is the filter: once you've been picked up, the driver has already established themselves as a one-in-a-thousand. They don't believe you're going to murder them, they ignored the media, their brains are still alive. Looking out the window, Aaron remains silent. He seems distant, bored, and with his journey having no real destination anyway, the longer he talks and the further I'll be driven.

'You must be pretty unique, a black teacher voting Republican.'

Aaron turns nonchalantly. 'I don't like the assumption that just because I care about the environment, human rights, and am black and a teacher, I have to be a Democrat.' He shakes his head. 'This country it's just too, it's just *too* ...'

'Polarised?'

'Yeah! It's *so* polarised, man!'

'But do you think the Republicans are aware that the things you mentioned: the environment, unions, teachers and human rights, are the sort of things their potential voters care about?'

'No, sure they don't. They used to care about that, but now the party machine ain't listening to the ground, and they should be.'

Aaron waves a dismissive hand. 'But I'm not a Democrat when it comes to things like foreign policy neither.'

'You mean North Korea and Iran posing a threat to world peace, things like that?'

'*Exactly!*' Aaron looks at me with a keenness that takes me aback. He gleans no hint of irony, it's like I just nailed it in one and now we understand each other. 'That's exactly what I mean. But most people don't get it,' he looks round, comforted to have found me, 'they don't follow international diplomacy like I do. I watched a really good documentary that explained it. People don't get that history runs in cycles.' Aaron's hands shift left to right, leave the wheel to fend for itself. 'Power moves from west to east. Nobody sees how we need to watch these guys, before it's too late.'

My ears drift away from the conversation, pick up Interstate hum. Aaron's still talking, but descending rapidly into noise from a history teacher who watched too much History Channel. I don't begrudge him any of that, nor his views, but if there's such a thing as right and wrong, he starts sounding increasingly wrong.

On Hitchhiking

Thin trees spread sparse: paper birch and oak, branches bare, dead leaves like cleaved hearts all around, collapsing underneath as I move. Applause. It's quiet, really quiet. Some splashes of red and yellow are still in the trees. One car passes and then, once again, it's quiet. My brain takes stock: Where is this? Where did I sleep? Where am I? A few flakes of snow, white crystals, rest in the folds of my sleeping bag, piled neatly. Pennsylvania, The Wide State, gets closer … waits just a few more New Jersey rides away. My body's warm, face cold: cold face looking up at blue sky, split to mosaic fragments by the bare branches of the trees, twisting black against the blue. And I smile, breathe a deep and happy peace. I remember exactly where I am. Warm body, cold face, beneath blue sky. My favourite place on earth.

While I pack my bag, begin a new day, you should know all this: the context to what is coming. Let me explain it now, before we really get under way, because once we are out there together, there simply won't be time. Those rides won't all be like Aaron. A context of the wider world will evaporate from conversation, so many thoughts will seem like only a slow-moving chaos. It'll be challenge enough just to stay afloat, to keep my head in one piece and you along for the ride. Most of all, as is always so, we will hear all kinds of lies.

The old Indian owner of the petrol station points down the road: 'Four hundred metres away from here, I see a lot of hitchhikers. I think very good junction for you.' He'll usher us off, a smile and a wave with his nod of encouragement. Five minutes later we arrive at his junction, to nothing: no hint of traffic, perfect peace in any circumstances other than needing to catch a ride. To think I have given up the halfway decent spot we had on his forecourt, for this. What did he even mean? And then it hits. That's it. 'Four hundred metres *away from here*'.

'I'm sorry, I can't give you a ride. It's company policy not to pick up riders.' That much is the truth, then he goes on: 'I'd love to if I could.' And now he's a liar.

A flicker before his answer, he scrabbles frantically: searches the potential lies for the one most truth-like. 'I'm not going that way.' And off he drives. My way.

A car full of family pulls in: 'I'm sorry, there's no space.' This one's got a point. Sure, there *could* be space, but no question it'd be cosy for the three of us in the back. He looks relieved at the get-out, an *I'm-a-good-person* smile spreading over his face. He continues: 'Otherwise I'd definitely give you a ride.' He pushed it too far. Now he's a liar too.

She looks at me, looks in earnest: fair enough, her child is in the back seat. Mothers driving with their children, I'd never begrudge them not picking me up, empathise entirely. She shakes her head slowly, more emotion than I believe sincere. She mutters it, mutters as if I'm a sorcerer with a spell and she can't but must break the moral bind of my request. 'I- ... I c-c-can't.' But what she really means, the truth, is only that she won't.

Each one is different, that's part of what keeps you going: the potential diversity of rejection. Some will veer gently away from the kerb even though they are not stopping, as if the very inert metal of their car were offended by my presence. I've moved an eighteen-wheel truck with a twenty-ton payload across two lanes of highway, just with the power of my flexing thumb. Some indicate into the lane towards you, and your heart jumps with the prospect that at last it's here, it's about to happen, only to sink with realisation that they were simply going about a lane change in proper accordance with the highway code. Others still will give a slight lift of fingers from steering wheel: an apology, embarrassed, as if I've just seen them naked, stripped of all airs, because they like to count themselves decent folk, but realise they just left another human stuck at a roadside in a desert. Sometimes I resent these guys the most, those without even the conviction to snub you properly, but in truth it is hard to dislike any of the responses because the variety interrupts the monotony of the ceaseless traffic. The very fact that it is a response at all, well, that's more than you get most of the time.

Sometimes, walking the highway, I'll pull my thumb back in. I'll take the *hitch* out of the hiking and suddenly I'm just a human being who's walking again: not asking anything of anybody, restoring my dignity. I'm autonomous, risen back from my rank of mile beggar, highway pauper. Now and then, I'll walk a few hundred metres just to regain a little pride, but a few hundred metres will take you from a good spot to a bad one. The reality of hitchhiking is standing still, waiting, and being rejected. And rejected. And rejected. You can't read a book, can't write, because you have to be paying some attention to the road, you have to be making eye contact, have to look like you care. All we are allowed to do is stand, to stand and maybe – now and then – walk, with a thumb out. Though, that said, we are less likely to get picked up when walking because this demonstrates – push-comes-to-shove – that we can move by ourselves.

When we're bored of all this thinking, of roadside psychology, to kill the time we'll play a game: guess how many cars will pass before the one, the *one* that spirits us along. You start out with thirty – *come on, man!* – be precise, make it interesting! OK, say *thirty-four*. A few hours later you're into the three hundreds. Often you lose count. Misanthropy rises with each passing hundred. The resentment is the only thing you can keep track of, or rather, the resentment starts to keep track of you: it starts to own you, you become nought but your bundle of rage, struggling to fathom why it is they all dislike you so much. Sure, I did some rotten things, I'm not proud, but do these guys know about all of them? I'd like to think I learned my lessons. Was I really such a bad person? Sometimes, after dark, in order to take back a little power for myself, distress them as they've distressed me, I'll stick out a thumb, even where I don't expect or want a ride, but only to terrify them, to strike some fear within their metal boxes. My night-time silhouette stalks the highway, thumb in air – a murderer for sure. Ten cars pass. I feel them shudder, rocked with dread at the thought that such a fell and devilish creature even exists. The Hitchhiker. He smiles blackly to himself – and I feel better.

The sign. The sign is key. I didn't always think so: thought a driver who will pick up riders always stops regardless. The truth is that, almost like an election, hitchhiking is about the centrists, swing voters. There are die-hards who will and (many more) die-hards who won't pick you up but, in order to really get moving, what you need is to win the middle ground, a group as precious as it is small: that legion of waverers of no firm opinion, the sort of people who – in your highway microsecond together – notice some good waterproof clothing as a mark of respectability, a neatly cut sign as a solid work ethic. A sturdy panel of cardboard, with no torn edges or damp spots, counts for about thirty miles a day. It is the equivalent of tucking your shirt in properly, showing some self-respect.

Hitchhiking will make you a master of communications: after this, I promise we'll be able to teach media agencies and campaign teams a thing or two about general public. Writing a destination on a piece of cardboard is as near to the bare minimum effort as you can get in the world of hitchhiking: shows about as much initiative as the roadside often allows. Taking some time with your font, colouring in some letters, adding a smiling face. In all those hours, from time to time staring hopelessly at your apparently futile sign, you'll consider the amendments that might improve the thing. You'll grow wary, lest you rashly add letters that cannot be incorporated into another, longer word, wary lest you draw an image badly, fill the last of the space on what was your last decent bit of cardboard.

The lone female hitchhiker, who once told me of putting tinsel around the edge of her sign as she hitched home for Christmas. She's sitting pretty, a Learjet in human form, there will be no stopping her. There again, I have to say it: she is also a girl, has breasts and long hair and, whatever the attractiveness, given her physical strength, people mostly suspect that if it came to it, they could murder her before she'd murder them. With me it is largely the other way round: I could murder them before they could murder me. The grip of my fingers around their neck would most likely be stronger than theirs around mine, not to mention the added strength of my uncompromising, pathological psychomania. They would turn blue before I would, their eyeballs would get bigger than mine. In America, after a while you realise that the possibility of larceny or violence often feels like the starting point for calibrating interactions with a stranger. But I digress. Back to the sign.

A destination is important: it is an expression of direction, signifies that I have a purpose somewhere on planet earth, separates me from all the bums with their plain pleas for help, dollars and mere escape. It also expresses belonging: shows I esteem a point of geography in the same nation to which the drivers belong. If you are aiming for a specific town, or even a neighbouring state, the name of that place will help you get a ride because by the name alone you share some slight connection with those driving there. Sometimes, the smaller the town the better, because that name means something in their heart: it is a home, a memory, a heartbreak, an old job. It is evidence that you are a human aware of the world around you, and perhaps – just maybe – therefore an ordinary person, possibly someone as mundane as a local in need of a ride home.

Some people pick up a rider even when they are evidently somewhat afraid to do so and even if only to drive a few miles together. I respect those guys, though they do make for strange, uncomfortable company. I like that they are determined to be *good* people, to keep the institution of hitchhiking alive. When I get out of the car, however, I feel them cower from me a little, as if *now* is the moment, my last opportunity to strike. And I just shake their hand and shut the door. I walk away, and wasn't a murderer after all. Sure, they didn't exactly *want* me to club an iron rod over their head, but at least it would've made sense. This way, leaving politely, it is as if I've disappointed everybody. I see their mystified faces, staring out through the glass and I feel awkward: like I'm not who I was supposed to be, a good-for-nothing imposter. I really did just want a ride after all. Not a bit like on TV.

The whole thing forms a long catalogue of human nature. People are more receptive to you when you are eating, because the law of the jungle dictates that a feeding animal is vulnerable rather than threatening. It also reminds people that you are human just as they are: you get hungry, and then you eat. The key is to be eating outside an establishment where you've evidently purchased something, because then you're also a consumer. You make transactions like everybody else and participate in that economy cornerstone of our existences. Suddenly the drivers can relate to me, a real, genuine human with some modicum of spending power and a receipt to prove it. The most rides I was ever offered was during a thirty-mile walk along the southern ridge of Grand Canyon. Car after van after car after jeep would stop. Some even turned right round for me, offered to drive back the way they'd come. It didn't matter that I wanted to walk and my thumb had not once lifted up. A dozen times at least I had to insist, fend off the rides. For a whole day I was set for big-time, and all because I was a valid participant in the consumption of Grand Canyon, *Experience of a Lifetime Ltd*: the venue that unified us all, humans under the sun and doubly validated by the fact we'd all coughed up the entry fee to see an empty hole in the red rock ground. Come next morning, the national park boundary had passed, the Experience of a Lifetime was over, and I was just a bum again.

Endless deliberation becomes commonplace. Do I hold the sign under my face, so that they have to look me in the eye, or at least close to the eye, as they reject me? Three cars pass … *Vroom!* … *Vroom-vroom!* … Is this maybe too much, too candid, emotional blackmail? Perhaps, but there again, I should consider that emotional blackmail works better in the US than it would in Europe. The whole American welfare state is based on emotional blackmail: hustlers at roadsides and outside every bus station, definitions of 'blackmail' round here are different to mine. Two more cars shoot by … *Vroom! Vroom!* I put the sign back at my side. I hold it with two hands to show that I'm willing and able and that I carry myself with honour, take myself seriously, a pride in the way I ply my trade. Three cars pass. *Vr-Vroom-Vr-oom!* This two-hands thing, maybe it's sycophantic? Overeager? Trying too hard? I hold the sign out, arm's length and in one hand, the thumb of the holding hand up in the air, casual like, as if hitchhiking were the most natural thing in the world and I do it all the time, picked up by average Americans just like the ones looking at me through the glass.

Then there's skin. My skin is cold. Of course it's cold, it's November in Ohio and so I'm wearing gloves, my jacket is done up tight. Somehow, I ponder, perhaps this is just a little inhuman, especially dressed in black as I am: it's all so melancholic, a droid of the highways. I take off my gloves, show hands, skin, human flesh, soft and not even so blemished if they ever cared to look. I've got hands just the same as the ones resting on their steering wheels. We've got hands in common, and that's only the beginning. Please, just give me a chance.

The entire population passes you by. Average America. The guys, all shoulders and biceps, driving in the most militarised pickup trucks: headlamps for tracking the hunt, two sets of wheels at the back, bull bars to take down a bison, enough horsepower in the engine to pull an artillery battery, ten seats to spare and room for thirty workers in the rear. They'll never pick you up. What you want is rust and mud. You want small. Full of boxes. Junk. Animal hair. That's where you'll get your rides, with an old guy of slight build who has to shove three Chihuahuas off the front seat for you to get in. Not all animal lovers are so forthcoming. I stand beside the traffic lights: a large car pulls up, waiting for the green, a woman driving and nobody else inside. From the back seat, two big black eyes are shining out at me, a tail wagging at the human through the glass: a coiffured, curly fringe of poodle hair, the dog sitting across two whole seats to himself, paws forward. Me and the hound laugh together, the lights change, poodle is chauffeured away. Human waits, and waits.

One last pointer you should know. Find a good place to stand. We have to get a good spot. It is important that the traffic should be moving slowly, or else have to stop altogether, because then we get face time and every second of that works in our favour: it trickles through their consciousness, their social filters, their reticence, hurry, natural caution, and finally, in some cases, it strikes heart. Just as important is a place that allows them to pull safely to one side: it needs to be safe and effortless, because 'there's nowhere to pull in' flashing momentarily in their head will lose us a lift.

Every ride you get is a moment of faith restored. Whoever it is that stops, however shabby the car. I'd say that – with huge variations between states and regions – around 0.5 per cent of the US population picks up hitchhikers. Technically, this means all you really need is to be passed by two hundred cars. The 199th drives off, then headlights and windshield face appears, and here comes your ride. Hitchhiking is just a numbers game: for each that stops you are passed by so many hundreds of cars that the increase of the number that have ever stopped for you – your total lift tally – from one ... to two ... to three ... drastically improves the ratio of rides to passers-by. Your second ride is a 100 per cent increase in strike rate. Even your tenth is still a 10 per cent gain. Each one becomes a type too, another *type* of person who could potentially stop. Alternatives, hillbillies, students, straight-laced surprises, youth, loners and the nihilistically wealthy. Often, even when you have a ride, the pastime can pull away at your patience: so annoyed by everyone who has driven right by that you end up taking it out on the one guy who picks you up. I'm irritated by his taste in music, by his air freshener, his run-of-the-mill ideas on fracking for shale gas, and – more than anything – the mere fact that he's the first person in a day who's let me close enough to form any of these judgements. Either way, they're all rides, they all go in, all count. Ultimately, you're grateful, deeply grateful, every time.

Netcong, NJ – November 10

SMS : 'It was really nice to meet you, maybe see you again. Stay safe.'

Sirens squeal. Loudspeaker: 'Stay where you are.' My boots stop, the hard shoulder of a quiet Interstate and I turn round to cops. The car is slung low, sits just over its axles, a white-black-gold colour scheme. I see his outline: Stetson behind windshield. Loudspeaker: 'Step over to the crash barrier, sit down with your palms against it.' I sigh with a smile, follow his instruction towards the barrier, moving a hand to remove pack from shoulders. Loudspeaker screeches fast: 'Don't touch your pack.' I do as I'm told. I sit. Out he comes: boots, dressed in grey, a hat with a wide brim, a white holster. He comes over with a smile, one hand on the holster. 'You armed?' Cops always ask that here, but the notion that I might be is still entertaining. I shake my head and he stops, toe to toe, before me.

'You mind if I check?'

'Be my guest.'

A hand comes round: checks under the front of my jacket, in the top centre at the back of my jeans.

'Where you from?'

'Britain.'

'Got a passport for that?'

'In the bag.'

'You want to take it off for me, slowly?'

Back to that old ritual of US cops asking once a day for my passport. A country where there's less documentation and suspicion attached to carrying a gun than walking along a roadside with a backpack. I sling down the bag, open up – 'Do it slowly', he repeats – I pull out red binding, gold insignia long-faded. Hand it over.

'Stay there.'

He turns back to the car, where I watch his outline moving behind the glass as he speaks in and out of the radio. He enters information on the computer beside the driver's seat, returns after five minutes, at ease and satisfied that I'm no threat to anybody.

'You're not supposed to hitchhike on the Interstate.'

'It wasn't the Interstate when I started on this road, and the cops in New York told me it was the one I wanted.'

He nods, believes, but believes with scepticism. 'I'll take you to the next town. Put your pack in the trunk.'

Following the clip of his boots to the rear of the car, he opens up to reveal a large, long black case, stretching one end of the vehicle to the other.

I look up at the officer: 'That's a rifle in there?'

From under the brim of his hat he looks down, seems happy with the question. He's clean-shaven, a smile of big white teeth comes. 'Don't you go worrying what's in there.'

Through a black shadowed window, countryside passes by. A metal grille separates me from the police officer, the coiled cable of his radio hanging beside the outline of his head with its close-cut hair. He lifts the mouthpiece from its compartment in the side of the radio, voice crackles: 'Travelling with hitchhiker now. Taking him to the next town.'

He turns to me: 'Where are you headed to anyway?'

'California.'

'You got a reason?'

A good question, but it makes me bristle. I make up my mind whether he's asking as an officer, in which case I'm not sure he's any right to know, or just as another person, curious.

'Not really, no.'

'Well, you be careful, that's a long way to go.' His tone softens, I thaw.

'You pick up many people from the Interstate?'

'Now and then, but not many. It's pretty quiet in this part of New Jersey.'

I look at the enclosed space around me: the boot of the car shuttered off, the metal grille keeping me from the officer, the daylight outside dimmed by tinted glass. I wonder who else sat in this seat before me.

'The state want to get rid of a few of us, or at least stop hiring new officers to replace the old guys that are retiring.'

'Is that Chris Christie, the big guy?'

The officer straightens his neck, looks at me in the rear-view mirror, as if odd to have found such an engagement in someone picked from the roadside.

'Yeah, he's Governor of New Jersey. Surprised you've heard of him.'

'He's pretty well known, isn't he, for not liking public spending? Didn't he cancel a tunnel that was about to be built between New Jersey and Manhattan? And I heard he was pretty tough on the teaching unions.'

'That's him. He wants to cut our pay, too. Broke a few of the promises he made when he was campaigning.' The officer makes pointed eye contact with me through the mirror. 'I don't know why someone promises one thing but then does another. If he wants to face the consequences of fewer police, so be it.'

The town nears up ahead, houses begin to replace the trees. I look out of the window and consider why it is that whatever job a person does, they can reliably explain the apocalypse that will follow the loss of it, but have strangely little concern for others facing the same fate.

*

One cop drops me, wishes me a good day as I stand at the roadside, thumb back out, and he pulls away. Five minutes pass. Another cop pulls in. A different one, the badge of Sheriff on the bonnet: the word written large, another in the endless and overlapping layers of US law enforcement, from federal to state to county to highway and everything in between. The cop leans out the window, growls.

'You're not allowed to hitchhike here.'

'The last ride I got left me here.'

'Hitchhiking is illegal in New Jersey.'

'But the last ride I had was a police officer. He dropped me here and said that although it wasn't permitted on the Interstate, it would be OK for me to hitchhike here.'

The officer is disarmed, didn't expect the bum to start stringing sentences together. US police pride themselves on manners: the idea that they're the well-mannered good guys probably helps them delude themselves about an awful lot of the injustices they perpetrate. Thing is, I'm better mannered than this guy. He's come at me and got more than he bargained for, as if – against his wishes – he respects anything that sounds so British and has no choice but to defer to it. I see confusion in his face. He points down the road.

'Keep on over that hill, by the auto dealership on the left. Once you're past that, do what you want.'

Obediently, I walk on up the road, pack to shoulders. I cross the top of the hill, reach the car dealership and a sign that reads 'County Line'. Sometimes there is surprisingly little law in the USA, only turf: an officer's patch and not losing face. Walking on, I begin to realise that the thoughts I feared on setting out are already coming to bear. The road feels tedious, nobody stops, the law seem set to hinder me. With only a map of the whole United States in my bag, I've little orientation for the direction I need to take, the specific turnings that will set me into Pennsylvania and then the fast arteries of Interstate moving west. I know that odd-numbered Interstates run north-south, and evens west-east, but that is all. Roadside conversations with those drivers of even the most passing interest in helping are non-starters: I don't know the names of the places they're heading to, nor how they correspond to my own journey. My confused, pondering pauses are long enough for them to lose interest, and you can't trust the impulse of drivers alone to get you where you want to go. Some want to take you out of only loyalty to hitchhiking, others will pick you up and drive you the wrong way just for the novelty of giving a ride. Sometimes, after enough hours, you are happy to go anywhere rather than nowhere, but I can't succumb to that urge just yet.

New York still feels frustratingly close: most major road signs still reference the place. The first law of hitchhiking returns to me: there is always more traffic on the other side. On the other side of the road, or on the underside of the highway bridges I cross. I begin to imagine all those willing rides driving by at a different roadside, and so it is that Greyhounds and buses begin appearing in my head, leaping through my imagination with an incitement to get this journey under way.

'Surely,' a small voice needles at me, 'a little trip to set you moving can't do any harm?'

My pride grits back. 'I can't. That's cheating. I have to hitchhike.'

'Cheating ...' the voice grows faint, almost disappearing, 'at what?'

He leads me into his office: 'Sure, let's look up places you could maybe get the bus ... I'll fix coffee too.' He's a big guy, but the garment industry is in the business of concealing that. A large, shapeless T-shirt falls down over the waist of jeans a metre wide.

'We're a family sign-making business. Mum does the bookkeeping, my brother makes the signs.' He puts a solemn hand on his chest. 'I work on production.'

He sits to an office chair, pushes a bowl of sweets my way. 'Let's call up the internet here, see you right.'

He taps a pen on the desk, blows air in and out of his cheeks and rolls through the mannerisms of a man processing a difficult task. The screen fills with the search engine homepage, illustrated by stars, stripes and banners: a township gathering of patriotic American beavers all standing proud. I consider what day it is: we're not July, so this isn't Independence. Thanksgiving isn't for two more weeks. What other days call for uniquely American celebrations?

'Why's the page all stars and stripes? Is that normal here?'

He looks round with a helpful face. 'Oh no, not at all. Today's Veterans' Day.'

Eleventh of the eleventh. Armistice comes back to me as I look at the US-emblazoned screen, thinking how a simple poppy has never looked more tasteful.

'You don't have it in London?'

'Yeah, we have it,' I consider how to put this, 'but it's not really seen as just a British thing. More of, you know, a general commemoration of the victims of war. Our allies too, sometimes even the guys on the other side.'

The man looks up at me with a furrowed brow and a squint not quite accusing, but sceptical of my patriotism, as if what I describe sounds suspiciously like aiding the enemy, and at best, cowardice.

Hackettstown, NJ

Back at the roadside I stand, watching dubiously at the ever-passing traffic. Humans, I decide in a latest grand judgement, don't like helping people who need help but aren't completely helpless yet. It does not provide the same glow of virtue. I think back to Crown Heights, so recent but already so far away. Political campaigning and hitchhiking have more in common than you might think, and both open the spectre of a stranger asking something of you without offering anything obvious or tangible in return. Faced with this scenario, and where society normally obliges us – against our primitive desires – to be polite to one another, people enjoy the tiny liberation that comes with having no real reason not to be rude. I pull my bag back to my shoulder. Who was I trying to kid? Hitchhiking across the US in this twenty-first century of fear and med– ... A car stops. A small jeep, sporty, window down: spectacles peer out, coins and cassettes across dashboard.

'Where you going?'

This is why it's hard to give up on hitchhiking, why it's addictive and why you're loath to move on from even the worst spot because, from experience, you know it only takes one car to change everything. The one-in-a-thousand person always arrives unannounced, can come at any moment, and is always possibly the next person. The windscreen up ahead could always be *the one* ... make all the difference between stranded and full steam ahead.

I lean down beside his window. 'West, anywhere west.'

He leans across to the passenger door, unlocks.

New Jersey moves quickly. I remove from space, place and time, wind down the window: a little noise comes in, the flap-flap-flap of squashed wind. The outside world relaxes me. Movement is good, it exercises the imagination. Derek looks round. He's young, I'd say my own age, but perhaps I've reached that age where now I'm meeting adults younger than me. He sticks out a hand.

'I'm the President of Old Jersey.'

He looks at me, gives an earnest laugh and angles in, as if waiting for a response, as if there's something for me to say to that. There is thick plaque on his teeth, his eyes are small behind the lenses of glasses. The jeep is messy around me, seats shine pink and green with discs of the trance music Derek will go on to tell me he mixes at home, each night when he can't sleep. I still don't know what to say, but he saves me the need.

'And you, I guess you just might be an assassin from England,' he pauses, contemplative, 'but if today's the day I die, then so be it.'

Eventually you have to just get on the fairground ride, suspend reality and join in. It's his car and automobile sovereignty says he can be whoever he likes inside the box. I'm not going to be around long enough to change this head.

'I'm Emre, from Britain. But don't worry, I'm not an assassin.'

We shake hands. Derek gathers himself up, closes his eyes and looks frustrated with himself, as if he's neglected to mention something obvious.

'I'm sorry,' he goes into a pocket, pulls out a gold coin, 'this is our currency, and that coin is now yours.' From the glove compartment he takes two silver nickels. 'And these are two coins I stole from the Rothschilds, to give to you.'

Right you are, Derek. Much obliged to you. I join the fun, play the game.

'So, is Old Jersey a kind of independent state within the US?'

'You could say that. America was a great country once, and it's soon to start getting better again, at which point we'll accede back to it. At least that's what I hope.'

'What makes you think it's getting better?'

'You know, I think people are finally waking up to what their government are doing.'

That's on its way to sanity, reality, that much I can relate to. 'You mean the NSA? Surveillance, spying on people's communications, things like that?'

Derek's delighted with me, his face opens in a smile, looks like I've paid my fare already. 'That's *exactly* what I mean, Emre.'

He nods towards me, like I'm a nugget, a real piece of work. He smiles, disbelieving the fortune that brought us together.

'You got lucky today. My transport ranges from poor to opulent, and today I was feeling poor, so I drove.'

'How do you travel when you're opulent?'

Derek looks over to me, calm as you like. 'Astroprojection.'

He turns nonchalant, downplays it. He repeats, 'Mostly astroprojection.'

Sure thing, Derek. I return to the previous setting, file Derek safely back inside the lunatic category, take my mind off the speed of his driving. New or Old Jersey goes rushing by ever faster, roads banked up and along the edge of ridges, through woods stripped by winter. Minutes pass, miles receding and it's too quiet, we need a question, if only to slow him down and take the edge off his zeal.

'Do you follow either of the current parties in politics?'

Derek shakes his head angrily. He doesn't even look at me, like I've asked a stupid question, having previously shown such promise.

'I see myself as a rebel.'

He's straight-faced. Rebellion might well have been written into his constitution, but still, it sounds odd.

'What's a rebel, though? Surely the day after the revolution, the rebels all become conservatives.'

Derek's perplexed. 'I don't follow.'

'You know, the old saying: that rebels become conservatives after the rebellion. I mean, I understand that it's attractive not to conform, to resist, but are you doing it for its own sake?' Derek's glazed. 'I mean, are you rebelling *against* just anything, or *for* something else?'

There's a small thud: a little dust of earth floats up where the rock landed, Derek's back on planet earth for a short, complicated moment. He looks at me, looks at me hard: eyebrows down, mistrusting, as if I just might be the British assassin he spoke of, as if I'm a gatekeeper asking him riddles, dangerously smart and far too curious.

He mumbles, ponders. 'That's an interesting question,' he speaks softly, 'I'll have to think about that.'

White, NJ

'I saw your sign for Ohio and I thought: "Hell, I'm driving to Ohio next week. I'll pick him up".'

He remains in the driver's seat as I swing my pack into the rear of the truck. The pickup is old and shabby, full of the scattered tools of an electrician's trade. Any vehicle in which you get a ride will always be this way. The mentality that allows for hitchhiking in an orderly, paranoid world, is also one that tolerates clutter. From a plastic bag behind us spew spare polo shirts, the chest printed with the name of his business.

'I'm Fitz,' he offers round a hand.

'Nice to meet you, Fitz. I don't think I know anyone called Fitz.'

He looks over, pleased. 'Short for Fitzgerald.'

Fitz is Guyanese, French Guyana: his skin a deep, dark black, but lips and eyes both thin and sharp.

'From Cayenne?' I ask, the only place in French Guyana that I know.

'Yeah, Cayenne.' Fitz looks over, seeming to take a liking to me. 'Not many know Cayenne round here. Where you headed after Ohio?'

'California.'

'California? You looking for work?'

And as with Aaron asking if there's a girl involved, or the state trooper asking if I have a reason for it, there is a weight to these first questions people ask about my journey and what motivates it. I suspect the question reflects back a little of the character of the person asking, and time and again I will eschew the true answer that I don't really know why I am going to California, other than it being the place where the US comes to an end, and so the obvious place to head for.

'No, I'm not looking for work, not really.'

Fitz looks round with a reassuring smile. Intuitively, there is no doubt in my mind that here is a good man, one glad to offer help but wanting no glory for it.

'Right,' he looks at me, like it's nothing to be ashamed of if I do, 'cos if you need work, I can find you some, here with me.'

Pennsylvania opens in front of us: barns and houses separated by ever more grass. The hills flatten to fields dotted with copses and dusty woodland. We go on talking, straight to all the big points, as you always do when you hitchhike: the intimacy of a stranger who knows nothing of your life, and won't be around so very long to judge by what he learns. Inviting someone into the private space of your car cuts all formality from an interaction, sets you to talking life, talking world. We turn a single corner, the movement sending a shining apple rolling across the dashboard.

'How long you lived in Pennsylvania?'

'Near enough all my life. Used to be Philadelphia though.'

'You ever been to Guyana?'

Fitz looks over at me, flashes a smile of happy memory. 'Oh yeah. Not for a few years now, but I been.'

'You like it there?'

'Know what, I gotta say I do … ah mean … I know this sounds

funny, America's a rich country and all, but life there it always seemed a whole lot better to me.'

'Yeah?'

'Yeah,' he leans over to repeat with ardour, 'Yeah, man. Ah mean, kids there they've got the freedom to play out in the streets, people are a whole lot nicer to one another.'

I'm smiling in agreement, but can tell Fitz thinks I'm just amused by his suggestion.

'I mean it!'

'I know you do, I can believe you!'

A dairy flashes by outside, cows chew cud, we both start laughing. 'And folk in Guyana, I tell you, they're actually happy and they'll leave their doors unlocked, and if you don't know what to eat one day for dinner, then you can just go over to your neighbour, see what they're cooking and eat with them.'

Fitz cocks his head over his shoulder, smiles again, as a grey cloud sets drizzle down on the pickup windscreen.

'And the food, it's so good. *The fruit!*' He blows a kiss off his teeth, as the windscreen wipers clear spots of rain. 'They've got mango, papaya … man … you wouldn't believe how good the pineapple is there.'

I smile. 'Think you'll ever go back?'

Fitz takes a hand from the wheel, rests it on his thigh. 'My wife is an American. And she ain't so sure about it all, but I keep trying.' He gives a laugh, 'She don't like her job much, or the place we live, but she's still pretty sure here's the best country in the world!'

'People here always do.'

Fitz gives a start, like I've just said something wise, when in reality, the words 'people here' just did that rare thing of introducing a notion of the outside world.

'You know, you're right. They just don't see that all over the world people are just wanting the same thing.' I listen, happily, truck rattling through Pennsylvania. 'An American person,' Fitz goes on, 'is just the same as a person in Iraq.'

Inside I glow. Such sweet, wondrous, downright un-American heresy. You'll travel a few miles in this nation before someone tells you an American is the same as an Iraqi. 'And all this war, man, it's just so senseless!'

I nod. The drizzle relents, large trees wave slowly against the wind.

Fitz looks round, all of a sudden intense. 'I been doing some reading. I'm really interested in stuff about God, and you know, I'm just not sure he exists.' Fitz straightens, says it purposefully, like it's the first time he's said it out loud. 'You know, I think I might be an atheist.'

The pickup flashes quickly past a gathering of high barns, tractors parked out front, before the fields open again. With the rattle of the road, disappearing east behind this old, red pickup, we speed out between fields lined with long furrows of dry, ploughed earth. Fitz turns to me, dark eyes and his mouth set serious.

'What do you think about God?'

Nazareth, Pennsylvania

Out in the countryside the adverts grow parochial. Big Time doesn't bother with these places, no stage schools on the billboards. The only celebrity here is George Washington, his head swapped for a large silver coin as he helps someone to skydive: *It takes courage at first, but saving helps you fly!* From a bus stop poster in rural Pennsylvania, a sad, tearful rhino looks out at me, courtesy of an animal charity. *I'm not medicine*, he says, as the organisation adds: *Every day a rhino is killed for the mistaken belief that tusk can cure cancer or hangovers.* On the opposite side of the road is a bus stop advert for obesity care. Facing an advert for hotdogs. The two coexist in harmony in this best of all possible worlds, always with a new product to remedy the problem the initial product created. Once a social problem has two industries attached, one that causes and another to accommodate it, pretty quickly the thing is normalised, and you remove all incentive to change the initial facts that ensure millions of Americans, for the foreseeable future, will stay obese. After a while, I gather up my bag and walk further down the street, suspicious that the rare presence of bus stops may be killing my prospects of a ride.

*

We shake hands. Ron's an old guy, the first over the age of fifty to pick me up. He's got maybe a week's stubble, drives an eight-seater people carrier with only the driver's seat occupied. His hands are small, dry skin over the knuckles, a gold wedding ring: he's short, wearing a checked shirt with an open collar, a fur neck around the top of his jacket.

'Nice to meet you, Ron. Thanks for giving me a lift.'

'You just having yourself an adventure?' he asks, releasing the handbrake and pulling away.

I think a moment, then nod, Ron as near as dammit to the truth.

'Why do you think people are so afraid of picking up hitchhikers?' I ask.

Ron shrugs. 'These days it's totally different to the way it used to be.' He speaks slowly, heavy and tired by years. 'Used to be less traffic, lots of people hitching rides. Now there's a lot of traffic and nobody hitching rides. Got more unusual it did. Not owning a car in the US these days, that used to be quite normal.' He breaks off, waves a hand dismissively, 'People's manners changed too.' Ron looks out the window, speaks almost quietly, irritated.

'These days, really, a lot of people are pricks.' He pauses, 'There are still helpful people too … but mostly pricks.'

I look out the window, consider whether I've just heard testimony of how the world has changed, or only another example of the changes that intensify in a man as he passes over middle age, when politics and society start having to answer for the injustices of the years. With all of the discomforts produced inside an ageing body, eventually government becomes responsible for the three pisses a night, for the prostate leaning on the bladder. Rotten politics, across the world, can always be explained by the inexperience of the young and the resignation of the old.

'Were you born round here?'

'Lived in Pennsylvania all my life, apart from a few years in Maryland, near Ocean City. I like it here. Here's home. I live five minutes from five state highways. Can't see even one of them from my house, can shoot sport in my back garden.'

I smile at the fact that in rural America you're never more than one question from a gun. 'What you shoot? Do you have deer or something, passing through your land?'

'Huh?'

'You said you shot … in your back garden?'

'Oh, I don't hunt, just target practice, but I've got over thirty handguns and pistols. I've not shot an animal since we were in Maryland.' I wait for Ron to explain the connection. 'Maryland, it's chicken country see, and when the rich folk buy their kids a puppy, every time the kids get bored of the dog, they put 'em out.' Ron looks solemnly at me, 'End up with a lot of wild dogs. The things start turning back to wolves, and they eat the chickens.'

Ron's tone turns positive, cheerful. He looks back at me, 'You ever fired a gun, Emre?'

I shake my head, and Ron starts telling me about his first time, the day he lost his virginity.

'My friend back in Maryland gave me a pump action shotgun to deal with the dogs.' Ron smiles warmly, remembers her, a wistful look moves over his face. 'I'd never seen one like it before, and I was sitting in a chair, butt between my feet, looking down the barrel. I'd no idea it was loaded, and I don't know if it was consciously or sub-consciously, but I ended up shooting the thing.' Ron laughs, his grey hair lifts on his raised brow, his smile wrinkles. 'Went whistling right by my face,' he takes his hands from the steering wheel, palms facing one another. 'That gun blew a hole this big in the ceiling. My ears didn't stop ringing for three days. It was like church bells up there!'

Highway 22, PA – November 12

Keep walking through the night, back roads of Pennsylvania encircled by Interstate. I can hear it, can hear it roaring. Tyres on damp asphalt, exhausts popping. Truck mufflers and engine-braking on a downhill. The tarmac river is flowing, flowing fast if only I can find a boat, a raft that floats with the current and has room for one more. First I have to get back to it, give these minor roads the slip and find a junction where I can hitch a ride with someone moving big distance. I've already walked five miles this evening, five miles in the name of this goal, but still unsure this is even the right direction. Up ahead shine the lights of a petrol station, a man filling up his car: the vehicle as big as ever, silver jewellery around his neck. He must be middle-aged, a lord-of-all-you-survey gaze over the dark landscape, a hand rested on the roof.

'Excuse me, sir, but is the junction with the Interstate up ahead?'

'Which junction you looking for?' He's cheerful, I grant him that.

'The one in the direction of Allentown.'

'Oh, Allentown.' He takes a certain pleasure from offering assuredly grim news. 'You're still a way off of there.'

We back-and-forth. I'm noticing myself getting better at sounding positive, friendly, even when inside I suspect perhaps I may be talking to an asshole. He gives me directions, works through details: it sounds convoluted, it sounds far, sounds like a different set of directions to the one I was first given, not that I'd put all faith in what this guy's telling me either. People everywhere take such pride in an ability to give directions: their own, unique directions. He gives me ditches, bridges and brooks, old oak trees and a particularly large stone at the roadside. Asking directions you'll never be told the same thing from one person to the next, even where two people stand just metres apart. We talk more. We talk New York to San Francisco. Talk London and accents and England and ancestry. He's still leaning on the car as the fuel line clunks finished. The guy seems to have started to like me, values my polite yet curious conversation during his petrol-refuelling experience.

'Yeah, I mean, that's quite a walk you've got there, to the Interstate. Sure wish I knew a way that could get you there quicker.'

He goes on, right on, the whole time leaning on his car, evidently not wishing all that hard. Leaning on his car, trying to think of some way, while leaning on his car with its wheels and spare seats and combustion engine, of some way, in all the wide, expanding universe, that could help shorten the second half of my ten-mile walk. 'Well, good night and good luck. Nice meeting you.'

I watch him drive away, my way, down the road.

*

White robes fly with the arc of the sword: a green belt around his middle, the wind tugging at the material of the belt as he runs through the villain dressed in red. A second assailant fails to accost him. The enemy falls to the ground, a red sash around his middle, the body disappearing: another vanishing, unconsequenced death as our hero sheaths sword in scabbard, swings it to his back. He jumps, pulls his weight up on to a ladder, climbs into the roof where another villain lunges terrifyingly at him. Swords flash. Steel gleams against night, they duel back and forth on narrow rafters. Fearlessness is everywhere, exceptional swordsmanship from both, though soon it emerges that our white-robed hero is the more skilled ninja. The black-robed foe is slain, falling down to die another unconsequenced death.

The driver hasn't seen me at all. I stop waving. I tap the window instead, ever so gently. This one's another enormous pickup: a war machine, humongous, military style, a vulgarity of excess and power.

Wheels made for deserts and riverbeds, huge treads. The man looks round from the screen in his hands, one more robed enemy oncoming, but now frozen in time by a tap of finger.

The driver snarls at me, disturbed, interrupted, put out at the stranger at the window. How dare I? The man's got large muscles, is fat under his tight shirt: a fat neck, a face that looks like it couldn't smile even if the owner wanted to. Reluctantly the man reaches for a button, the window drops. Only a little. He can't hear me. Window drops ever so slightly more.

'Don't suppose you could give me a ride?'

'I'm not prepared to do that.'

Window up. Screen unfreezes, hardman resumes his life as ninja.

*

My head turns towards the far-off sound of a dull thud, a scraping of metal: perhaps a car toppling and then a quiet, slow, unspectacular crash. I stop walking and look around into the night. Only the grey shadow of the road stretches ahead, looping off in the distance and surrounded on all sides by thick, black trees. Nothing moves. The noise comes no closer, is not repeated or followed, and so I return to walking, pick up my pace, striding across grids of wide, deserted highways and their slip roads.

Right now, truth is, I'm ready to give up a while. Ready to cheat Pennsylvania, to head for Greyhound and start hitchhiking proper once I've reached the state of Ohio, Appalachia. The East Coast seems too densely populated with suspicion, its countryside forever interrupted by unpleasant development, by strip mall: an endless stretch of shopping centres, supermarkets, drug stores, car parks, car dealerships and identical café buildings towering the size of warehouses. The Greyhound idea comes for me with a wagging tail: so warm and comfortable, sidling against my leg, looking up at me with big, wet eyes pleading. Only a simple bus journey and I can travel fast, convenient and trouble-free. Looking back now, thinking Greyhound an easy option, well, there's never been such a laughable, European failure of local knowledge.

Ahead comes a light: a tiny fairy dances on the highway, exploding in gunpowder sparks and then a red glow. Forward I march, straight into that light among the woods, waiting patiently for the apparition that now comes to play its tricks on my tired mind. Closing on the glow, scarlet turning crimson, I wait for the vision to fade before realising it won't, that this one is not a trick. Some fell presence, a dark and distant silhouette, blocks my path all dressed with sparks and bathed in blood. I make out gauntlets on hands, a helmet with the visor lifted above the head, boots steadfast and legs planted, clad in armour and set into the road as if trees in the earth. I scurry up the bank from the road, stalk the edge of the tree line, my shadow moving in and out of thin trunks. Below, nearing, the scene reveals the cause of that sound of crashing metal. In the asphalt, warning any approaching traffic, a sparkler shines bright against the road and illuminates the firefighter standing tall above. His face burns without any movement, and I scramble over tree roots, turning a corner to see sirens blue and red wash the ground in a puddle of emergency services. A car waits on its side, wheels up in the air and as helpless as some upended insect. Flashlights cast long shadows as fluorescent figures disappear inside the bodywork of a mutilated frame. Morbid fascination takes me, *Crash* and Ballard as Vaughan flies the scene and my gaze is locked in that moment of maybe death, maybe life, and then the terrible seductiveness of human destruction. My own life gives a stir, a kick. But what really can I do to help the many workers and plant machinery already circling the wreck?

Without taking any conscious decision, my feet carry onwards, revealing a second centurion standing guard above his own sparkling flare: a plume of pink smoke carries free, shot with the shifting shadows of emergency workers. The scene and its activity recede behind me, get swallowed by night and then disappear as, from the corner of my eye, I see my own unfolding journey and, for the time being, a destination. This is what I've been looking for, the landmark for the bus station that the sign maker told me of. I look up at a church silhouetted by moonlight: at a rusting, ruined cathedral to forgotten industry. The blast furnaces, the chimneys, the pipes, the valves that once stoked the fires of America, before the Chinese started doing the same and cheaper. My head rolls up and beholds the ghostly old organs of a steel mill. I've reached Bethlehem.

Greyhound – Bethlehem, PA – November 12

In the abandoned shadows of the factory, I waited for the Greyhound, watching as the subtle glow of dawn picked shades of red from walls of corroding metal. A man, walking an Alsatian among the gravel and long, wild grasses, stooped with a plastic bag and retrieved a pile of gently steaming faeces forced out by his squatting dog. I waited beside a small sign, sunk into a lump of concrete and doubling as a bus stop. The man followed my own gaze up at the steel mill, tied a knot in the plastic bag as he spoke the mournful words.

'Sure is something, to think that once they made the steel for the Golden Gate Bridge in that place.'

'Here in Pennsylvania?' I asked.

The man gave a nod, 'You bet. This was steel country once. We built America here.'

*

The orange dawn disappeared into sheer, black geometries as the sun rose brighter, then dimmed for midday and, eventually, the gunmetal-grey panelling of the Greyhound bus came pulling up. In a hiss of hydraulics, the door opened, steps descended, and a short man wearing a company tie jumped to the roadside. From inside the bus, an old face appeared, calling meekly after the driver.

'Excuse me, is this Thirtieth Street?'

The driver turned with rolling eyes, 'Does this look like Thirtieth Street?'

He opened a luggage berth beneath the windows, a line of sunlight slicing across the metal as pistons sighed and the hatch rose up and out. I held my rucksack out towards him, stepped forward and offered myself as the next victim of his short temper.

'Can I take this on board?' I asked.

He looked at me, once and then twice. An untidy moustache of long stubble grew over his top lip, the sunlight shone where hair had fallen out from the black skin of his bald scalp. He looked me up and down, as if momentarily trying to figure out who I was, what to latch on to and on what terms to justify the instinctive dislike he had found in yet one more insufferable passenger. In the end, he simply snarled: 'Do what you want. I don't care.'

Columbus. Columbus, Ohio would be the town to satisfy my irrational desire to clear Pennsylvania, without being a place so distant that it would take any more of the dollars I was able to part with for a fare. The journey from Bethlehem began aboard an almost empty bus, first heading south for a transfer at Philadelphia. The swaying of the highway and hum of engine slowly pulled my tired head downwards by the chin, and then in and out of sleep.

Under the shades of a late afternoon, my eyes opened to a billboard, shouting down: *Be Fearless!* The large head of a child looked down from behind a pair of gleaming sunglasses and the name of a business school, locals apparently ready to start thinking about bigtime again, as we moved out of the countryside and closed on Philadelphia. Under hues of a final pink upon the sky, the Delaware River ran beside the bus, and wide, concrete storm drains, spotted by puddles, slipped beneath the highway and out over the riverbanks. A few seats behind, a woman shouted loud into her phone, singing exclamations of surprise with a powerful accent of Philadelphia: 'No shit, ma man, you kiddin'!? No, tell me. You. Kiddin'?!'

Once I'd have been enchanted by the force of it: by the large uninhibited vernacular of the USA. Now all I wish is that she'd speak quieter. From out of the window, and peculiarly for the lifeless Interstates, a man in denim jacket and jeans hurried up the dimly lit stairwell of an overpass, then clumsily scaled a fence and disappeared, leaving me to wonder who he was, what stories he carried, and what chain of events – the breakdown of a car, or perhaps an entire life – had taken him, like me, to scurrying on foot in a place of only automobiles.

As the city streets folded around us, the bus began a string of unannounced stops. Uncertain where to get off, I made my way to the front, where the driver bounced up and down on the generous suspension of his seat. Gloved hands gripped the wheel as he rolled it through sharp, right-angled turns. Sitting down beside the front seat, I leant over.

'Is this next stop where the bus terminates?'

He doesn't look at me. 'Depends if you want the bus or train *terminal.*'

Wiseass, obnoxious answer to a question he hasn't even understood. This guy is a real piece of work, nothing but snide aggression, and yet I'm too tired to care. I go back for more.

'That's not what I'm asking. I'm asking if the next stop is the last stop.'

Deadpan, sullen. 'Yeah, it's the last stop,' he retorts, before his attention shifts to an amber traffic light turning red. Impatiently, with a fast and determined press of the pedal, he rolls through the lights and blocks the path of a woman driving her small car across the intersection. The two vehicles jar to an abrupt halt, passengers behind us shake and, down in the car, the woman stares in frightened disbelief from beyond her windscreen. The driver shouts down at her, waves his arms wildly and fires a loud horn: 'Just drive, lady, just drive!'

Exasperated by this man, the words fall out of me with some vague duty to remind him what he's become.

'You know, it's not that woman's fault, or your passengers' fault, that you hate driving this bus.'

Were he not so hard to find the least bit likeable, I'd say the man needs help: energy is pent up inside him, his stressed shoulders sit hunched at ear height, a pair of tweezers holding a tiny pressure cooker of a head right where they want it. The man feels like a killing spree waiting to happen, a tiny illustration of the untapped and colossal rage that sleeps, mostly unreleased, in the bosom of modern America. His ill-tempered dismissal of everyone around him starts to make sense: he hates his passengers because they have created his job, and because he hates his job beyond all bounds, he cannot help but hate his passengers. Travelling through this country on a bicycle, able to keep largely to yourself, you don't see all this. When you are forced to interact regularly with people, however, when you watch as they go about their days, things soon become apparent.

He ignores me flat, fires the horn at another junction. He curses, 'Philadelphia – *damn!* – I hate Philadelphia!'

'Didn't seem like you liked Bethlehem much either.'

He looks round, even the slightest interaction has softened him a little: my eyes show him who he is to the world outside his head.

'I *live* in Bethlehem,' loudly he bursts, 'I hate Bethlehem even more than I hate Philly.'

He sighs, shifts tone. 'Drive this route every day, every day. *Man,* it grinds you down.'

We roll steadily down a boulevard, the driver now timing his speed for the changing traffic lights. Asian people walk the streets around us in what looks like Chinatown, old ladies pulling groceries in canvas shopping trolleys that trail loyally behind them up the sidewalks. I offer something positive.

'Couldn't you change job?'

He straightens, pride rises in him. 'I'm a teacher, a teacher by training, over in New York.' He looks to me, 'New York was where I was born, but my teaching certificates aren't recognised in Pennsylvania. I don't have the money to train, and anyway I refuse to go back to school at the age of forty-six when I already know damn well how to teach.' He shakes his head as he hears himself. '*Man!* How did I get to be forty-six?'

I try not to leave him in his despondency. 'How come you came to Pennsylvania?'

The story won't get any better, they rarely do round here. He answers soft.

'My mother got dementia. I had to come out here and care for her, then when she died, took it pretty hard.'

The lights of the city glow on his face, dark skin beginning to wrinkle with a life passed by and the sense that he knows it. Telling a stranger is both solace and rock bottom: a confirmation by having someone else bear witness to his rut. He laughs out a sad smile of resignation at his own expense, a sort of comic tragedy.

'I taught literature in New York. Always hated school when I was a kid, but literature was my favourite subject.' He shakes his head, 'I *loved* becoming a literature teacher. I read all the time now, books keep me sane these days.'

Into the forecourt of the bus station, there comes a hiss of brakes, a second hiss of doors, of plastic seals pulled apart in the sound of what I think might be my heart cleaving for him. We hold one another's eyes a moment. He stands up in his seat and calls over my shoulder, down the length of the bus. '*Philadelphia! Philadelphia!* Bus terminates Philadelphia.'

I stick out my hand, he removes the glove from his and takes mine, places his second hand to my elbow.

'My name's Shaun,' he tells me, and for once, it seems somehow important to learn a man's name and find out that fragment of identity, a piece of who he is to all those, however few they now are, for whom he is more than only a bus driver.

*

At Philadelphia the journey found rhythm. Inside the station, suitcases rattled away, relatives hugged, and a handful of us huddled in a cold line, joined by other passengers bound for Pittsburgh, for

Columbus, for places as far west as Chicago. The next Greyhound rolled in, filled up, rolled out and, heads down, we slip beyond the city. Dusk creeps over, looms, then starts slowly passing with sleeping faces lit by the lights of plugs charging phones, charging screens of all different sizes. On the opposite side of the aisle another light is on, where a woman sits reading a book. Presumptuous or otherwise, and no idea what she's even reading, again and again I can't help but look over and adore the fact that in her lap is that collection of pages and not a glowing box of electronics. She uses a dollar bill as her bookmark, folds her jacket around her legs to stop the cold air that blows around us. There is no computer beside her, no headphones in her ears: only her book and her own head.

The Greyhound lurches west, races after the set sun in its pink sky. Bare trees line the horizon as the lights of Philadelphia are snuffed out by woodlands. I check myself, realise suddenly that I'm riding a Greyhound into the American night, headed first for the West Coast and then for San Francisco. I'm twenty-eight years old, and at least half of the words in that sentence would've set Kerouac chills all down my spine less than five years ago. I look out at the evening: the firmament in yellow, then a clear violet, and finally a bank of grey snow cloud that slices the sky at a heavy diagonal as it moves steadily in. The bus rocks and I hear axles squeak below, with everything just as beautiful as ever it was. Thickets line the country lanes we fly above, with churchyards and the hills of Pennsylvania coming out of the night to meet us. And yet, and yet – even in all this – my heart is still unmoving, so that perhaps I've just become an adult, have let off all my fireworks already, learned to keep my powder dry but forgotten how to have it spark. Pennsylvania or otherwise, suddenly it is simply still more space that I'm moving through and I'm all out of myths and romance, the tank has run empty. Beside me, the reading woman lifts out of her seat to resettle herself more comfortably, and I glimpse her book's cover: *The Battle Belongs to the Lord.* On the spine is the publisher's name: *Evangelical.* And I am obliged to remember that books were once no marker of spirit but only the latest, scandalous technology for people to consume the thoughts of others. Still, at least she is reading it herself, is active and not passive.

In a remote rest area we pull to a halt: a woman in cassock and bonnet stands in a pool of lamplight, waits, before stepping through the darkness and into the bus. Her body is ushered up by that regular hiss of the door. Amish, pale-skinned, head and hair wrapped tight inside the bonnet: she walks slowly down the aisle, clutching a large, leather portmanteau in both hands as she bounces between the upholstery of the seats. Our Greyhound returns to highway, with only the Amish woman and me going about journeys undisturbed by all but the window. Together, we forty strangers accelerate, bore a hole for ourselves in the dark as headlights open white on the night. I see the yellow lines of the coming road from down an outlined corridor of heads, necks and shoulders. Some rows in front, a man stays awake with his screen: watching first car crashes, then space creatures. And I wonder what he'd have put in his head before those images. How would he have spent these hours of Pennsylvania and what part of the night would've soaked in to form thoughts of his own?

One by one, sleep takes the rest of them and heads droop and then hang from necks. I look at all of those peaceful faces, think of what they dream now that their waking sights and thoughts have already been filled with so much fantasy. The bus rocks on, a giant crib of adults. Sleep picks at me, tickles my eyes with dust and lullabies, only I know that it will never settle. Tonight the insomnia doesn't trouble me, it's a friend, for in its company I watch the world passing. The cars scream by, possessed of such purpose towards who knows what end. The underpasses and flyovers we constructed: concrete glowing orange in the streetlight as it rises in and out of this earth, chartered so that humans might never need sleep again. Above the seats, I crane to get a look ahead of us: see the driver lost in trance, talking to the highway, his lips murmuring a dialogue with

Interstate 78. From behind comes a snore, then a kick, hard in the back of my seat! I swing round, we face one another: eyes meet, a fierce stare filled with fear as the cold breeze keeps on pressing at the windows, blows a night terror out of the bus and back to the darkness with a squeal from the asphalt.

Getting comfortable in his seat once more, the passenger behind slips a headphone back inside each ear. Our eyes break from one another, and here upon Interstate, surrounded by titanium and circuits of tin and cobalt, human history is suddenly nothing but the invention of new technologies: the moment at which human society intersects each new invention is what determines the path it will take thereafter. My mind moves back to old journeys, and I think of China and the zeal of its people for that nation refounded in 1949: an age of telecommunications, heavy industry and mass movement, so that a new nationalism was to be put down with more totality than the nations of Europe were able to achieve in all the nineteenth century of horse, cart and steam. In a matter of decades, the Chinese were able to do what took two European centuries, with the resulting nation baptised abuzz with energy and optimism for what would come in a land without space for dissent. In Turkey, substantial roads were only built as the automobile was invented, and so cars dominate those spaces. In Britain, early roads emerged with horses, walkers and bicycles that were only later joined by cars, so that the new technology of the automobile had to fit within a culture of rules and the less powerful vehicles that came before it. On a bus through the Pennsylvania night, surrounded by sleeping faces that illuminate in the soft glow of a screen each time they wake, I think what will become of our democracies, parachuted down to a society with no idea where they came from, what to do with them, how to preserve them.

Outside the window, America flashes. Warehouses float beyond the glass and I see myself and all these passengers hurtle through space and time, rocking slowly back and forth like the curled-up, dusty forms of dead spiders blowing on drafts inside factories long closed. The future lurks ominously at that point where the distant horizon reels in the highway, and for a moment I forget the technology of physical invention, and think instead of the technology of our systems: the structures that govern us, which are no less designed than any electrical device. Where a population has not participated in, or witnessed, the emergence of a system, then the nuances behind that technology and how it changes society become meaningless to them, so that only the easiest or most powerful versions of that system will prevail. Our democracy stems from an age when humans, their innovations, labour and their consent, were needed to achieve the functions of a society that now, in a glut of energy, technology and control, can be either automated or ignored. It is to that accident of chronology that we owe our liberty. The printing press, electronic telegram, steam and then jet engines made nations possible by allowing the transfer of standardised images, ideas, versions of events, across once unimaginable areas. Steadily, the internet destroys these nations, creating instead a broad, autonomous frenzy of information that must be collected into whichever aggregation of meaning will be accepted as fair by the greatest number, and meanwhile do humans least harm. Looking out on an America dressed in neon, I sense that soon, nations as we knew them will be made extinct. Where once the idea of a nation was impossible because peasants could not imagine places and people so distant, one day they will cease to function because we can no longer imagine anything so coherent, nor deserving of our shrinking, individualised reserves of empathy.

Up at the head of the Greyhound, the driver blows hard and close into his microphone. The blast of feedback lifts me up and alert, sets sleeping passengers stirring all around.

'Ladies and gentlemen, this is Pittsburgh. Pittsburgh, Pennsylvania. You've got one hour. Next stop Columbus. Columbus, Ohio. Ain't nothing positive here 'til Columbus Ohio.'

Pittsburgh Greyhound Station, PA

Snow and darkness fell on downtown Pittsburgh. Steadily it settled beneath a small row of skyscrapers, built from the profits of the state's steel, and from where they once shuffled that deck of money made in Bethlehem's blast furnace. Out on the street I stood, taking in night air as the other passengers waited in the warm lobby, gathered around vending machines of soft drinks and arcade games loaded with toys, from which people steered a metallic claw to try and retrieve cuddly animal toys. Beside me, on the wall of the station, a poster showed the Greyhound dog, lurching over the glowing lights of Las Vegas, and promising cheap tickets for passengers tempted by the idea of a trip to a casino and the better fortune waiting there.

Stretching my legs, I made my way across the deserted road, my feet leaving a dark trail through the thin carpet of snow. Further down the street, a truck had pulled in, with a driver eating a sandwich beside the cab. The man braced a little as he saw me near, the time well passed 1 a.m., and I gave a sort of come-in-peace wave as I passed him.

'You waiting for a bus?' His voice, gently concerned, came from over my shoulder.

'We've got an hour break.' I turned back to him, 'Heading for Columbus.'

He gave a nod, happy at the opportunity for conversation. 'Why Columbus? You don't sound like you're from round here.'

'No, I'm hitchhiking, west, for California.' And then I research my prospects. 'I got the bus, to get me started, because it seemed like I wasn't getting any big rides covering many miles.' I gestured at his vehicle, 'Do truckers still pick people up?'

He shrugged, 'Sometimes, sometimes we do. Been a while since I took anybody. A lot of the guys aren't allowed because they don't own their own truck and the companies they drive for say it's prohibited, normally cos of insurance.'

I nodded, the driver continued, 'I'll help people if they need it, but you get a lot of hustlers out here.' He pointed to a space across the road. 'Two weeks ago, I was driving this same job, a guy there told me he needed twenty bucks to help get a bus fare back home to Harrisburg.'

'You gave it to him?'

The driver nodded, pulling his hat down further over his ears. 'Yeah, I gave it to him. Then last week, I came back and I saw him here, asking money for a fare to Cleveland.'

The driver smiled a warm smile, at the expense of his own trusting nature, opened his palms, with one still holding its sandwich.

'But I'd rather be fooled by a hustler than have someone who really needed it tell the truth and me not believe them.'

He shrugged, the man just one more dignified soul in this vast land, holding a life together, and obliged to pick through the lies of desperate people that America permits fall through the bottom of its society. The driver finished his sandwich, scrunching a ball of plastic paper into his pocket and climbing back up the door of his rig.

'How's your ride on the Greyhound going?'

'It's an experience.'

'Yeah, even for us, those buses can be quite something.' He laughed, ''specially this time of year, lot of folk go in to the terminals at night, just to keep warm.'

*

Twenty minutes before departure, the truth of his words is plain. Pittsburgh Greyhound Station. 2 a.m. And I realise, despite trying hard to suspend all judgement against people based on lower incomes or lesser educations, I have to call a spade a spade. I'm up to my neck in Underclass. Enhanced flavourings, additives, sugar and colourings: the salt of the earth are turning to monosodium gluta-mate before my eyes.

Above us hang six televisions: the televisions live in pairs with no corner left un-televisioned and no brain unsupervised. I scan screens: cops chasing robbers. Plain clothes cops beating one another across the face. A commercial break ends and the next thing up is a documentary, something educational, a moment of promise. And then it comes: *The History of* – I can't bear to write it, but I must – *The History of Bacon in the USA*. Each screen is flanked by a second: showing adverts, weather, so-called news and other light relief to contrast this weightier programming. The worst thing is that people are actually watching. Only me and the religious loons are impatiently queuing for the bus to get us out of here. The Amish lady clutches her bags, seated right beside the heavy, sliding door that demarks the parking bay from the terminal. Nervously she looks up at the digital clock, checks it once a minute, desperate to get back on board, back into our shuttle of dark and silence, comparative paradise beside this terminal.

The music, loud and pounding over my head, is killing me. Sure I'm a long way from home, sure my life could use a few more prospects right now, but personal state of mind aside, none of this feels natural. Nobody told Greyhound that it's 2 a.m. and there's nothing remarkable happening for hours in either direction. They think it's a party, like everything else in America – one, big party – and we're all waiting on a bus to go win big in Vegas. The synthesised disco sinks in, the audio pulse that makes you feel there's cause for excitement when you're actually just waiting for a bus in the Pittsburgh night. I cover my ears but the asinine, saccharine words slip through my fingers like sand: *'Tonight's the night for fun … I see you and your moves on the dance floor … My love for you, and all those things you do.'*

Across the hall, one man keeps marching up and down, his chin dancing in and out with the beat: dreadlocks high on his head, boots with trailing laces undone, jogging bottoms to his ass, a hook tattooed as a tear on his cheek, a bottle of Gatorade in his hand. For a while we seem to size one another up, read eyes: me and one more *only-god-can-judge-me* badass. '*Trust nobody*' is the slogan writ large on his T-shirt, and I think of Harriet Tubman and the safe-houses of the old railroad, taking slaves to freedom in Canada. How would they have fared in that T-shirt? All these twenty-first century heroes, basking in the glory of other people's sacrifice. Damn, but they piss me off.

A couple stumble up: he's in a leather jacket, a short guy, dwarf-ish, long beard, hooked nose, he squeals as the metal claw fishes down into the arcade machine full of teddy bears. '*I missed it!*' he yelps, and then turns my way, towards his partner. I see him, full in the face: see his blotched red skin, beady eyes, big, white trainers on his feet. Why does this whole country wear such big trainers? With a steely gaze, the man beckons a slender finger and long fingernail to the woman: coaxes, implores and in a high-pitched, nasal whine he feigns a seductive voice: '*Come here, snookums. Why don't you come here? Of course I missed the teddy, why don't you come watch?*' She gives a sigh and storms over: dyed black hair with a dyed pink fringe, hair thin from all the dye, matching pink trainers, pink laces. She pulls up her trousers, pulls them back over the loose crowns of her buttocks. She marches to him: a bottle of sweetened orange juice in one hand. What exactly is it that everyone here has got against water? Together, the two of them press their noses to the glass of the teddy bear trough, as the claw goes down again. '*Ohoohoh, you missed it again, stoopid!*' And she hits at his shoulder, pouts and sticks out her tongue as I feel the air jostling with scents of sugars, flavourings, aftershaves intended to charm and hair prod-ucts that gel.

America, suddenly, is just one giant crèche for six-foot kids. I look around at the nation that wrote the Declaration of Independence, that was thinking about intellectual property as early as the 1770s. A man strides by me: forearms forwards, biceps out of his T-shirt. Happily he watches his polished, pristine grin reflected in a window and strolls by another passenger, who goes shouting furiously into his telephone.

Opposite, the Amish woman beneath her bonnet peers out with a hint of fear: her feet are up on her beaten old case, she crouches as if sheltering behind the thing. Nearby I see the evangelical, blanket over her legs, and by god, if I lived in this America then I'd be counting on heaven for a bit of hope too. Right now it feels there's a lot to be said for life in barns with conservative Christians in rural Pennsylvania, a damn sight better than what's waiting in mainstream culture. I look around, my thoughts deafeningly loud, ears screaming at the volume from my brain. I put my head between my knees, hood up, hands over ears. Rock yourself, child, rock yourself ... Cover your eyes, close the open book of your face before someone reads you and all of these poisonous thoughts. I glance up, mesmerised with disgust and sleep deprivation.

For the first but not last time in this journey, it's coming: I have nothing in common with these people. Here there is no public, no humanity, nothing to connect us. I'm somehow coming to understand killers, that sustainable feed of Americans willing to act on the feelings now rising in me, the whole country defending the right of those people to own the implement of murder that allows them fulfil a cold, numb, destruction of others. Even the conservatives and survivalists, the miscellaneous patriots so full with bluster and rights, they'll settle for disempowerment and this human mess in exchange for a gun to shoot, a barrel and a trigger to allow themselves feel mighty in their own yard.

In this instant, misanthropy has never been so obvious, so reasonable, such a well-thought out position. I want all of the lives around me to be so much better, more tastefully fulfilled, but only for my own sake and so that I don't have to look at them, to smell them, to listen to them. Then I rear up fast. Hold on, hold on, Emre: 'Look to the raft in your own eye.' And I realise that, actually, it's me, not them. I am the aberration, freak, oddity. These guys are all doing fine, they're happy. I look around at faces and, again, it hits home: they're all only children. No, that's not quite it. They're not children. Children are more innocent. These guys are all teenagers. Only one in ten Americans ever pass their nineteenth birthday, and I may again be fabricating statistics right here in the Pittsburgh night, but fabricating statistics falls right at the heart of modern America. Go large or go home, round here is the land of the free and I can make up whatever I like. Truth is only a sensation, accuracy a tyrannical imposition of bureaucrats.

Loud, the sound of sweet saviour cuts the music and screeches from the speaker. '*Columbus!*' I breathe relief for that word so terribly dear, my favourite place in this whole country. '*Columbus, Ohio. Leaving now.*' We shuffle into line, like a chain gang, all of us shackled together as slaves to that shared destination and the waiting Greyhound the only way to get there. I fall in with this crew of passengers, my nose to the floor and in my head that line of Henry Thoreau, so loved in this land: *That government that governs best is that which governs least.* I'd hate to see this lot with less government than they've got – they'd be eaten by the Koch brothers, turned to pâté, American *foie gras* made from the country's one-time blue-collar and then sold all over the world. Thoreau, in his defence, wasn't thinking of my companions when he came out with those lines: he had in mind a well-nourished, educated, principled, spiritually enriched and Spartan people concerned with nothing more than the order of right and wrong. It is not that modern America is the worst country in the world, but where it reigns supreme is in the gaping gulf between the way its citizens perceive their country and the reality. In few places with such entrenched troubles do people believe themselves possessed of such splendour.

Aboard the bus, at long last my head lolls. It's coming for me, the sleep, at last the sleep. I lift up, I float, I look down: see myself, one arm on the top of my bag, knees up against the seat in front, feet dangling in a vertical foetal position, a Greyhound's womb, the fans humming as I see my hands twitch, my eyes looking around the backs of my lids. I leave the bus, I take flight, tour the world and then resettle, blink. Bright lights of Interstate and again screens glow all around me, we throb and pulse like a tiny glow worm crawling into darkness. From nowhere, we hit a rut, one more tarmac crater in the great, crumbling infrastructure that is the USA. I bounce up off my seat, then land back down on its springs with a fearful, waking thought. A realisation: My god, but America is the third world.

Columbus, Ohio – November 13

Scarcely awake, I stand in the main hall of the bus station, some-where between bewildered and happy just to have arrived. Outside, snow is falling once again, starting to settle, carpet the pavement. Inside, a man stands in a pair of shorts, talking at an attendant, firing out thoughts. Disjointed, incoherent he talks … The whole country is falling apart, but slowly. Before anything else, you hear it in their voices, the faculty of speech is the first thing that goes.

'I'm from Las Vegas. I looked out the window, had myself set for the sun, and … an' … *I see snow!*'

The attendant dodges him. He has a gun on his hip but, given that he's not about to shoot the fellow, doesn't know how else to handle the situation. He's cautious, jumpy. The man in shorts is tall and well built, athletic, erratic: he's shifting his weight, hopping between feet. He shuffles another direction with each change in his thought process. 5:30 a.m. All I want is a diner. I want to sit in com-parative peace, to stretch my legs away from the seat in front of me and the telephone conversation of the passengers around me. The last four hours I've spent imagining the bowl of chilli I'm going to eat. It's dark outside. I should've asked my question elsewhere, kept my diner enquiry for someone else, away from the man in shorts. This accent works a treat in picking up attention, bad as well as good. Like an idiot, I open my trap, ask the attendant. 'Excuse me, is there a diner near here?'

And the man in shorts turns my way. You can tell he's a hustler by how quickly his attention switches to the new audience: a hustler always wins their pay in the first few seconds of the interaction, when momentum is found and the element of surprise either has you cough up or dig in against the advance. The security guard is replaced as a prospect by a stranger passing through foreign waters. The man imitates me: opens up his vowels, over-enunciates, speaks deliberately clearly in that way Americans do when they mock a British accent: 'Yes – Kind – Sir. Thank you … I can take you to a diner, don't you know!' The security guard leaves me to it, lets me secure myself against the madman in shorts in the black night of Ohio. The man follows: tails me down the street, jacket open, hands in shorts pockets. He returns to his own, excitable voice, 'Name's Mark.' A hand comes out to me and in a rare breach of my own etiquette, I leave my glove on to shake it. We walk the street together, Mark disregarding how hard I assure him I'm fine.

'It's just that you're downtown here and I don't want you walking into the wrong part of town. I just want to look after you in my town at least half as well as you people looked after me in your country.'

'You've been to England?'

'Sure have. I was in the military. I'm a veteran.'

There it is, the V-word. And if the ending of this exchange hadn't been a dead-cert already, it is now. I'd rather Mark just cut to the chase, ask for his money so that I can say no and he can leave me alone. I slow down to trail behind, he marches ahead as I insist on my own pace, allow a gap to open and make a point not to directly follow his lead.

'Where d'you go?' He looks round, disturbed. 'Oh, *there* you are. *Behind!*'

'Mark. I'm happy walking by myself. You're wearing shorts. You should go back inside.' I look up at him, tall above me with dark eyes and a tight-curling crew-cut of black hair.

'It's OK, I won't hurt you, and you don't need to be afraid of me.'

I'm not afraid of him, I just want some peace and quiet at five-thirty in the morning. Now I'm annoyed he's started bringing fear into all this. He goes on, 'I'm wearing shorts because my leg is just out of plaster. I was in the war,' – he doesn't say which one. 'These people,' he points to the state senate on the far side of the road, though the building probably doesn't matter, 'saw fit to send me off, but by the grace of God …' Mark signals to an old stone building on our side of the street, invoking, I suspect, a church, but in fact pointing at an attorney's office, 'By the grace of God and my mother, I been raised a good man and I won't hurt you.' Jeez, I wish this guy would stop talking about hurting me.

The two of us walk wide boulevards, small humans together, though no more than that for me to share with Mark in this hour.

He goes on, 'My head, it might be a bit strange, and I'm so tormented by these dark images.'

Mark, grinning, taps a finger on his skull and it *ra-ta-tap-taps* to let me know where the dark images are kept, nice and cosy. Mark sure could learn a thing or two about putting people at ease on deserted streets in the middle of the night. We walk under the red glare of a traffic light, fire in his eyes.

'It's ever since I was caught in that explosion I wear shorts, cos I have to put cream on my leg: really thick cream, ever since the accident and I guess my life's ruined now and I never got to take that NBA scholarship.'

American dream-disaster comes at me, condensed into five seconds. There's so much detritus round here that people have to be quick, attention spans are shortening.

'Say, there's the diner, under the green lights on the corner.' He pauses, points, here it comes. 'And I don't suppose you could help me, could help me with a dollar, could help me get some food?'

We stop. We face one another. At last. Mark from Las Vegas, who seems to know Columbus, Ohio remarkably well for a Nevada man, gets to the point. I feel for the guy, of course I do. Hustler, veteran, liar, all three or just plain misfit, one way or another, being Mark doesn't seem such a hoot. Is there a principle here? There are dollar bills in my pocket, I could spare one for a guy who's got fewer than I have, but then what? This guy needs professional help, needs support. My head screeches it at me: 'Who provides the goddamn mental healthcare in this place?'

And then I realise. Oh. I do. Mark is one more eternal outpatient and I'm the nurse, the psychiatrist, the institution, funding and the hospital all rolled into one, right here. I'm the mental healthcare system, just like I subsidise the poverty wages of the waiters and bar staff. So what next? What happens at the end of this dollar is what I want to know. What does it buy other than my own short reprieve from guilt and awkwardness? I'm deliberating, quick and invisible, I'm figuring out what to do, but it doesn't matter. It doesn't matter what I decide because Mark's making up his mind for me. He's still human, still remembers. You can sense he still remembers how it felt not to beg. He's ashamed, his broad shoulders slump as he turns on his heel and goes back to mumbling the hardships of his life. He turns quickly. 'I'm sorry, I didn't want to bother you.' He walks off fast and 'Have a good time in America' recedes with him into the distance.

*

One after another, I've been passed over. Hours on end. Been passed and passed and passed up by hundreds of Ohio motorists. It must be five hundred and going strong, setting records, a scintillating performance. Ordinarily I'm optimistic, the next car could always be *the one* that makes the difference. Sometimes, though, like now in Columbus, things turn on their head and I start thinking back instead, thinking back to the last one. Fitz: dropping me down in Pennsylvania. Perhaps this time there isn't a *next one* and Fitz was the last American driver ever to pick up a hitchhiker. That's it. We're through. Hitchhiking has been cancelled and either I adopt new methods or I'll be living out my days in Appalachia. The end of my tether is nearing, that phase of the journey that began with Greyhound has sapped me dry, wound down my humour.

Four Interstates and even more railroads connect at Columbus: the city is a transit hub with nothing in it but changes of direction that leave an awful lot of space among rings of tarmac and rail. They filled that empty space with Columbus, made the place big: one more large American nothing. Across the road, a banner stares me down: 'Workplace Freedoms Act'. The thing is blazoned with red-black-yellow: hazard colours, hammer and sickle either side, the banner affiliated with an organisation called *Keep Ohio's Heritage* and the intent to stop direct donations from salaries to union funds. Workers' rights are for Commies, un-American. Nothing should come between a US worker and his or her right to be summarily dismissed without recourse to representation. The hammer and sickle are printed there larger than all the words combined, and I'm curious how far into the twenty-first century those Soviet icons and twentieth-century horror stories they invoke will be used to scare people away from sound political ideas. Beside me, a café begins a busy morning trade, the door opening ever more frequently and blowing out warm breaths of air that eventually pull me inside to rows of suits in morning meetings, then students, and more students.

A long line waits ahead of me at the counter: bags are open on tables with lengths of cable looping up and out. Electrical devices charge from sockets all around. They have headphones, tablets, laptops, telephones, a few cameras, a pair of curling tongs next to a hot metal rod for straightening the curls back out if you overcurl. *Columbus State* is written on each chest and I wonder what any of them are studying. Makeup is applied, screens above us show replays of American football video games. My snide suspicion grows that I'm not in a cathedral of learning and education isn't what it was. And then someone shouts, over my shoulder, passionately, positively booming: *'Marx was right!'*

Oh my god. I swing round. There's a saint in here, a raging intellect and partisan is right behind me. Politics and ideas are alive in Columbus after all. Damn right Marx was right! I could faint. My knees go weak. I'm going to hug someone. Loud and clear in middle America, the first intelligent thing I've heard in forty-eight hours.

I've given them all short shrift, I've been harsh, I've written these guys off far too early. My god, I'm such a prick, so presumptuous. The smile is all over my face as I turn, looking them right in the face. I'm looking at them, positively gooey, as one says to the other, pointing hard in the chest of the third, 'But it's true, Mark was right, he *is* right, that restaurant was never *good*. It was always just, you know, kinda OK.'

My face falls as despair hits. They look at me, looking straight at them with the remnant of a warm smile still on my crestfallen chops. Luckily this country's full of lunatics, so right now I just look like one more and there's slim cause for alarm.

Self-reflection comes back over me: stop casting blame, look to the raft in your own eye. It's me, not them. *It's me, not them.* I need sleep, once again, and I don't know what I'm doing out here: who I thought I was kidding with this idiotic hitchhike across America. These guys are only living what they know, and that might be little more than a quest to acquire each newly released distractor coming on to the market, but you have to blame the adults before the kids, they're the ones who orchestrated this as a vision of progress to sell to their own children. Some patience is restored to me. It's always strangely calming to recognise your own mistakes, they're the only things in this world we actually have any control over. Besides, things are looking up: I'm fourth in line for coffee. Third. Now second, but it's taking a while. Half the problem is that none of them really want coffee. The orders coming through are more like shopping lists. Vanilla syrup, chocolate chips, cinnamon, double syrup (how did anyone *double* syrup?), gingerbread crumbs … it's a baking class before a coffee shop. At the end of all that, the thing has to be made with almond milk, because without almond milk you run the risk of double syrup and chocolate being bad for your health. The girl in front of me is worse than the rest of them, or perhaps that's just because I'm next up and so the waiting becomes harder. I've been standing still for three Columbus hours, all I want is something other than plain waiting. They make her coffee dessert as she talks to a friend inside her phone. 'I just really didn't like that movie, it kinda sucked.'

'I don't know, I just thought, you know, it was just really sucky.'

The barista interrupts the review, asks for $4.75. 'I'll call you back,' she says quickly as she goes into purse. Counts. Counts. Counts coins not quite there and the silver thinning out against the leather hide. She looks up.

'Oh no! I'm sorry. I only have four fifty!'

The barista smiles, 'That's OK, we're good for twenty-five cents.'

I watch as the girl lights up, 'Really? Oh my god, you guys are *so* awesome, that's the nicest thing!'

My head is grinding, grinding, spluttering. Really? The *nicest* thing? My head is overheating, needs coolant, can't take much more. Under my breath:

'Well, technically, it's twenty-five cents.'

Did I say that? Hard to tell, but anyway, Emre, close down your ears.

'I love,' she emphasises, swallows air, pops, 'thewayyoudothiscoffee! It's like totally the best thing in the world.'

'Hardly.' I snark, although again, I'm not sure if this mutter is between my ears, as was intended, or out of my lips. She looks round at me. I hear more words I had no idea I was saying.

'The greatest thing in the world is hardly double vanilla syrup, almond milk and chocolate chips. How about Higgs Boson? The Three Gorges Dam?' She's looking at me, looking at me like I'm really mean. I snap. 'Why can't you just calm down, breathe, and be a bit damn *balanced* for once? Jesus fucking Christ, what the hell happened to your brains? Don't you get tired of being so damn stupid?'

Cheeks quiver, she bites lip and then the meekness catches fire. She remembers Saratoga, Shock & Awe and she slap-slap-*slaps*. A hand comes right at me, straight across the face. My head flies to one side, following the trajectory of a wide, open palm. My head comes back, comes back slowly. I can feel my cheek stinging, the lights overhead are flicking in and out, swirls of pink and magic are jumping out of the bottles of flavoured syrup as I look at her and hear music, hear drums. I feel my fingers clench, fist appears at the end of my arm, relaxes back to palm and – *thwack!* – I slap her back, set her head flying on the end of a long, elasticated neck: the soft, empty head floating off – *jack-in-a-box* – to the far side of the room. She takes a moment, then starts wailing: gives a howl, a choke, and head after head looks round across the café. I hear men, hear boys, hear college football team shout. *'Man! Did you see that?! That guy just hit that girl!'*

The thunder starts up, the thunder comes a rumbling. Biceps and knuckles plough my way. Chairs scrape and floorboards quake as the quarterbacks line up. I stand there, feet together in Columbus, waiting on my fate as a wall of chests and shoulders and forearms comes right for me. They come, I gulp as the first fist flies, and closely I watch the arrival of knuckles on the end of my nose. *'We'll teach you a lesson! You think you can behave like that in America?'* Knuckle after knuckle comes flooding, I'm dizzying, colours spin. Stars and moons fly and I glimpse heaven as they pummel me into the ground with fists pounding. Feet first, I disappear, my mind softening and head nailed to the pillow of my forearms where, on a tabletop, I sleep.

Logan, OH

Mercy came. My Ohioan Beatrice. The thing is that in a country so far gone as America, those able to keep their hearts and minds intact have been required to do so with a tenacity that is hard to find in Europe. To survive this abomination, day in day out, takes a spirit of the most joyous proportions. Delicate hands grip the rim of the steering wheel. Slender fingers drum up and down in the corner of my vision, a few of them dressed in silver rings, and one thumb remarkably short, surely smaller than it should be. I look at it, trying to work out if I see something deformed or just an oddity: the fascinating form of a body part that just doesn't look quite right. The thumb nail is small, is hardly there, a thumb truncated with its nail shaved towards an oblong. The shortened length of the thumb above the knuckle goes tapping at the wheel as we drive. Linden looks over, sees me checking out her thumb and gives a sideways glance as if I'd been looking down her blouse. Caught with wandering eyes, this is embarrassing, but she's from Ohio and I'll learn they're not precious up here.

'My first job as a teenager was in a meat-slicing factory. Hundreds of ham hocks every week, pushed through a circular saw and cut thin for salami.' She looks round with an unconcerned grin, wiggles the thumb stump. 'They're pretty forceful in those places, insist you slice right down to the end of the hock. ' She cocks a nonchalant shoulder. 'I misjudged.'

Linden drives quickly. Woods, copses, crofts and townships with thrift stores flash past us. Shops selling chainsaws and workwear, with sit-down lawnmowers parked out front, are replaced by trestle railroad bridges across the winding Hocking River. The water meanders through the dawn, morning is risen and Linden speaking so wonderfully smart that the waters carry memories of the Greyhound off into the Ohio and then Mississippi rivers. She looks over at me: thick and angular glasses, lengths of black hair cut to shoulder length and falling over dove white skin.

'It's a beautiful river,' she says. I nod and she goes on, 'Pretty polluted, unfortunately.'

'Yeah?'

'Out here is old mining country. Ohio is the coal state, and there was always a lot of run-off into the rivers.'

A billboard of the morning roadside returns to me: a man in orange overalls, soot and an honest expression across his face.

'I saw some posters earlier, saying that the mines were under threat.'

Linden laughs, 'They talk about them like they were endangered species or something, but they do provide a lot of guys with jobs, and there are more people here who value our history as miners than care about climate change.' She watches the road ahead, sun scrolling across her face as we pass in and out of the shadow of trees. 'Because culturally people are so attached to mining for energy, that also means there's a lot of fracking for oil and gas here, and people support it because it brings jobs.'

'Is there any opposition?'

'Yeah, a lot, but so far they keep drilling anyway. Around Athens it's a really poor part of the state, so we get lumped with more wells. It's really bad in a place like Ohio because the ground is full of holes and tunnels, there are so many lost mineshafts, and the chemicals that companies use for fracking leak into them, then into the rivers and water supply.'

Out of the window I watch the countryside move by, so picturesque above whatever invisible works below the ground. In silence we drive south, straight towards the sun in its cold autumn sky, framed by the walls of valleys up ahead.

'Do you think things are changing?' I ask. 'I mean, you seem really informed about this sort of thing.'

'Things move slowly out here.' She sighs, 'And people always think things are changing, but rarely in the ways they actually are, or need to. Take Steubenville. Steubenville, Ohio. A girl was raped when she was drunk, by guys on the college football team.' Linden looks over at me, her tone rising. 'And people talked about how things were different, like this lost American golden age, back when things were wholesome and people apparently didn't behave like that. So people think something's changed, but they just talk about how sad it is that two young guys have ruined their lives and their stupid football careers, and now go to prison.' Linden straightens, electric. 'And so many people don't even see that, in all this, a young girl has damn well been raped!'

She looks over at me, shaking her head with an anger I share but know it is not my right to express like her. 'Athens, my hometown, the college there did all right in all that. They made it firmly into a women's rights issue, and it was so good, in what has always been a very male-dominated culture to hear people talking about rape culture being legitimised, to see a poster up in town that said "*If it's not welcome, it's harassment*".'

'And people are starting to talk about it?'

Linden shrugs, 'I guess I'm not the regular person. I live near Athens, which is a college town, and was always pretty liberal for that. And then, I'm different again,' her tone cools, she smiles, 'because I spend a lot of time with a community up in the woods.'

'A community?'

'Yeah, a group of anarchists bought some land off-grid. You know, the usual.'

'To get away and start again?'

'Guess so.'

I'm intrigued. 'You see yourself as an anarchist too?'

With a smile she looks over. 'I take parts of the idea and leave others. Obviously I don't just believe in smashing the system and all of the cliché stuff, but there's a lot I'd rather opt out of.'

'You vote?'

'Yes, I vote.' Linden is deadpan, as if she knows I'm testing her and doesn't appreciate it. 'But I don't like the idea that you can only be political at elections. I think that, in society, we have power on different levels and I wouldn't want to exclude myself from the power that comes with elections.'

I feel myself loving America all over again.

'You always thought like that?'

'Pretty much.' Linden accelerates, her car growling as we pass a milk tanker on the crest of a wide bend. 'It's going to be different for different people, but if you take *Roe v Wade* and a woman's right to choose to have an abortion, that's being eroded by conservative state governments across the country.' She knocks the indicator and drops back into lane. 'Ohio now only has three clinics that will perform an abortion. So that's why, yes, I'm an anarchist, but I'll still vote Democrat, because *Roe v Wade* is important.'

I start to say something, find a finger stuck straight out, demanding I wait. 'But what I resent most is this liberal idea that we should all just fall into line and get behind the Democrats because they ain't so different to me. And that's not true, because the Republicans might be falling apart, but the Democrats aren't a patch on what they should be.'

The car strafes by a cluster of barns, a lone horse, a large billboard showing men standing tall with chainsaws. Clouds move on a strong wind overhead, their shadows passing dark shapes across the road and up the side of a grassy bank. We move alongside the end of abandoned rail tracks, old wooden boxcars with their doors left open, their metal braces rusting and timbers rotting away to give me that same pang of railroads I always had. With a shake of the head I half-whisper the words, 'Jeez, I'd love to ride those things,' and Linden gives a small nod but says nothing. A tractor, its trailer piled high with bales of straw, comes towards us, golden lengths of grass blowing behind it in a dusty haze.

'Living out here, do you ever feel disconnected from the world?' I ask hesitantly, wary of sounding patronising.

'I used to be in a city and I will be again in future. For now, I think I need to be out here. And it can be a bit isolated, but country people are part of society too. What they think is as valuable as anyone who lives in a city.'

Linden cocks her shoulder once more, a mannerism she flashes again and again. Her upper lip lifts in the same direction from one corner of her mouth and we're overtaken by a large jeep, tyres to the height of our heads, a muffler howling. 'The internet helps because it makes you aware of the good things happening. And then it harms too, because you can just surround yourself with that, and your own life, and start to think it's the world. But anyway, we don't just have to talk about the place,' Linden looks at me, playfully. 'You want to come?'

Athens, OH

Under a cloud-set night sky, we sat around a bonfire surrounded deep in heavy woodlands, the glow of flames brushing at the circle of trees leaning over us. The founders of the community consisted of four regular residents: one a teacher and three of them carpenters, one working away on timber frame structures out West, so that I was given his cabin with a loft bed in which to make myself at home. A gentle drizzle fell steadily, the minute forms of droplets caught in the bright firelight and then steaming upwards in a gradual mist. From the nearby towns of Athens and Amesville, a wider group of maybe two dozen friends had come up to the smallholding for the weekend, and a line of old pickups were parked at the top of a rutted, muddy trail that wound through the hills to the community, perhaps half a mile from the nearest tarmac road.

Linden sat beside me, all of us in a circle of sawn logs and tree stumps. To our left was her boyfriend, Sammy, leaning forward with a bottle of beer between his knees. Sammy talked and laughed with a tall, broad-shouldered man who Linden had introduced as Kuzey: another regular resident, with a braid of red hair hanging over one shoulder and into the long length of his scarlet beard. Above the fire hung a heavy, cast-iron pot, steam bubbling from it, leaking the rich smell of game.

'That pigeon?' A newcomer pointed to the pot.

Kuzey got to his feet, lifted the lid so that a plume of steam exploded in the white light of headtorches and the glow of the fire.

With a large spoon he stirred at the pot, a smell rising, as a drunken voice rang out loudly.

'*Pigeon!* I ain't never eating no pigeon! I mean, *hell*, those guys are monogamous! Ten years those birds stay together, you'd be shooting someone's wife!'

Kuzey laughed. 'Relax, Maceo, it's venison in there. And it's ready.'

The drizzle kept falling on a pyramid of light, lifting up from the fire and between the trees with a small corona pulsing around its top. Tin mess cups and chipped enamel mugs were held in hands, the rattle of metal as many hands reached towards the stew, thick and sweet, curling onion and cubed carrot with the leaves of a bay tree among them. Linden had told me more of herself: that she had studied environmental and agricultural security, while Sammy liked hunting, guns, his carpentry. Buying a share in the community had been his way of finding a place to get away from the parts of society he disliked, and Linden's occasional visits to the settlement had become more frequent since their new relationship. With a smile and quick lift of her eyebrows she summarised: 'He liked that I was smart. I liked that he was practical.' Beside me, her face lit by firelight, her button nose and cheeks rose red, she gestured to the bubbling pot.

'I spent about two weeks solid out here this month, without much research work. I told Sammy I had to go home and study.' She blew on her mug of stew. 'Sammy knows I'm into anything with sourcing your own food, and he knew I wanted to help butchering the deer.'

From the corner of my eye, I watched Sammy not exactly listening, but certainly hearing what was said. His eyes gleamed mischievously at the story. Linden continued: 'So the very day after I left, I get a call.' She hits him playfully, impersonates his voice, "We got the deer, if you still want to come help butcher it." And I'm like, "Did you get up at 5 a.m. to shoot a deer just to get me back out there?"'

Again Linden hit at him playfully, hard playful, then followed through a second time. 'And he just says,' she exaggerated his drawl, "*Ah might have.*"'

Sammy looked over at me, shot a comical glance and raised his palms as if to ask what else he was supposed to do. The drizzle kept on, spat out of the flames and dried fast on heavily smoking logs. Two bottles of rum arrived, while Kuzey drank towards the end of a can of beer, raising his hand a moment to set the blue handkerchief tied over his red hair. Someone offered up the rum, to which Kuzey just shook the almost empty can in response.

'I'll just fill this with water in a few hours, fake-drink with you guys until I go to bed. You won't know the difference.'

A pregnant woman walked out from the main cabin, her large belly shown in outline and pushing from between the folds of an old coat made from hide and with fur around its collar. She passed beside the terracing cut out of the hillside, where vegetables and herbs were growing. Deliberately loud, Sammy asked, 'Mean you're not getting drunk with us once more before Erin goes into labour?'

The woman came up behind Kuzey and made a throttling gesture, before sliding her fingers down to his shoulders and resting them there.

Kuzey tilted his neck backwards, looked up and kept the smile. 'Took me long enough to convince her I was cut out to be a father.'

The rain seems to get heavier. Hoods go up, but everyone sits fast. A quiet, calm voice asks, 'Aren't we all getting wet?'

'It'll pass,' Maceo yells theatrically, half-falling backwards with his bellow, then pointing his can of beer and foot at the bonfire, 'Put some more wood on that thing. That'll keep us dry!'

I look quizzically upwards, as Linden gives a knowing shake of the head, as if to tell me not to consider it. Wood is thrown into the fire, hot on our faces with my back growing wet and drips forming on the peak of my hood. Maceo sits opposite, red in the chubby face, a physique of too much drink: young but with lank hair thinning and falling into his eyes, so that irritably he blows it up and brushes it back to his head, only for it to fall again. He keeps on talking, shouting in good humour as if there are things to get off his chest and the conversation with his immediate fireside neighbour needs to be made more public.

'Of course we're all screwed!' he screams in a good-natured madness. 'Haven't you heard about Fukushima? You know the radiation count in the fish on the West Coast is about a hundred times what it was. Man, I ain't gone to be eating sushi again in the next fifty years.'

A voice puts in, laughing kindly, 'Shit, Maceo, you never ate sushi.'

With a smile, Sammy leans in and I begin to get the impression Maceo is a regular act and that we're his audience. Someone hollers, 'Tell us about spinach!'

Maceo laughs, throws up his arms, 'Don't even get me started on the spinach. Basically,' he puts down his hands, levels with us and says it, deathly serious, 'there ain't nothing you won't get cancer from eating now. It's getting a whole lot worse than just those chem trails in the sky. Only good news is that the banks will take us all back into a war,' he points at all of us, waves a finger across the circle, 'and that'll get you before the cancer does.'

The audience laughs, Maceo taking long mouthfuls of beer, so that you feel he's in character, performing his role with a contented smile. A pause settles around us, silence but for the fire, logs smoking with the rain but the blaze burning bright. We sit a while more. Rain. Fire. *Rain*. Rain and then larger puffs of steam lifting like hot air balloons off the burning logs. Finally a voice. 'Anyone else getting wet?' A ripple runs all round us … yep, yep, yep. Hands are put to knees, headtorches lift, and everyone gets to their feet as we make our way back to the main cabin.

Gradually, the night rises with the drum of rain on a tin roof and drips falling round the perimeter. All of us stand indoors, pressed together with our bodies warming the building. Someone sits off to the corner with a ukulele, and high-pitched strings pluck notes that bounce between the walls. A girl, sitting on an upturned tea box, begins to slap rhythm at its plywood walls, knocking out a tune as another man takes up a guitar and the three of them start to play, the voice of a crowd rising to shout out a chorus as the dancing starts up. Feet stamp floorboards, which spring up and down so that the cabin, windows aglow, begins to jump among the hills. Kuzey comes towards me, a beer moving my way in an outstretched hand, knocked suddenly from his grip by the elbow of a man clapping his hands in hillbilly glee. The can flies through the air, then glug by glug spits itself on to the floor.

Sammy looks around, asks with a smirk, 'Where's that flag?' And he hands the beer up to me as Kuzey turns and unties stars and stripes from the doorknob and throws it in a ball at Sammy, so that I watch the star-spangled banner become damp: red-white-blue, frayed ends push through the puddle of beer as Linden rolls her eyes and Sammy grins. He squats down, the puddle, turning fast into a pool of polished floorboards, shining in the light and then, one-by-one, marked by the soiled treads and the mud of the boots that close in on all sides and begin to dance once more. From the margins I watch, looking in on the scene of this community: built in its own, heartfelt resistance to the country that swarms outside. Hoisted up in the apex of Sammy's elbow and forearm, Linden lets fly her feet from the floor, the two of them spinning together with an orbit of hands clapping all around. A few figures sit happily in the corners, rolling large joints of cannabis. As the bottles of rum are passed and then begin to run empty, Kuzey comes back up to me, rattling a large jar full of silver quarters and greenbacked dollar notes.

'Wanna play?' He asks.

'Play what?'

'It's our game ... you throw dice, six dice. If they land one through six then you take the pot. Someone always wins before it hits three hundred.'

From my pocket I pull a dollar bill, and Kuzey opens the stopper in the jar with a pop, his arm extending up to me as he drops at the knee in a pretend curtsy and invites my dollar for four plays. Faces turn to watch as someone else's dice rattle the room … six cubes of wood, each the size of a small apple. Maceo is up before me and whispering, whispering on the things … blowing numbers, dusting the wood with one-through-six prayers before he lifts his heel and sets them fly. Wood sets hard on wood for ping, pack, *rat-a-tat-tat* across the floor, bouncing – *three* – across cupboards and – *five* – a chair leg and – *five, five, two* and … *six*. Maceo curses, clenches fist and spins in the agony of a near-miss, as if he'd been out by only one. I take my turn and the blocks of wood rattle through the cabin, off floorboards and doors, coming to land between the dancing boots as the crowd cheers one not so near-miss after the next, and Kuzey slaps a broad *better-luck-next-time* palm against my shoulder as if in welcome to Ohio. The rain picks up harder, grows into storm proper, as dice join thunder and water spills over the edge of the roof, yellow light pouring from the windows into the dark mass of trees leaning over and around the cabin as if in protection of its sacred space.

The party grows as hours pass. The rum finishes, is replaced by new bottles as cupboards are rummaged to unearth undrunk spirits from parties past. 'I was saving that!' And similar other protests, time and again, disappear up only to submit beneath the laughter. I abstain from the spirits, watching as people dance, music plays, in this cabin at the end of a long, secluded trail beneath the fallen leaves of autumn, all hidden away in a remote corner of this remote state, the money in the betting jar climbing patiently towards a new number everyone's soon too drunk to count or care about. Again and again I drink, then begin to slow, introspect as forgotten thoughts return and I think of times where once I would have been so full of life, elated that here was the secret and unspoilt world of stories for which I longed. I remember the days when I'd have drunk the last drops, slid a dry tongue into the sticky neck of an empty bottle. But that person he is such a stranger to this man standing in Appalachia and so suddenly reserved, for here I am in their escape, but not yet in mine.

Athens, OH – November 14

Dawn, first light and then full morning woke nobody but me. One of the members of the commune had a British heritage, told me soon after my arrival where in the kitchen to find tea bags. On a ceramic urn I turned a tap, letting a flow trickle slow through the filter, pulling out the fracking chemicals and giardia bacteria I had been warned were in the water. I warmed a cup on the stove and set a pan to boil. With those cabins buried in remote Appalachian hills, the shelves that covered each wooden wall around me held boxes of Italian pasta, a Spanish liquor, green and red lentils, while preserves and Bonne Maman jam jars waited on the counter beside an old copy of *The New Yorker*. At that moment, more than any other, when you see the keepsakes and indulgences of a faraway cosmopolitan society, you realise that up there in the hills you have found something little more complex than a contented group of refugees, still more of those US citizens who also reside in cities across Europe and further afield. Millions like them are dotted around the world: people who either escape altogether or hunker in Appalachian woodlands, or the deserts of New Mexico, unable to abide the consumerism, corporate power, supine politics, media distraction and under-education that has ridden roughshod over lands and people they left behind.

Outside, I sat beneath the lip of the roof, bleached green by copper running with old rain. A vegetable patch and long line of harvested beanstalks stood opposite, behind a few leeks waiting to be dug from the soil. From the rafters of the porch hung four haunches of venison, the blood drying in the sacks of translucent skin remaining on each muscle, shaped in red harps set with black strings. The wind blew eerily through the valley and so came the gruff sound of a length of twine pulled down by the weight of dead limbs, sliding slowly against the metal hook that held each swaying haunch. Beneath the hanging meat, an old hurdy-gurdy with a broken leg sat under a covering of dusty soil.

'You about ready to get back on the road?'

Kuzey passed between a pair of trees, walking along the winding path towards me. I smile a hello, shrug that I'm not really sure.

'Linden said you were thinking of jumping some freight trains, that you might want some pointers.'

I nod.

'You sure you want to?'

Again, I nod.

Kuzey sits beside me, and slips something out from the inside pocket of his denim jacket.

'You might want this.'

He unrolls a paper booklet and passes it to me. A title in Comic Sans font, and a title that he'll tell me before parting that I'm not allowed to write or reproduce in print: this censorship the one condition of my being given these pages.

Kuzey looks at me, friendly firm. 'Keep it hidden. Don't mention it to anyone. If anyone catches you don't tell 'em you have a copy or ever saw a copy.'

I nod. 'Thanks. What is it?'

'It's *the* guide book.' He takes it, flips over its pages of small, typewritten lettering, dense from corner to corner. 'Put together by regular riders. It'll tell you the approximate schedules for all the major railroads: BN Santa Fe, Union Pacific, Norfolk Southern … You name it, it's got it. What's running which way and how many times a week, where the fence is barbed and where there's a gap, and where the bulls are known to be aggressive.'

'Bulls?'

'Railroad cops.'

'Right. I heard those guys have a reputation for being rough.'

Kuzey strokes at his beard. 'They do, but often they're fine. My advice would be, if you seem 'em in a yard, don't hide unless you're sure they won't find you. They're worse if they find you by surprise.'

He pulls his jacket round him, sniffs back the cold. 'Best thing is never to approach when there's more than one. That way you're putting them in a tough position, and a guy who might be OK with you riding will start worrying what his workmate thinks and if he's going to get reported for being cool with it. You could be with two bulls who are both OK with riders but won't say so in case their buddy isn't.'

'I get you.' I scratch my head. 'You ridden much?'

'Not for some years, but yeah, before that I went back and across the country a few times. If you have time and don't mind waiting, it's a good way to travel. If you want to give the road a miss, go straight for trains, then I can come with you to Cinci. I know the railyard tracks down there pretty well.'

'Thanks, but I'll stick with roads a while, try and move fast to warmer weather before I give it a go.'

'That makes sense. And really, most places you'll see where to ride. There'll be hobo jungles at the tracks. Certainly are some south of Cinci.'

'Hobo jungles?'

'Where the tramps hang out together, waiting for trains to catch a ride.'

'There are a lot of them?'

'Some places more than others. The rails heading south this time of year will be busy for just the same reason you're trying to cover ground, a lot of the homeless have to ride rails. They're too far gone for hitchhiking, nobody would ever pick them up.'

'Those guys must know what they're doing.'

'I guess, but lots of them learned the hard way. You'll see them, missing limbs,' Kuzey breaks for a black smile, 'a hand, or a finger.'

'They take more risks?'

'Often, but I s'pose the more times you jump a train and probability starts doing cruel things to you all on its own.'

New and pressing questions keep coming to me. 'And do I catch a train when it's moving or when it's stopped?'

'Up to you really. Often they'll stop completely, sometimes not and you have to catch 'em on the fly. Only do that if you're comfortable with it, and if you are running for a train, make sure you throw your pack up first, don't try jumping with it.'

'Makes sense. What else do I need to know?'

'Take plenty of water, food too, warm clothes … You'll get cold for sure.' He says it lightly, then grows stern. 'Never go under a car, even if it doesn't look like it's moving. Always get on the ladder and climb over. Never walk between them either, just always climb over, even when it looks like it's all clear. You got me?' I nod. 'Often, what they'll be doing is called "bumping", when they put a line of cars together by taking an engine and shunting one to the next, and they send the things rolling down the rails into one another to build the train. You don't want to be on the rails when that happens, especially if there's a downhill, because the cars appear out of nowhere, and they'll be moving fast, and it's goodnight before you know it.'

In my head, it all gets filed away.

'What sort of car do I look for? Can I ride all of them?'

Kuzey grows enlivened, like he's back on the rails himself, reliving a life of his own, from before days when fatherhood beckoned.

'Some are better than others. The boxcars, the old wooden boxcars,' – my eyes sparkle, wait for what to expect of that word still so magic to me – 'they don't exist any more, you won't find any of them really, certainly not in use. What you need are intermodals. You can tell them from afar. They've got ribs running down the outside of the cart. They're the ones with enough platform space for you to get down on. Lots of the others don't have anything, just beams for containers to be loaded into.'

I realise from this point it's simply down to me, at some moment in the future, to make the jump. Kuzey snaps a finger at me, 'And don't ride dirty-face!'

'Dirty-face?'

'Make sure you're at the back of a container, not the front. That way the container breaks the wind for you, otherwise it's all gonna come right at you and you'll find out what dirty-face is soon enough.'

We smile at one another.

'You nervous about setting out?'

'Not really. Kinda keen to, really. You done much hitchhiking?'

'Used to. Not any more. I got this big, red beard,' he tugs at his chin, 'and I don't want to get rid of it, or cut my hair, and I'm a tall guy. Last time I was doing it, and I had to wait three days for a ride, I figured that was it for me and hitchhiking. I'm glad I did it at the time ... got some stories. For sure, it's the only way to appreciate how strange the people in this country can be.'

'Yeah?' I ask uncertainly.

'Yeah, I mean, they're the minority, but they're out there. I remember a time, hitchhiking in Northern California, around the cliffs that dive right down to the Pacific and then climb back up the hills,' I smile at the memory of once riding that road. 'I got a ride with a woman out there. She was on her own, and that's a bit unusual to start with. She seemed a bit troubled the whole time, but I was heading for San Francisco and needed to make time. Her skin ...' Kuzey squints a little. 'Her skin was breaking out in a rash, and I remember her hair was real thin, greasy. She told me a few times that she was having a rough time of it, seeing a therapist, and that's not always what you want for a comfortable ride, but I think it's good for people to talk about this kinda thing. Then we get to this hairpin in the road, with a bridge going above the ocean and the rocks.' Kuzey leans over, earnestly, 'And she just drifted off a moment, her voice became really faint and she just said,' – Kuzey whispers – '"This is where he always starts following me." So I just play along and ask, "Who starts following you?" and she tells me about a man on a motorbike, with orange hair, who always starts following her at that point, trying to force her to the edge of the road and into the ocean. And then,' – Kuzey leans in on me – 'she screams! She screams so loud, and we're going over this narrow bridge along the cliffs, and she takes her hands off the wheel, hits the accelerator, and covers her eyes, "It's you! It's you! You're the man with the orange hair!" She won't stop screaming, and I have to lean over and take the wheel, and I'm shouting that it isn't me and she's shouting that it is. I had to keep shouting at her, tell her to take her foot off the gas,' – he leans over and pilots an imaginary wheel – 'and all the time grabbing the wheel and steering the car with the cliff face right next to us. I grabbed a length of my hair and put it right in front of her, "Look at it! Look!" I had to shout, she was so mad. "My hair's red, it's red-brown, not orange … I'm not him. I promise I'm not him." And she uncovered her eyes. "You sure you're not him?" and I nod. Man!' Kuzey laughs, 'I thought we were both going to die, but she got herself together and took the wheel back, then drove on until I asked her to pull over and let me out.'

'And she did?'

'Not really. She pulled in and asked if I was leaving, and I say that I am. And then she covers her eyes and just starts crying, real howling, and she sobs, "You're abandoning me! Everyone abandons me!"' Kuzey puts up his palms in defence, 'Erin will tell you, I'm real soft, and I put my hand on her shoulder and said that I wasn't abandoning her, that I just needed a different ride, something like that.' Kuzey gives a relieved sigh. 'She cried as I got out, and I just walked the other way up the road and didn't look back.'

'That's the worst of it?' I check for reassurance.

Kuzey strokes his beard. 'I'd say … 'part from that time in New Mexico.'

'New Mexico?'

'Yeah, that was different. That one was sinister.'

Part of me doesn't want to hear it. Part of me mistrusts those who bill a story as sinister, but I sense Kuzey is not one to sensationalise.

'That time was with Erin, down in the desert. We got a really bad ride, left us in the middle of nowhere, just the classic landscape of a highway stretching into the sands, and absolutely nothing. We must have waited there a few hours, and then, from far away, a figure starts walking towards us, from nowhere. And he wore a long black coat, boots and black jeans, and a black shirt. Lean-looking guy. And he keeps marching towards us like he's just headed for the horizon. As he gets closer, he starts to slow down, and me and Erin are both looking right at him as he puts a hand in the air and raises his palm and calls out in this totally flat voice … "Wanna catch a ride together?"'

'That's not normal.'

'You bet it isn't. I mean, that's never going to work, and I could tell Erin was getting really spooked. He came right up to us, stopped and asks again, just the same: "Wanna catch a ride together?" I told him no and he insisted, so I kinda stood up to him after a while, asked him to give us space. He tried to suggest harder, "I been waiting here all morning, and yesterday evening too …"' Kuzey impersonates a hushed accent, "I tell you … it'd be better if we wait together."'

Eventually he backed down, turned and took a few steps, but then he stopped, crouched and waited there in the dust a moment. I backed off, could feel Erin standing real close to me, and then the guy leaps up and turns, spinning, so that the tails of his coat kinda swept around him and left him standing there as I saw something flash with the sun. He stood there right in front of us, grinning crazy, clutching a nickel in his hand that I guess he'd just picked up.' Kuzey holds finger and thumb tight in front of him. 'And he held the thing there, and kept on staring at us and said, sort of threatening-like, "Looks like my luck is already starting to turn."'

There is a rustling from the bushes in Ohio as Sammy walks up the trail, calm but somewhat groggy. He sits behind us, on the terraced ledge of the vegetable patch. Kuzey looks over his shoulder, then continues:

'We watched the guy walk away, get smaller, but it seemed like real quick he'd disappeared, and then, in the distance, there was just a silver van driving towards us. It got bigger, came up to us with a driver and passenger up front but not looking round. The side door rolled open, and in the back was a guy in just a vest and jeans, real scrawny and sitting with loads of tools and other junk. He had fair hair, cut like a bowl, and he just leaned forwards and said, "Get in."' Erin was half behind me, and I just looked at him and froze, and he said it again, "Get in."' And I shook my head and he said it a third time, "Get in."' That was when I realised I had to do something, even though there was nobody else around.' Beside the cabin, Kuzey lifts up to a fuller height and sticks out his chest. 'So I just stood tall, and I grabbed at the handle on the side door and I took it and shouted, "Get out of here!" and I threw that door shut, and there was a screaming of tyres as the driver floored the gas so that the vehicle pulled away with loads of smoke off the tyres. Across the back of that van were loads of bumper stickers, real nasty shit. Stickers like "Watch out hippies … I love my country", Confederate flags, skulls, crosses.'

My eyes boggle. We three stand in silence, Kuzey shaking his head at the memory. Sammy eventually chooses to end the silence with quiet laughter and a memory of his own.

'One time, I'd ridden with a trucker, from North Carolina or somewhere, four hours all the way up to D.C. I'd been waiting a while, and it was a really good ride. The guy was pretty ordinary. We didn't say hardly a word to one another the whole journey. He had a dog in the cab, and now and then the dog would come for you to stroke his head or something. We arrived at this truck stop, just outside D.C.,' Sammy breaks to a laugh, 'and I thank the guy for the ride, and he just looks round, real calm, and he says to me, "Got another ten minutes and I don't mind suckin' on that little dick o' yours."'

Kuzey laughs, smiles and nods knowingly. 'Yep, I've heard some of them can be pretty affectionate with guys.'

'They're gay?' I ask.

'Nah, I wouldn't say they're gay. Just lonely, and not choosy, like in the military or prison, I guess.'

Inside the cabin we cooked breakfast together, frying bacon and eggs while a pan of tomatoes, canned and preserved from the summer harvest, bubbled on top of the wood burner that quickly brought warmth to the room. Morning became afternoon and then evening, and together we spent long hours, talking deep into the next night, about their lives and visions. Excitedly, Linden told me about a small town they had visited near Big Bend, Texas, a place of musicians and storytellers, craft breweries and organic farming. She talked of how, when the US census had come through collecting population data, half the town had left, gone up to the hills so as to deny the census any accurate information about them. It occurred to me then how much of the US is defined by opposition: that even where the values might be for solidarity, togetherness and unity, so many will take even those inclusive ideals and prefer to live away from the nation, isolated in the hills and free from the unwanted interferences of a country they mistrust so heavily.

Gradually the conversation turned to Erin's job as a teacher. She placed a protective hand to her large, pregnant middle as she lamented that the students at her college had no idea whether they were in education to learn or just because it was the correct thing to do to get ahead and earn big. 'Inside a generation, we've totally destroyed the idea of learning and education as a good thing in its own right, something with a higher value.' Now and then the conversation took in guns and insurrection. Kuzey announced that top-down control simply would not work in the long term, and that even if the powers of corporate America were too strong to overthrow: 'If you're going to lose, it's important to resist, to go down fighting.' Sammy gave a slow nod of agreement, at which Linden put in, sighed frustrated words as if with the return of familiar conversation.

'Guns are just a distraction. You can never take anything down with guns, the state will always have more firepower. You need to win people, and win ideas.'

'How many guns are out here?' I asked, thinking about it for the first time. Heads turned to Sammy.

'Sixteen,' he said, holding the intent looks of the others, as if he were the only one to blame, 'but they're not all mine.'

At the words, Kuzey let out a belly of laughter. 'Sammy! *You liar!* Fifteen of 'em are yours and one's your sister's.' Kuzey wagged a finger. 'And you got her that as a present and now you're looking after it for her because she doesn't want it at home with her kid.'

Everyone became all smiles, Linden showing Sammy a moment of solidarity, perspective as she pushed her hand affectionately at his thigh. 'It's not that guns are a problem up here, but the issue is always so split, and it always becomes some debate of city people versus country people. And everyone starts arguing about which one of those groups they identify as, and not talking about what they need to be discussing.'

'Isn't that kind of problem inevitable in any democracy?'

Even as the question left my mouth, I watched as each face gave a sort of sad smile, looking back and forth as if to see who would field it. In the end it was Erin that spoke, her hands around a cup of tea held in front of her. 'In Louisiana they've got electoral boundaries drawn up like horseshoes, they'll draw lines any way they can to bunch Republican voters together and make sure they get in. I wouldn't call this a democracy any more. Last election topped a billion dollars … how the hell can you spend a billion dollars of money, from corporates and rich donors, and still call it a democracy?'

Three days I eventually stayed with them up in the Ohio woods. Finally there came the time when I had to refuse their kind protests that I remain as long as I liked, as long as I needed, that I didn't have to press on for California if I didn't want to. Eventually, bound by nothing more compelling than that vague plan to keep moving west, I was dropped back at the roadside by Linden, who left me a phone number and told me to get in touch if I needed to. I waited a luckless hour, then took to walking a mile at a time between the slip roads on what I'd been told was the Appalachian highway, Route 32. I'd wait a while at each junction, few cars passing, then pick up my bag and walk on to the next.

*

He pulls up in the area between highway and slip road, blocks the on-ramp, which counts as erratic to start with, but the road's deserted. The truck's in the normal state: all magazines, hay and paint cans, its bodywork rusty and driver with a thick beard cut away from his cheeks but long on the end of his chin. He wears a baseball cap. The skin of his hands is stained grey, the grip feels like sandpaper. He nods a few times when I say hello, doesn't say anything in return. He doesn't inspire confidence, not my ideal ride. The moment of turning from new friends back to the road and its strangers needles at me, and somewhere inside me lurks a question: *What kind of person picks up strangers at the roadside?* I take stock, chide myself: oddballs are the nature of this mode of transport, you can't be choosy and if you paid attention to each minor uncertainty, you'd never get to San Francisco.

Finally, after a silence of a few miles, he says quietly, 'Name's Manny.'

He's not from round here, the accent is South: quicker and higher pitched, jumps like a bouncy ball, the string of a steel guitar. I ask if he's an Ohio native and Manny gives a slow shake of the head: 'Tennessee.'

We drive on a while. Eventually, he turns to me.

'So … where you going?'

'California. Probably Cincinnati first. Where you going?'

Manny shrugs, as if I'm not helping much with Cinci, and so I rephrase: 'Where can you take me?'

He looks over to me, 'I can get you closer. How's that?'

Along the ridges of Ohio we drive, Manny opening up some more as I decide that what seemed like suspicious behaviour was probably just caution mixed with maybe not so much of an education. The fact is, truly, Manny's just a regular guy driving home from work in a truck he doesn't trouble to keep clean.

'I work in catering. You know them rolls, filled with cheese sauce inside? Although,' Manny ponders, 'guess nowadays some of them are also filled with ham and cheese sauce, maybe you know them ones. 'He points proudly at himself, 'I put that in there, then we ship 'em all over the country.'

I look at him: steely grey eyes, tangled hair, the colour of his checked shirt fading and material thinning into holes at the shoulders. He reaches for the glove compartment, takes out a pack of cigarettes.

'You smoke tobacco?'

I shake my head as Manny lights up.

'Mind if I open a window?'

He waves the cigarette in approval, 'Go right ahead.'

The smoke winds up from his cigarette, tightrope-walks along the thick lip of the glass window, before being pulled out on to the highway. Forested, wooded banks stand up and down each side of the road, the pickup moving apace with a whining from the engine and a rattle from loose bodywork.

'Do you prefer it in Ohio or Tennessee?'

Manny considers. 'Prefer Tennessee ... but seems there ain't no work for me there.' Manny turns to me, throws up a cigarette hand. 'I just can't make a living.' He laughs a little at this fate. 'What's it like in London?'

'London is different from the rest of the country, but I'd say people get paid a bit better than here, and they don't have to pay directly for things like healthcare if they get sick.'

Manny looks round as if I've just mentioned a promised land.

'You don't pay for healthcare?' He takes a long inhale of smoke. 'I pay two hundred dollars a month, another two hundred for my wife, plus the first thousand of any hospital bills. Who pays for you in London?'

'Well, we pay for it, but in taxes, not when you actually need to see a doctor or go to the hospital.'

'That so?' Manny chugs his cigarette. 'Sounds a good system.'

I give a little nod. 'Yeah, it's efficient, and it saves money too, because there's not so much need for bureaucracy in deciding who gets what treatment and how much they pay.'

Manny's nodding, thoughtful. I drive home my universal health-care home run, 'And, I mean, it's OK to make profit, but I think it's wrong to make so much money from people being sick.'

Manny straightens, alert. 'Oh yeah. Now I sure agree with you there. Business is business, but I'm sure some of these insurance companies don't have to charge so high.' He looks at me. 'This London sounds like a good place.'

Casually, noncommittal, I nod, eager not to take too much credit. I back up. 'The current government are changing lots of things, making it worse, probably.'

'What they doing?'

I flick through my mental notes of grievances with the government, think of the one that irks me most. 'Well, they're letting private companies take over the health service. And in the UK people really need jobs, and they're doing things like forcing unemployed people to go and work for free if they want to receive benefits payments.'

And as I say it, I hear the words in my own ears and realise what I've done. Manny lights up and I realise I pulled the worst example. 'That sounds all right to me' goes pinging brightly across the truck, but at the same time I detect that there's a question mark in his tone. Manny looks at me, as if for guidance, approval. I re-manoeuvre.

'Well, it's pretty bad, because it means big companies get a load of free labour paid for by the taxpayer.' Manny makes a face, nods agreement and I realise I've clawed it back. 'And people are unemployed because there are no jobs, and finding work is almost like a full-time job, so someone can be a university graduate with a lot of potential, and they don't get a chance to find a good job because they've got to go out and work a bad job.'

I feel like I'm campaigning, talking in sound bites a few words ahead of my brain. I catch up with myself, realise I've just talked about 'bad jobs' to a man who injects cheese and ham filling into bread rolls for a living. I've suggested that some people are too good for jobs like that. I look over at Manny, Ohio moving past, and I suspect I got away with it. Perhaps he lost my thread anyway. Still, I try to finish on a high.

'Although, obviously it's good for everyone to experience hard work.'

He straightens up, '*Ho yeah!* That's for sure.'

After driving a while longer, I ask if Manny votes, curious as to what party politics exist in a white man from the Republican red state of Tennessee, but living in the red-blue swing state of Ohio, and with obvious social values. He keeps on looking at the road, as if before we were talking about life but now we're just talking of an irrelevance we can no more control than the weather.

'Always voted Democrat. Haven't bothered at all these last few elections. All the same, I say.'

Manny looks straight ahead, says it all with a finality that invites no further comment. The wooded hills keep unfurling either side of us, dusk begins to beckon, and I consider the path of his views. Manny lights up another cigarette, takes a long drag, and I wonder if his parents were once Republican, wonder if they resented his voting for the Democrats and if he himself now misses the sensation of having a political party he feels represents him. The shifting history of US politics and the South is that the Republicans delivered the abolition of slavery, so turning the furious and defeated Confederate states Democrat for a century. At that point, in the 1960s, the Democrats delivered Civil Rights, simultaneously giving – with some dog-whistle racism from Nixon – the blue-collar of the white South back to the Republicans. Now, as big business and Republican money, the party elite, develop a more cosmopolitan worldview at odds with the blue-collar, conservative white Christianity of the South, those votes come up for contention once more, as half-century loyalties shift back to a sense of betrayal. If Democrats make a compelling case about social justice, about low pay and inequality as more important than racial divide and supposed religious purity, a lifetime of Republican voters could swing back to them. Meanwhile, the African Americans who in the twentieth century moved out of the impoverished South and up to the industrial Northern states – to Michigan, Ohio, Pennsylvania – as jobs dry up, as the motor and steel industries splutter and fail, those families drift back to their roots in the South, but take with them cultures of Democratic alignment, unionism and workers' rights, that developed in the factories of the rust belt. Forever it changes, back and forth, the challenge ever to read changes before they come, and so make those changes for the better.

Perhaps an hour and three cigarettes after he first picked me up, Manny drops me at a junction. He leans across, turns round at me, hand out.

'I'm glad I picked you up. Feel I been educated on a few things.'

We smile at one another. With the opening door, the front of the car bathes in a slight, yellow light that spills out into the dark. 'Thanks, Manny,' I call in and wave through the closing door, 'me too.'

Jasper, OH

'Sure, I don't mind helping somebody out with a ride. Hop in the back. Gone be cold though.'

It's a red pickup, open at the rear, just a platform with the tail-gate to hop in over. The guy must be younger than me, beardless. Smooth, white cheeks, shaved head, T-shirt and jeans. We're at a rest area: he and a friend ride up front, only two seats. They move a cool box into the back and I watch as they secure it down with straps. With pathos in their eyes, and I presume considering me home-less, they hand me a Styrofoam tray of leftovers: macaroni cheese, mashed potato, gravy. 'Have that, if you want dinner.'

Evening is by now well under way. This will be my last ride, but if they're headed all the way to Cincinnati, I'll take that for a good day's work. As they prepare to depart, I dive deep into my bag: retrieve my thick, woollen jumper, my windshell, a peaked cap and a woollen hat to go over the top of that. I pull on my gloves. Just standing still is brisk. When he says the back of the pickup driving the highway will be cold, I believe him. I jump in, hook my bag to a corner, push myself to the opposite corner, hold the cool box's strap with one hand, the side of the pickup with the other. I slip the cardboard sign for 'Cincinnati' between me and the cold metal. From inside comes a tap on the window: two heads are looking round at me, the driver showing me a thumbs-up question mark. I give a thumbs-up in return. We roll out on to the road.

It falls by us, Highway 32: the Appalachian Highway with forest still thick both sides, the road leaning left and right, always banking at an angle as dusk comes heavily at us. Along and down the long spines of mountains, riding crests, I look down the length of my body, the length of the truck. My legs stretch out in front of me, central on the road. My nose and cheeks chill fast. My nose drips but the layers of clothes work, everything else stays warm. The boy drives fast, fast but safe, I suppose. He passes traffic, the drivers of family cars seem to look over at me with disapproval as they realise there is a rider in the rear of the truck. Part of me agrees with them. Another part of me read *On the Road* when I was nineteen and I owe this ride in the back of a pickup to Kerouac. This ride in the back of a pickup, speeding across Appalachia.

But in spite of that, once more, nothing takes me. It's all left back there and aged 24, all the other side of his dying. I ride the back of a pickup down the Appalachian Highway, driven at 70mph by some kid headed for Kentucky. The forest flanks us, dense all around as I feel us riding along and over the contours of America, of Appalachia, two words that in themselves would once have been enough to set me smiling giddy. The moon comes up on me, slow and large and impossibly full, but nowadays I'm only a manic depressive of landscapes and – once again – nothing moves me. Moon climbs low into a pink sky as road flies away from between my outstretched legs, like I'm giving birth to the highway, or like it's a long, unravelling rope with me tied to its white lines and then thrown overboard. And I'm numb, and I don't feel a thing, simply a little closer to Cincinnati and then California, the reason for which I'm headed for I still don't even know. The moon lifts up some more, half an hour passes, pink turns black, the moon glows, and inside me is so much death and nothing but an uncontrollable sadness. I feel my face, as set and solid as the asphalt, skin cold above my warm neck. And it's over. Is this the moment I find it out, realise for the first time? Is it at an end at last? Yes, that's it. I'm only numb.

Mount Orab, OH

Swinging under the doorframe, I board this bonus ride, pulling in after I thought the miles had run dry for the day. My bag falls down across the rear seat as I slam the door closed and a warm, wet palm slides soft into my hands, gives beneath my handshake, which wasn't meant to feel as assertive as it does.

'Nice to meet you, Dan. Thanks for picking me up.'

Dan pulls away. He's pale: mild-mannered, long-necked, straight-cut ginger hair, drives a hatchback, which in this country looks conspicuously unassuming. He speaks softly, whispers at me. *Excuse me?* I can't hear him. *Excuse me?* I put my finger in my window-side ear, in order to hear him a bit clearer, block out the wind. He repeats:

'I've been there. Waiting, I mean. I thought I should pick you up.'

Dan is, in some ways, the model ride, in the sense that he seems slightly scared of me, and so I needn't for a moment worry about him. Dan is excited by what he's doing, as we listen to the lounge ambient music playing from the corners of his car. Nervously, he goes into questions of my route. I tell him California, San Francisco. Three minutes later I'm still talking, conscious of it, give Dan a turn, ask what he does. He whispers as gently as ever, quiet but sure of himself.

'I'm a convenience store manager in Cincinnati. I run stores that aren't doing very well, failing stores. I come in and turn them round.'

'You drive to Cincinnati every day? Why don't you just live there?'

'Oh, I don't like cities, they're too fast-paced.'

Dan catches himself, as if he doesn't like the image of himself he's just projected, as if he's more exciting than he's letting me see. 'I always planned to hitch cross-country sometime. That list of things to do just gets longer though.'

I smile, reassuring. 'What else is on it?'

Dan turns from the highway unrolling ahead of us. He smiles, nervously, and then answers.

'Skydiving. I want to go skydiving.'

Eastwood, OH

I put down behind a line of trees, prepare for sleep to come like someone waiting for a train. Chin rested on hand, time passes slowly, disturbed by noises as eventually consciousness disappears. Hours pass. Once or twice I awake to the sounds of cars, once to the scuffling of an animal, a *humphffffing* of breath and a shuffling that sounds like perhaps a wild pig. I sleep. I wake. And inside the bivvy bag, rivulets of rain upon the back of the hood trace in my mind the words of the scrawled note that had waited with it in the New York bar: *Really good bit of kit. Not used it for a while … keep it as long as you need.*

As it rains, I ponder how long that while was. A length of metal wire keeps the plastic lining away from my head and face, allowing me to breathe a little clearer through a thin mesh. Sleep maintains a good hold of me as the rain goes on falling centimetres from my head: the fast and regular candour of raindrops, dotted with the heavier drip of water that the leaves of the trees above can no longer hold and so let slip. It makes me anxious about how waterproof I really am. I fall back to sleep. I awake. The night is pitch: the bivvy bag cold against my skin. Wet? Who knows. Hope not. Lethargy takes me, and to the sound of heavier rain, I return to sleep. I awake: and no doubting, there is damp inside my sleeping bag, rainfall gathering, but the night so black and the rain so heavy. Perhaps it's better here all the same. I fall back to sleeping. I awake. Wet. Bona fide wet. Shit. The seams are all gushing, breached. Headtorch on. No let-up in the rain either, streams are running inside bag and I've got to beat it. Clock reads 4 a.m. I've got to get out of the wet, out of the bivvy, out of the *really good bit of kit* and into the equally wet night, walk until the Ohio woods will yield and give me shelter.

Rain falling, double-quick I pull on waterproofs: roll up bivvy bag, pull on boots, pull on waterproof trousers, pull the hood over the old backpack that, so it will soon transpire, was not waterproof either. Hood up, the peak low over my forehead, I scramble out of the woods: all in black, the sound of rain on plastic swishing against itself. Marching down the highway, rain falling I go: my pack high on my shoulders, my hands tucked between the straps and my chest, head set with purpose, eyes down, unflinching lest my mind wander and begin to curse. I march.

Desolate, remote. Looking through the night yields nothing but trees and rain above me, the leaves letting slip the water. Miles must pass. Billboards appear, though with no offering of cover beyond only the width of a girder. Occasionally comes a streetlamp, a pool of yellow glowing in the black. Under the falling rain, waking dreams conjure Nathalie, she the only soothing thought but back in New York and getting further away with each step. Imaginations of a comfort I'll never know come through the night. I see our wedding day photo on the wall of our home: we rushed it through, only the closest of family. She was looking up at me, wearing a dress of brown calico and white geraniums in her hair, but the pollen set off her allergies and so she sneezed uncontrollably: six blasts on her whistle, one after the next. The photographer took the shot mid-sneeze … we laugh about it, our children went crazy at the fact we'd always tell every dinner guest the same story. The kids they've grown up now, children of their own to embarrass, old enough to realise that their mum looked beautiful when she was young. The make-believe helps me stay dry. I keep at it, still too close to the start of this journey and Nathalie the only sight in all America it feels like I want to lay eyes on.

Cars appear a shade of grey, the roar of tyres pulling water and throwing the contents of a puddle high across my path to fetch me from my dreaming. I entertain myself, lighten the tone with the old thumb trick: all in black, walking possessed, through the woods in the middle of night and pouring rain. Even I think myself a little odd for finding myself in this predicament. The Americans will be convinced I'm psychotic. Using only a thumb I'm able to make other people even more uncomfortable than I am. They'll be shitting in the front seats, icicles forming on their skin as I quite clearly go about escaping the scene of the murder, eager to find a next victim and, though in the safety of the car, films have taught them exactly how to extrapolate and they know in their heads that next up could be them.

An hour passes. Still no sign of any built structure with more shelter than a tree. My marching keeps up, regimented: determined, purposeful strides towards a hoped-for dry place. The rain relents, or else I've just got used to it, and the sky begins to lighten so that the edges of clouds appear in the wet, blue haze above. Ahead, surrounded by still more nothing, lonely stands the shape of a petrol station. A cylindrical storage tank of gasoline rears up: pumps, a roof, a blessed roof, the whole scene planted down on a wide, concrete runway. Wet hair in my face, drips of rain falling from my nose so that the rainwater gathers out the guttering of my cheeks, and runs into my mouth where I blow it away.

A quick secret, let me say: the key to adventure, indeed, perhaps the only thing that qualifies as an adventure at all, is terrible kit. Bad kit is the least contrived route to the life affirmation that comes when you wind up marching an hour through Ohio's pouring rain in the middle of the night. Adventure is borrowing kit because you can't really afford your own, for a journey you are making for almost no reason other than idle idiocy, a journey that seems more stupid the longer you think about it. Anything else is just sleeping outdoors. Ten years' loyal service I've given to this whole discipline, have done my time, the only payment – where it's done properly – are the stories you amass and the vague hope that some person younger than you also winds up smitten by the idea that that's what their life was meant for, and so passes the infection to another generation. Marching, riven wet, I stride towards the petrol station, jump over a flooded ditch beside me. Everything is sodden but, emerging from out the woods of Ohio, there is a small bright smile on my face.

Afton, OH – November 17

He talks, animated, to the cashier: 'Darn me, I knew it, I just knew you were Tracey Phelps. It must be, what, twenty years since we saw one another … fifth grade … Oh my! Fifth grade!'

I overhear the Sunday morning reunion as I stuff folds of kitchen towel into wet boots, the fleeting smile following it down there, the fun and thrill now damp and over. Today will be miserable. The next forty-eight hours will be miserable. I need warm states, need south, need desert warm and dry. I put the driest garments into plastic bags, leave the wet outside them, place layers of kitchen paper beside them as across the counter the reunion continues.

'What have you been doing? You're on the radio, right?'

He goes faux-modest, a self-effacing version of delighted. 'You've been listening?!'

'Yeah, I tune in now and then. I always thought it was your voice.'

'It's me all right. And how about you, what have you been doing?'

Tracey waves around at the petrol station. 'Running this place, fifteen years at least, I guess.'

Scott bowls over it with a wave. 'I stop here now and then. Your coffee's better than the next place along.'

Tracey smiles, 'We try and keep it fresh, change it often, you know.'

'Well, I noticed!' He rocks on to heels, re-tucks checked shirt over stomach and inside belt. 'You run this place on your own?'

Tracey fixes a firm nod, 'Sure do, look after two boys too.'

'You're a mom?!'

'Youngest five and eldest nine.'

'And you live here with their father?'

Tracey gives a proud shake of the head. 'He cleared out some time back, went to Indianapolis, but we three we do all right.'

Scott glows a little, the feel-good story goes right in to the open heart. 'I bet you do. You always were a fighter!'

And they laugh together, warmly, before Tracey asks if he's got children. Scott pushes spectacles up his nose with a bashful smile. 'Oh no, not me, just me and the radio show, that's more than enough to look after!'

They talk classmates, talk time passing as I walk over and prepare to ask for more kitchen paper, so as to absorb more water from my clothes. 'Excuse me, could ...' falls out of my mouth as Scott interrupts my third word.

'You're British!'

He laughs, shakes his head in disbelief as we drive. 'Sure are lucky you ran into me.' I hear a lot of this, they all do it. Most of those who give me a ride are similarly convinced of my good fortune, they pack an absolute surety that they're the good people, manning the last post as the bugle call sounds on the wave of human scum all around them. Gently, oh so gently, I try to tell them there was no luck. Without wishing to seem ungrateful, to insult this sense of unique goodness, I try to say that – had I not found Scott – I'd have found others of similar heart before too very long and likewise convinced I was lucky to have met *them*. This is only the very nature of the world, and, really, it's not such a bad place. I shudder to think how strong we could be if we had a little more faith in those we live alongside.

Scott tells me he's from Mount Orab. 'I'm just out for a drive really, get some gas.'

I remember Mount Orab from the night before, I see a wet Ohio passing by the small grey truck, miles counting down to Cinci, Mount Orab the opposite direction. Halfway between wanting the ride and confused, the thought flutters.

'Isn't Mount Orab behind us?'

'Oh yeah, but don't you worry about that. I spend enough time there, it's good to get out.'

I smile, 'You always been there?'

'You bet. My parents too. It's home. I'm happy there. I was born there, and I know the land I'll be buried on too, organised my grave, the lot. Sometimes I tell the boys at the cemetery to make sure they keep my grass cut nice.'

Scott turns to me with a remarkably cheerful smile for a man, perhaps not yet fifty, announcing that he's planned his death. He keeps looking, as if inviting a reply to his foresight. The leather of his chair squeals under his large figure. How to respond? I simply grin and he turns back to the road.

'So where are you going?'

'San Francisco.'

'*San Francisco!?*'

I nod. Scott shakes his head, like he's disappointed in himself. He clicks tongue inside jowl.

'Now here you are going to San Francisco, and I've never left Mount Orab!'

What to say? 'But you sound like you're happy there.'

'I am happy there! But I meet that woman at the gas station, and I see her for the first time in fifteen years, and you know what?'

The question sounded rhetorical but, without my responding, Scott's just watching the road ahead silently.

'What?'

'I've not done a thing.'

Here we go, confessional getting under way. I smile. 'You've got your radio show.'

Scott bats that away, 'But I've never left Mount Orab! And here you are, hitchhiking to San Francisco!' Scott leans over, shows me his scalp, points to his receding hairline. 'I used to have hair here!'

He points again to the empty space on his scalp. Skin. Some freckles. Scott invites me look at a corner of his forehead. I don't know what to say. He's got a point. There's no hair there any more, that much is true.

'And now, I realise, I've got red in my hair too. Some of my hairs are red. I don't like it.' Scott turns from the road, straight at me. 'I don't think women are attracted to me.'

Involuntarily, I breathe deep, fill cheeks with air, let it back out slowly. This one's quite a catch. I return to San Francisco: easier territory, a note of optimism to help him through.

'Don't you worry about it.' I talk American a moment, speak his language, chat Hollywood. 'Everyone's got someone out there waiting for them,' (*ha, yeah right!*) 'and hitchhiking to San Francisco isn't all fun.' I cock a thumb to the rear. 'It involves walking through the woods with a bag of wet clothes.'

'But it's an adventure!' Scott is delighted by the bag of wet clothes, he's intrepid all right … my bag of wet clothes leaves his ideal of adventure intact. 'And you know what, the worst part is that two weeks ago, I went down to the local automobile dealer, and I spent three hours looking at camper vans so that I could figure out a vehicle for going cross country.'

'*Great!*' I mean it too, Scott's not all talk after all.

'Yes, but after three hours, asking every question you could ask about a vehicle, I left and went home.'

'That's all right, you can always go back again.'

Scott shakes his head. 'I know I won't go back, I knew it when I was leaving too. I'll always find an excuse.'

I pause, unsure what my role is supposed to be. Does Scott want inspiration, motivation? Does he want quotes from Einstein, Nietzsche and Buckminster Fuller, one of those talks the professional motivational, self-help adventurers hash out at five hundred bucks a pop? Or does Scott just want ears? The truth that I can't tell him is that people do the things they want to do. The things they don't end up doing it's because, really, they didn't want to do them. They liked the idea more than the reality, or else talked about them enough to realise they no longer needed to follow through. That's the bottom line. Now belt up and get on with your life.

'Don't you get scared out there?'

'Not really. People are good. They're just people, like you.'

'But have you ever done anything like this before?'

Truth is the easiest answer. 'I rode a bicycle across the US ... a few years ago now.'

Scott looks at me with an open mouth, holds the steering wheel with one hand and hits his thigh with the other. 'You didn't?'

Nod twice.

'Isn't it dangerous?'

'If it is, then only because of the traffic, and not for the reasons most people in the US think it's dangerous. There aren't so many killers out there.'

We drive quietly a while: woods giving way to regular housing, strip mall. A short line of match boxes is assembled on the distant plain up ahead, clouds moving through a skyscraped horizon where Cincinnati stands and waits. The half-dozen buildings that lift above London are commonplace in the US, so that a full twenty or more cities must have a similar number of skyscrapers. Pittsburgh the other night, Columbus off the Greyhound, Cincinnati today, each one with a central business district about the same height as the Square Mile. My head leans on the window, fingers hooked to the handle above. I look sideways at Scott as he peers ahead through thick-rimmed spectacles, the depth of the glass hitting me with a pathos at how bad his eyesight must be and perhaps always was. In the side-by-side architecture of a car, close but never needing look each other in the eye, one life after the next spills its revelations. Scott sits calmly, both hands on the wheel, clean shirt tucked smartly over his large stomach. For all his lack of resolution, here's a good guy and no less: one more who's just the child of his parents, a boy who became an adult and stayed innocent.

'You still like your job with the radio station?'

Scott gives a sad smile, like he's thinking of an old love. 'I used to, you know, I loved my job *so* much. Sometimes, sometimes I'd get so excited about work the next day I couldn't sleep at night. I loved the records, the music, but the records especially. I loved the vinyl so, so much ... choosing what to play. But now it's all CDs. Well, *now*, it's not even CDs.' Scott pauses, still watching the road. 'They don't need a DJ any more, nobody has to play the records, to take them on and off the players, because the computers line up all the tracks.' He looks at me, as if he's been emasculated, redundant in the truest sense. 'You don't need anyone.'

Scott lowers his spectacles towards the ball of his nose, wipes a finger to the side of his eye as his large heart goes brimming. His voice takes on an emotion different from the breezy cheer of everything he's so far said: 'You only need to do a thirty-minute session to record a whole six-hour slot of radio.'

He turns solemn, confesses money. 'Getting by is harder than it used to be. All I have to do is go in and say a few words about the next songs, and something about the town, and perhaps the football team, and that's all. They can play the recording and the songs without anyone in the studio.'

Scott looks at me, his small eyes shining, a short shrug of an apology on his shoulders, as if he's guilty that he's no longer much use to the rest of us. Out of the corner of my eye, I look at him as he drives. He's totally silent, no more than a man driving his pickup because it relaxes him on a Sunday morning, because he enjoys leaving the town where he grew up, works, and plans to be buried. I see him, with his job that used to keep him awake at night in excitement, and I wonder about the algorithm and the robot that replaced him at the radio station, that since rendered him useless. I wonder who they are and what their personalities are like, what fears and excitements keep them up beyond bedtime. I wonder, who is it, who took this DJ from a local radio station and turned him into a human being for which the world has no further use.

PART III

PALA

Cincinnati – Flagstaff

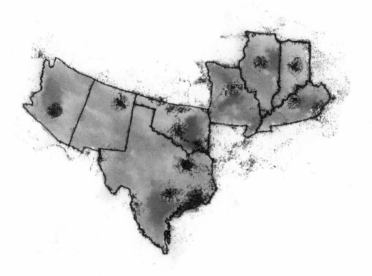

Dow Jones: 15976.02 (+0000.00)

I-275, Kentucky

Tough crowd. Articulated haulage apathy. I stand back, look around the runway: eye height with wide-open, laughing radiator grilles that shine to show the sorry sight I cut, their gleaming teeth and the same names over and over: *Mac, Kenworth, Peterbilt, Mac …* then me again. Off to one side a cab door is open: a black-yellow paint job at the front of a black trailer and pulled in beside a flatbed truck. A brown, Mexican face waves me over, cocks a head with its neat, short-cut silver moustache. Lots of truckers have moustaches, facial hair means a lot out here. The poorer people are kept the more important moustaches become, a proxy for dignity.

He calls down, 'Where you heading?'

'West really … anywhere west.'

He lifts his head to gesture across the forecourt. 'Some of these guys are going your way, for sure. They just don't want to take you.' A bag of orange peel hangs from the inside door. 'I'm driving Florida – Cincinnati – Florida, or no problem I'd give you a lift. I'm not heading back 'til Tuesday,' – three days off – 'if nothing comes your way before then, see what we can figure out.'

Any truck, whatever cargo it delivers to Florida from elsewhere, will always be leaving full of either oranges or orange juice. In return, the biggest import to Florida from the neighbouring state of Georgia is dirt, just dirt, aggregate to shore up Florida as it goes on sinking into swamps and the sea. The driver reaches down to a box beneath his seat, pulls out an orange and with a kick of the wrist he tosses it my way. My palms clap shut around it. It's not the best route to California, but it's perhaps a little closer and, crucially, it's warmer. Just to have a ride in the bank, a hedge on Florida, is not so bad.

*

Fidgeting through from the end of an aisle, I shuffle out towards a till. Pale-skinned kid, a few spots on his chin, a face without a smile wipes down a counter, sees my bag on the floor.

'Where you going?'

'California.'

He nods a sure approval, like it's the right answer. 'Wish I was.'

Even one and a half centuries after the Gold Rush, still America is convinced California offers some sort of promised land. They've even less idea than me of what's waiting down at the end of my road. However potent that fantasy, it seems sad, to have a kid so young seem so jaded with his life.

'It's not that bad here, is it?' I rally him, smiling as my question conceals my own opinions.

He nods a dead face. 'I'd say Kentucky has to be just about the worst place in the world.'

That's some verdict. 'Really? You mean worse than all the other states around it too, not just California. Worse than Tennessee, Ohio or Indiana?'

'I'd say so.' He goes again, 'Pretty much the worst place in the world.'

'You plan to leave?'

'Soon as I can.'

'How old are you?'

'Eighteen.'

'Where you going to go?'

'I dunno. Probably like you, California, I think.'

'Is that the good life there?'

'That's what everyone says.'

*

Smartly dressed, sharp Stetson, proud of his demeanour. A pair of polished cowboy boots, a neckerchief. Piercing blue eyes shine and then – with the smile – what look like teeth too white and square to be anything but false. Beside him in the cab is a much younger boy: black with curly hair, sitting up and along for the ride, but by his appearance, too junior to be a driving partner. Me and the Stetson have passed a few times on the way through the diner as I assessed rides or food. This time Stetson speaks, reveals a silver crown on an incisor.

'Where you heading?'

'San Francisco.'

'Shame. I'm goin' t' New York or I'd've given you a ride, no problem.'

'You think I'll find someone going west here?'

'Yeah, you should. You're a good-looking boy.' The dentures smile at me, 'You'll get someone soon enough.'

His eyes fix shamelessly, propositioning, as those words of Sammy's lonely trucker echo back to me.

'Another ten minutes and I don't mind suckin' on that little dick o' yours.'

*

There are whole volumes to write on the anthropology of the truck stop. We're going to visit a lot of them and you should make yourself at home, get to know them a little. Hours of our time will be spent waiting here and in other places, non-places, elsewhere but, location aside, utterly identical. First point is that, however grim, however beaten down the humans here can sometimes seem, these locations are impressive. The scale: refuelling lines, air compressors, repair pits sunk into the asphalt beneath ailing engines, long lines of diagonally parked, eighteen-wheeler rigs. You have to call them rigs, because this is America and nobody would be seen dead inside a 'lorry'. The stickers on the back of London's goods trailers, warning cyclists of left turns and blind spots, out here they put stickers warning of whole cars getting snagged in the right-turning equivalent: any vehicle could get swallowed by the length and height of the things. Plying my hitchhiking wares, I walk hours between line after line of trucks, appearing under a window or wing mirror, tentatively giving a wave that can be rebuffed with only the slightest flick of a hand. The truckers drive entire decades, motor mileages that would take them to the stars and back a hundred times and more, all at the beck and call of some broker or invisible consumer trend, so that an opportunity to reject a hitchhiker leaves a rare, precious sense of power.

Mile after mile of truck corridors I pass between, hearing only *No* and *No* again. Flanked high on either side it grows dark, long and dark, daylight deep at the end of the corridor with who knows what part of the US economy you're walking between: the ground-up bonemeal for fertiliser or animal feed, the three tons of indigestion tablet for after the humans eat the animals. The view between two trailers looks a lot like the last view of a coffin lowered to the ground: daylight receding to a distant dot. At another window I will appear, and another hostile hand waves me on. The setting is military: the rigs, the rigs, the rigs … stand assembled as if upon an aircraft carrier. Space is uniform, regimented, all at perfect, symmetrical angles and machinery shining as rose-petal dawn lifts on to white cabs. I walk down the grave between two more: so very long and dark above puddles shining up to sky. This style runs right through the culture of the truck stop: martial, angry, bad-tempered. A banner, on the wall above one more saturated-fat diner: *The US flag does not flutter with the wind, but on the last breath of all those who died for it.* Martyrdom is high currency out here.

The first thing an eye settles to in the truck stop shop are children's toys. Children's toys are stacked up waiting for the absent fathers of the road, plastic soldiers man a plastic tank in one more acknowledgement of struggle, a nod towards the idea that any US worker abandoned to a job so hopeless must at least be led to believe their loss of meaningful existence corresponds – however imprecise – to some greater sacrifice on behalf of US Empire. On the roads is similar evidence, and where in the past I'd seen Chinese trucks with templates of military robots stencilled to cab doors, their American colleagues have opted for the silhouettes of fallen soldiers. On one truck, the outline of a comrade leant over the outline of a body with rifle, helmet and the sombre, stencilled words: *We will honour their sacrifice.*

The dining room offers further evidence for this non-specific form of patriotic anger. Some reckless truckers might self-medicate with drink, others infamously pop amphetamine to keep impossibly long hours awake at the wheel in their automotive wilderness, taking up an altered state aboard the Interstate. For the most part, however, in a truck stop restaurant – where diners are also drivers operating their heavy machinery livelihood – the standard grievances of downtrodden, dissatisfied classes cannot habitually be tempered by alcohol. The same tone of chorus rings loud and angry from Atlantic to Pacific coast: *They've ruined this country.* The words sprinkle conversation as liberally as salt shaken to the fries. *Freedom!, Republic!* The only word repeated more than 'constitution' is 'unconstitutional' and in no time you learn that the United States is home to the world's largest and least-trained force of amateur constitutional lawyers. As shouts subside and one man walks away from inevitable confrontation, you see the danger in giving people weighty political words to throw around without demanding that their meaning should first be understood as complex and changing. 'They've ruined this country,' one man shouts after his departing foe. And while I agree that his country often seems to have been ruined, is he talking about the same *they* that I hold responsible?

On this subject of dining rooms, it is a footnote, but it seems an important footnote, and you should know that in each truck stop is no living thing other than humans and the very occasional pet dog kept by some drivers as company for the road. These places are the epitome of what is known in the US as a Food Desert, a place where nothing edible exists that is not packaged or fried and processed beyond all recognition. In a misery that compounds the rest of them, the only hope of vitamins you will find here – and even then its appearance will be rare – is an apple. Even where they are bruised and yellow, where the skin shrivels and lifts from the flesh below it, still, an apple in a truck stop quickly becomes the most tempting of creations, looks like Eden, no matter the wax on its skin or the pesticides it was certainly doused with in the industrial orchard where it grew.

Despite all this, the truck stops are innocent places, furnished with nothing more sinister than the trimmings of dignity that working men must be provided where they are deprived of all recourse to more sincere forms of job satisfaction and humane working conditions. *Professional Drivers*: those words are everywhere. 'Attention *professional drivers!* Will the next waiting *professional driver* make his way to shower cubicle number 3, which is now available for you.' So too is it writ large on the partition to one side of the café, the sticker on the door: 'Lounge for *professional drivers* only.'

You'll witness the way the cabs take them … not just the aluminium litter of heart palpitation-inducing caffeine drinks, so too will you notice the truckers walk bow-legged when they drop from cab, down to deadweight legs swinging from the hips, a wobble at the knee as, after hours at the wheel, men readjust to taking footsteps rather than the press of pedals and cushion at buttocks. Some of them strike up a conversation with me, apologise that they can't pick me up for they are but gasoline serfs, and the company who owns the cab does not permit it. 'They're watching me … caught once more with a rider and I'm finished!' The driver gives an apologetic smile before telling me, as so many do, and no matter how directly his own kindly nature contradicts the claim: 'You watch out with these guys, most truckers are assholes.'

They are not. Whatever the frequent angst on behalf of the country and parts of the world beyond to which their head might occasionally drift, the truckers are a wholly decent lot and if anything are – at core – absurdly soft-hearted. Dolly Parton, Don McLean, Glen Campbell and others like them sing consistent country music, anthems all full of Love. Love. Country, Home and Love. In response the truckers live out their tarmac lives as asphalt slaves, nourished fleetingly by the promise, the unbearable lie that elsewhere, some-where out there, they are moving the commerce for a world that is good, a world that is fair and just and impossibly beautiful, a world in which someone else is living the good life even if they missed out on it, and that even if this is not so in today's America, then at least it once was, and this is a thought no less dear to them.

Trucking is the archetypal American job. In it are the freedom of the open road, the undeniable wonder of the nation's landscape, and a strong dose of individual, noble sacrifice that, eventually, comes to replace the *money-to-be-made* promise that first sets drivers on their journey through perpetual poverty. Still lively with the excitement of youth and the riches that will come, at first it seems a good idea. Ultimately, by the time it dawns that the job is only treading water, living an all but stateless three square-metres, truckers can come to take pride instead in their obedience, subservience, rather than con-fronting the unfairness of the initial illusion of a system that would ever have enriched their small lives to begin with. They often come to resent those who ultimately have less, and are obliged by an ideol-ogy of wealth to respect those who have more.

As ever, the adverts provide the window to the soul. Time and time again, I am confronted with the same advert for engine oil: a large image of a hard plastic bottle, accompanied by what must be the perfect, prototype trucker, the image of a man the rest of the truckers would, I suppose, wish to resemble. The advert is an interesting one, because whereas most advertising rests on an ideal form – the most sophisticated, contented, attractive and healthy of beings – nobody in a truck stop would ever believe something so well-rounded, nourished and content to look like a truck driver. An attractive trucker would be too unlikely, the truckers would spot him as a fake and a phony. The image needs to be highly positive, but plausible. Beside the image of the alpha-driver, I begin reading the text and, seconds later, I realise I'm still reading. In truck stop advertising you find lots of text, for whereas advertising elsewhere is all images, and has grown too busy for words, has places to be other than reading, drivers have got time on their hands. Years and years of dead time is swilling around in truck stops so that something to read in the corridor where they loiter is actually a pleasant respite, a reason to stop their walking back to the cab that will hold the next twelve hours of their life.

The text of the advert belies the trucking fairy tale, explaining how this man, whose image sells engine oil so well, is what is known as *owner/operator*. Owner/operator is the term for a driver who owns his rig, a worker who owns the means of production which, in this apparently arch-capitalist profession, is ironically the outcome for which everyone strives. The image beside the text wears a week of stubble and a US Marines baseball cap in recognition of his – in other circumstances – military prowess. He wears a denim shirt, unbuttoned, to show his relaxed but hardy peace with the world, the front open to reveal a suspiciously clean, virtuous-looking white T-shirt. He wears a silver bracelet in humble beautification of his form and quiet reassurance of his earnings. The man is big, fat by European standards, but no more than a robust, assured weight here in the US.

I-275, KY

Eight hours going strong. Nothing. I'm starting to get rejected for second and third times, recognising familiar vehicle-faces: Louisville,

Kentucky: flatbed loaded with steel rebar. Oklahoma plates: wide berth flatbed, a fracking chamber the size of a small house, covered in dials and wheels to control valves. *CR England*: one of the corporate firms that owns a quarter of the Interstate fleet. *Hunt*: likewise. *Swift*: likewise, but with an overweight husband-wife team waiting in the cab, hour after hour, the wife giving me a sharp shot of disdain and a line of fat fingers brushing me away. Michigan plates: empty car transporter with chains draped upon it. New York State plates: no trailer, waiting on a load. Illinois plates: smashed wing mirror and a young, black driver with dreadlocks, seems inexperienced, like this is his first job and it's already gone badly wrong, he speaks nervously into the phone. Between one set of fuel pumps and two separate parking courts I circle, back and forth, fishing for my ride. A new prospect appears, I get a bite. Refuelling: window down, a real haunch of a forearm hanging out of it and a hand waves me over. The guy is driving a big recovery vehicle, a huge hook and two serrated-steel platforms to take the front wheels of broken-down engine rigs. I hop up the metal rungs beside the door, lean mid-air beside a man in a T-shirt stained with grease.

'Where you going?' There's empathy in what sounds a Slavic voice.

'California.'

He looks up, like I could've said something more convenient. Over his shoulder is a football scarf, Bosnia and Herzegovina, and an evil eye in blue-white glass, to ward off spirits.

'I've got to pick up a broken-down rig outside Nashville, then go west with it. Can get you two hundred miles.'

I deliberate. Somehow two hundred miles isn't quite enough on eight hours walking this place. He gets me, motions like it's OK either way.

'You from Yugoslavia?'

And he nods, gives his chest a thump with his fist, 'Bosniak.'

We talk Europe, he twenty years in the US, ever since he was a child. 'The war' is all he says by way of explanation. We talk a while about the difficulties and assumptions that come with being a Muslim in the US. Ten minutes later and he's gone, pulling out on to the highway, the Interstate spinning roulette below us in a whirling of on- and off-ramps.

It's then, from the corner of my eye, that I see it: a new truck's face pulling in, a red cab, unfamiliar presence on the forecourt, this one entirely new to me and – damn! – California plates. Fresno. This would be California within a week, would be Golden Gate. From Fresno I could almost spit to San Francisco, just too bad he's about to knock me back like all the rest. He faces the other way, his back to me as I walk on over. He fidgets in old papers under the driver's seat, standing on a step as the cold wind snaps tight between trailer and pumps. I keep my distance, don't want to be pushy, get off on the wrong foot, startle him as he turns back out from the truck. A fuel line goes into one of his bathtub tanks, pump rattling as the rectangular numbers on the display spin to hundreds. He looks round. Dark eyes: black iris set with black, shadowy rings, deep brown skin with age and wrinkles across it, purple-brown lips with – as ever – no trace of smile. His turban is up high on his forehead, just above a dot of purple scar tissue. A long beard is tied into a knot from his chin. The eyes are looking right at me.

'I saw your plates, for California, and I'm from Britain, hitchhiking to San Francisco. I wondered if you could give me a ride?'

Broken English, the guy's matter of fact, straightforward. 'I am here tonight. I wait for load tomorrow morning from broker.'

At least he didn't say 'No'. Time to get presumptuous, make my own momentum. 'OK. And then, tomorrow, to California?'

'Arizona. Maybe Phoenix, maybe Yuma. Maybe somewhere else.'

He still hasn't mentioned the word 'No' Anyone would think the chap weren't ruling it out.

'OK. And I can come with you … tomorrow?'

We sit inside the truck stop restaurant, opposite sits Pala. In this country, full of talk of its bravery, it turns out the last fearless American comes from the Punjab. Pala is across the wide rectangular table from me, framed against the plastic-leather of the cushioned back to our booth. He's pure Khalsa, a bun of hair under the turban under the woollen hat, a knot of black beard tied under the chin. Pala looks at me, looks at me straight and I stare back across the table at the human face of a two thousand-mile ride. I'm all set to strike hitchhike gold. He eats a sandwich while I eat the apple he had offered to buy for me and I gratefully declined. The yellow flesh of the fruit tastes terrible but the excitement of the proposition at hand is all that matters. On Pala's wrist rests the steel of a kara, a slight stain of green on the skin beneath it. He's eating his sandwich of cheese, peppers and salad, ordered with strict instruction: 'Everything salad. No meat!'

I've met the only vegetarian trucker on all Kentucky Interstate.

Pala is wearing a tracksuit: an Adidas shell jacket, loose jogging bottoms and trainers laced tight. His elbows are up on the table. I start the charm offensive. We talk vegetarianism. 'The way animals are treated in big farms – *terrible!*' I shake my head despondently, 'The amount of meat in the truck stops – *terrible!*' From the depths of memory I pull out rudimentary Sikhism. I begin to Guru Nanak, I Guru Granth Sahib, all set to build a gurdwara and even make a stab at my five Ks. Secondary school religious education is about to get me to Arizona, a real boon of unquantifiable returns on learning. I'm unstoppably Sikh, will sign myself up, shameless as ever: 'What I always liked about Sikhism ... was the way it really seemed to teach respect of other faiths.' Pala agrees, turban nods and I sense we're doing well. All I have to do is convince Pala I'm sane and decent, and I'll be set to steal four hundred bucks from the US economy, land myself free of charge in a seat already going my way.

'British people know a lot about Sikhism?'

Enthusiastic nodding. 'Oh yes.'

'Here people know nothing, here people think Sikhs are Muslims,' Pala says with disbelief. 'Here man in Wisconsin goes into Gurdwara and starts shooting people because he think Sikhs are Muslims!' Pala laughs blackly. 'President has to go on news to tell America that Sikhs are different to Muslims.'

Over our shoulders are screens of American football, beneath the television sets an endless cascade of orange-pink drink dances high, looping turns through a machine with a paddleboard. Pala insists I keep trying for rides, doesn't know what will happen for him tomorrow. He pauses, as if painted into a corner by obligation and his curiosity.

'I call my broker in the morning. For me is OK, but for him I not sure.'

'But you own your truck?'

'Yes, I owner-operator. For me no problem, you can come, but my broker give me work so he has to be happy too.' And Pala opens his hands. 'If no broker, I have no work.'

Pala looks at me, straight-up, right in the eyes again.

'I leave tomorrow. If nobody else give you ride, if my broker say yes, you come. If you still here tonight, you can sleep in cab. I have two beds.'

I deliberate. I suppose this is the start of plunge, the leap of faith. You can't get a four-day ride from a truck driver without spending four days alone in a truck with the truck driver. I smile awkwardly at the offer of the bed. Pala smiles hospitably, then his smile drops. He stutters out: 'Sh-should I be afraid?'

I look straight back into dark eyes, see wrinkles on that stern brow as I watch the backs of hairy hands on the table's edge, strong fingers holding the lip of metal. Good question, that's a good question.

Laundry Room

'When you tell me you cycle and you like riding bicycle, I know you are good person,' Pala smiles at me. 'Sport is good for a person. If person play sport they have ...' Pala thinks, '... good energy. They have life inside.'

I take the compliment, not sure about this universal truth but disinclined to talk him out of it. Pala waits on a tumble dryer of his clothes: nine minutes illuminated on an orange dial. Washing machines turn all round us, a row of Cyclops humming, their eyes staring down as bedding and jeans spin through suds in a two-storey line of domestic industry. In the otherwise silence, the sound of metal buttons and forgotten belt buckles tap against glass. Pala and I don't know how to talk to one another yet. Right now this feels like even in the best scenario of the ride coming good, it's still the start of a long four days.

'I play field hockey.' Pala grows animated. 'Field hockey is my passion always.' He begins cradling an imaginary hockey stick in a laundry room in Kentucky. From left ear down to right hip he practises his strike with utmost seriousness.

'When I was young, in Baihan, all night in my room, no sleep, I only practise ball control, so many hours. My mother would come up and make sure I was in bed.' Pala laughs at himself, voice softening, 'And when she leave the room, I get back out of bed and go back to practise. She so very angry when she catch me.'

I smile, happy to meet Pala's child. 'You still play?'

'When I am in America I must work all week to pay truck debt. My cousin in San Francisco he is successful architect, he co-signs on loan for this truck. I have to work to keep repayments or me and my cousin in big problem.'

Then Pala brightens. 'But every year I have other cousin who drive my trailer to keep up repayments, and I go back to Baihan to play hockey for two months.'

'For two months!?'

'Yes, two months, every day, because I no afford health insurance, I need to go home and exercise to keep body strong.'

My mind returns to a story from Brooklyn: the pink Himalayan mountain salt that Nathalie's friend sprinkled on everything to ward off ill-health with its minerals. Here in America, you soon find that everybody has their own herbal remedy, hocus-pocus or exercise routine to avoid the financial disaster that is getting sick.

'But new law means soon I will have to start paying for health insurance.'

'You mean the Affordable Care Act … Obamacare?'

'I not sure what the Act is called, but everyone has to pay so now this is another cost for me every year.'

I don't want to say anything, am instinctively supportive of public healthcare but do not wish to contradict the judgement of a working man worried about another expense just to stay poor but alive.

'But I think it is OK,' he goes on, 'I think because now *everyone* has to pay, I think price also gets cheaper for everyone too. And it good for me to have healthcare now.'

I smile, reassured. You can forget all the comment, rhetoric and opinion on the subject of America's Affordable Care Act, all the economist's justifications and counter-claims – right there in those words is the plain, abject truth. For Pala is a man who has deduced that his optimal fuel economy involves driving at 65mph, he will buy gasoline only in those states where tax regimes mean it is cheapest, he knows the value-per-acre of land depending on the crop planted on it. Pala is a walking algorithm of pure capitalism, the human best-interest version of it rather than the trickle-down lie that tells the average American that if the country were allowed to work in their best interests it would correspond to some lack of virtue on their own part. Without a care in the world for dogma, Red, Blue, Democrat or GOP, you can be sure that if Pala says the Affordable Care Act is a good idea that will save him money, it is a good idea that will save people money.

Pala waves a hand away, as if all this talk of healthcare is a distraction from the real issue of field hockey. 'I send money to Baihan for hockey team bus and for balls. A hundred dollar is six thousand rupee, so I send. It is little money for me and a lot for them.' He adds proudly, 'We have only six good hockey fields in all Punjab and one of six is in my village!'

I smile, warmed by the spirit of this global community. 'Do lots of people send money to pay for it?'

'No,' and a grin breaks to full smile at my naïve question. 'Regional governor is our friend. We vote for him and he pay for field.'

Pala pauses a moment as I laugh at my innocence. 'We always play on grass, but tournament is on AstroTurf.' In front of the washing machine, where bedding and underwear spin either side of his head, Pala holds up his hands, fingers taut with feeling and frustration, such anguish that his English becomes temporarily perfect, 'You cannot win a tournament on AstroTurf if you only play on grass!'

He shrugs with resignation, turns to check on the dryer and then faces away and out of a small window to resume hockey strokes. Beside us a woman stands, watching our conversation. She looks familiar, and then I remember I saw her, sitting with a scowl for me up front in a cab: blue-red lettering on a truck from Alabama. She sat alongside the man I guessed was her husband, both times the two of them gratefully taking the moment of dignity they were afforded by the right to dismissively reject the hitchhiker, someone lower down the pecking order than they. In the laundry room she seems gentler, now that somebody else is talking to me and she's alone. Against an overweight torso she folds the bedding, so that when she spreads her arms to bring the corners together, her own body reaches almost the width of both the washing machines she stands in front of. Now that she's alone, without husband in the cab or food in diner, no longer looking down from the altitude of her truck, all of a sudden and she's got time for me. She hears the exchange with Pala, belatedly wants in. She looks my way.

'Where you headed?' Something irritates me, only a splinter of grievance, but grievance nonetheless, from the fact that I sense she wants to talk to me but not to Pala, who turns – lifts from his hockey shot – and looks over his shoulder to check whether he's being addressed. The question's mine, he checks the tumble dryer and goes back to hockey.

'California.'

She nods.

'We're driving back South. Were driving for Maine, came back through this way because my daddy in Alabama had a stroke when we was heading north. He went into hospital and we didn't know which way he was gone go, so we turned round.'

Misery seeks company. I nod, mutter condolences as she goes on folding clothes and I watch, thinking how small she once must have been. I look at the woman: her bucket-sized head, her shapeless, moonlike body, her fat arms made of ringlets, like two giant caterpillars crawling out of her torso, flying as she shakes out blanket-sized T-shirts pulled from the washing machine. Her gut must be two and a half metres all round, about the size of the tyre on her truck. She's a sphere, just four planes that pull towards the crushing circumference at her middle. Sure, she's disabled now and deserves compassion, but still, this size ain't normal. As she stands there, it's as if I can see and feel her own arteries squeezing, fighting, waiting to disappear into themselves and give up ghost. I see her father standing next to her, just as I saw her ginormous husband in the canteen with her. And I wish heart attacks on nobody, but really, was anybody surprised, was cardiac failure considered bad luck and does she expect a fate so different for herself?

My spirit is hardening, I feel it. Age is getting me. I'd once have been all pity for this woman, but life's hard enough already. I've got my own plate to worry about and the injury of her rudeness earlier takes longer to heal. As you get older everything starts disappearing faster apart from the grudges. Those slights get indelible. Your own mortality, the anguishes and setbacks all become insulting enough without people taking each opportunity to be crummy to you into the bargain. There is little left to say. She knows it, gives a short smile, sad it worked out this way. She folds one more extra large T-shirt and places it into a holdall.

'Well, safe journey now.'

But before she gathers the bag straps and turns away, she looks at me for a final remark. The poor woman is so mired in prejudice and American-grade fear she can insult people without even realising it, even when trying to be kind. She somehow presumes she and I to have some degree of kin beyond that of me and Pala. Pala is beginning to empty his tumble dryer behind her, leaving us politely to our conversation.

'Don't go riding with anyone you're not sure about. *Y' know*, anybody who don't give you the *right* feeling.'

And she tips her head towards Pala, the bearded Muslim beside her.

*

Only thin slivers of blue light come through the curtains. Pala removes his turban and hits a light switch in the ceiling of the cab. A beam of solid yellow shines down with Pala at its heart. The bun of his crow-black hair sits proud in its knot at his forehead. Around him on the floor is the rubbish bin with its empty bottle of milk, the plastic cups of takeaway coffee, the trays of past meals. On the bunk, I look up at the ceiling half a metre above my head, roll to my side.

'Pala, do you feel American or Indian?'

Pala shrugs, reaches out to hold the headrest of his chair. He presses it and then lets go again, pausing for thought.

'I am not American really, but I am not Indian. I cannot go back to India, my brain is change.'

'You think you will stay here?'

'I think so. I think so, yes. In five more years I will pay for the cab debt, then there is less pressure, and I can make good money.' Pala gives a laugh, 'People in Punjab think life in America is easy … *ohmygoodness* … it is not easy here, here is only work. I worked four years for someone else. Only because my cousin give me money for this cab and trailer. Maybe now one day I make money. Without cousin, I work all my life for other people.' Pala leans towards me, ardent, 'When you come to America you have to work like three men. If you come and work like three men, then one day you are comfortable. If you come and work like one man, then you are always poor.'

'But without your cousin, helping to pay for the truck …'

Pala's nodding. For sure he's not yet an American, doesn't believe he made it simply because he was good enough, preordained. 'Yes, yes, you need help too. I am very lucky I have help. Without my cousin, I am nothing.'

'Do you think it's fair, the system here?'

Pala shrugs. 'Where I come from, if you have no money and no connections, you are nobody. Slowly, I think maybe because I am here in America, I get connections there, and respect.' Pala remembers something excitedly, a credential, 'You know Pagrat Singh?'

I shake my head. Pala looks disappointed.

'Pagrat Singh is field hockey superstar. He plays defence. In Punjab he is like a god,' Pala waves an arm, 'but he is famous all over the world.'

I listen for where this is going.

'When I go back to Punjab last year, Pagrat Singh know who I am. He has idea for trucking business and wants to ask me questions about trucking in America.'

Pala looks proud. I look over at him, give a smile back at his own: his with an uncertainty to it, as if smiling the smile of someone who doesn't dare hope for too much. My heart gives its small heave, as standing before me is a man of the noblest heart and yet taught to believe that without money or connections that virtue counts for nothing. Framed by the two seats he looks at me, the curtains drawn on our confessional booth in the cabin of the rig, somewhere at a truck stop off Interstate 275. The glimmer of the light shines in his dark eyes. Pala, a messenger misdirected in the sorting office of the cosmos and accidentally landed as some form of highway spirit. I look at him, and it makes me feel so sorry to think this man and billions like him will take pride in slowly, painfully, succeeding or not succeeding in a game built against them, that they will value themselves by whatever they achieve within that game, rather than the goodness that was in them to begin with.

'I think, here it does not have to be so difficult as it is. So much about money here! America is the only country in the world that really, *really* cares more for money than for people. And all our money spent for fighting!'

Pala touches his heart by way of confirmation. 'I think this is wrong.'

You don't find descriptions of the world so accurate as those made in mouths of broken English, spoken from a point at which a vocabulary has been stripped of all but its barest essentials. A few shouts come from the pumps outside: the clatter of a broom falling, the branches of trees hitting their sticks, one against the next, where they wait at the fence around a concrete perimeter. Pala sits on the edge of his tiny cabinet fridge, lifts a leg and unfastens the laces of his shoe. He turns to me, 'What you think about God?'

'I don't really think about God.'

'Why not?'

'Because I wasn't religious when I was young and I went to a school where they made us sing Christian songs, and I didn't like it.'

Pala gives a single, purposeful nod of support and moves to his bunk, his voice rising from underneath me. 'Religion is personal thing, you cannot make people be religion. All religions same principle. My cousin's seven-year-old girl, how I call it? … My cousin's daughter?'

'Perhaps your *niece,* I suppose. English doesn't really have exact words for relations with cousins and aunts and uncles.'

'Why not? Is family not important?' And I consider the question as Pala continues.

'My niece is seven years old. She learn about religion at school and she say it herself. One day she come to me after school and she say, "Pala, all religion one principle."' Half in light, Pala holds up a large index finger with purpose, and repeats, "All religion same principle." And I think, if seven-year-old can understand it, why can't adult?'

A truck horn fires shrill on the Interstate, a compressor hammers air, the hiss of brakes lifts up and trees continue to slowly tap branches above. I lie on my side, the two of us shut within the cab and a stillness settling, both of us suspended in a slight uncertainty, as if, for a fleeting moment, we are genuinely unsure why the world outside the cab doesn't correspond to the words just spoken. Sleep and silence hang inside the metal walls as I hear the sound of Pala's tracksuit, a plastic rustling as he looks for a comfortable position, tossing and turning on the bunk below. Finally, exasperated, Pala gives a sigh.

'What you think about globalisation?

I laugh, the first of so many questions that will cut straight to the chase.

'I don't know, Pala ... more power and money for fewer people? What do you think about globalisation?'

Pala sighs, frustrated, 'I not know either. Things should get easier but they get harder. Man buys a car and then he wants boat.'

The coffee is acid, goes right to the stomach, burns, and then to the brain. I was anxious even before it, sleepless. The sounds of the truck stop not yet familiar, a disturbed night's rest with the hiss and pound of constant activity. Tyres tearing, the rattle of exhaust stacks as the first combustion rips through and out the engine. It's early, dawn only just beyond blue, the sky a single cloud with sun trying to pierce through. Pala disappeared an hour or more ago to take a shower. I've a bad feeling. None of this is going to work. He's not going to take me. The broker will bust the plan. I'll be left with a lost day and having given up that two-hundred-mile ride with the Bosniak. Well, Emre, another fine mess you've landed yourself in. Hitchhiking to San Francisco and still stuck in Kentucky. Most of the adventure hokum boils down to little more than this. Kentuckied, junk time, days gone for good, and no feeling more intense than the heart-on-sleeve balls-up I made of all those job interviews back home. We must, by now, be pushing close to a week on the road and the majority of my miles covered by Greyhound. The clothes in my bag are still damp, my accommodation leaks and who knows when next I'll get a decent meal. Across the café, I watch a waitress wipe down the counter where customers add milk and sugar, and sugar, and sugar to their coffees.

Alternatives creep to mind. The only thing to do once you're stuck in a worst-case scenario is accept it and then figure out a better one. Staying here at this truck stop doesn't seem so attractive, that much is for sure. Even waiting thirty-six more hours for this potential Florida ride seems dubious, and besides, my feet are itchy. Walking at four miles an hour will feel a lot faster than waiting so much as another ten minutes at standstill, even if I'd eventually be driven out of here at seventy. With a steeling of my resolve, I lean to lace up my boots, decide to walk down towards the highway, another on-ramp, stick my thumb out along the way and see if I don't get lucky. Who knows, perhaps the police will pick me up for a ride again? One way or another, it'll be all right, I'll get the hang of it. The world's a tough place, Interstate even tougher, but I'm a match for it and …

'Emre! *Emre!*'

I look round at Pala, his head leaning in to the café and his body hanging from the door handle. 'Where you be? Come on! *We have to go!* Broker calls with load.'

Broker calls with load!? 'And I can come?'

'Yes, you come!' Pala's laughing at me. 'Enough writing! *Come!* We must go thirty minutes ago!'

Lexington, OH

We drove the wrong way. An hour and a half the wrong way out of Cincinnati. My last half-dozen rides, and a day on the road is undone, driving back north of Columbus, up to Lexington, Ohio. Pala's angrier about it than I am: burning fuel for free, waiting around to be sent the wrong way 'and still we not loaded!' He's looking sternly out at the Interstate and shaking his head in firm disapproval.

'How long to get loaded?'

Pala says nothing. I don't press the question, give the man some peace. A minute later, biting at a fingernail he mutters:

'Loading maybe two hours, maybe more. I have to lie in my logbook.'

'Your logbook?'

'Logbook for Department of Transportation. I am only allowed to drive eleven hours a day, but loading time counts as working, even if I am only sitting in my cab and not doing anything. If I have to drive two hours wrong way to Lexington, then that included too and broker still want load in Arizona in two and a half days.' Pala looks round at me. 'Logbook is big problem for me, rules are crazy. If I can only drive eleven hours a day, then what I do for thirteen hours in my truck? I can't sleep thirteen hours.'

'So how will you lie?'

'If we wait two hours for loading, I will say we wait three. I drive sixty-five miles per hour, but say in logbook seventy-five miles per hour so we can drive more hours. If we stop one hour for lunch, I say we stop two hours. Always has to be realistic numbers.'

'Does everyone do this?'

Pala nods, 'I don't want to, but DoT give fine if they stop me and logbook says I drive too long. Broker no give me work if I'm not in Arizona in time. What am I supposed to do?'

'Don't they have tracking on trucks, for deliveries?'

Pala's eyes widen. 'Not yet for me, because I owner-operator. Some drivers very angry about this.'

'And you?'

'I think OK if everyone has it, because some truckers break law so bad, and drive so dangerous, and lie big in logbook. And that makes brokers and companies think it is possible to drive faster than it is. If we have electronic tracking, then not possible to lie like this, and trucking gets fairer because everyone has to tell truth.'

Somehow the dilemma seems so familiar, for people always come to fear and dislike technology, but only really because of the system it enforces.

*

Chemical stacks rise out of the woods. Steel chimneys lift above the trees. Pala and I walk inside together, step into ten acres of plastic on rolls and reels and in boxes. A sign: *No food, gum, liquids or tobacco*. I ask why, when all they have is plastic. Bold and austere, the foreman lays it out, 'We're part of the American Baking Institution. Can't risk contamination.'

'Baking? But it's only plastic in here?'

'Yeah,' he rolls his eyes like I'm stupid. 'Where d'you think they get the plastic to wrap the bread in?'

The warehouse is a steel hull where ten trailers are docked to rubber umbilical ports in the wall beside us. The trailers are lined with chipboard, plastic-encased pallets are deposited in orderly fashion as if silk-wrapped bugs inside a spider's web. Around the corner, a conveyor belt drops small pellets of plastic eternally into a large mixing tub, and in a cauldron below the pellets are melted down to a liquid that is spread thin, poured on to rollers and then pulled to transparent sheets. 'Recycled plastic!' one worker says proudly. 'All of it recycled!' And I'm touched that he would be so proud to be recycling, though keep to myself a thought that perhaps it might have been better were this entire industrial process not devoted to wrapping bread and vegetables in packaging.

One after another, small forklifts go in and out of trailers, between the docked rear-ends of the trucks. The machines glide over floor and ramp, followed in their loading by the halo of an orange flashing light above the forklift operator. High-pitched electric engines whir, batteries buzz, as cubic metre after metre is packed inside and I look around at all of this before me: the two hours we just drove from Kentucky, the $400 of petrol Pala just bought, the truck stops, the next two and a half days of Pala driving to Arizona, all so that a muffin and perhaps a courgette can be wrapped in plastic. I count the heads around me: the whole notion is a curiosity of needless hygiene fear but still, the phobia and madness has created ten jobs in this warehouse alone, still more out on the road and all for a packaging that will be in landfill two weeks from now, with thousands of wasted miles locked inside it, biodegrading across the next two centuries.

Pala and I stand just inside a blue-painted line across the floor, denoting the difference between safety and hazard: as if all this were only mythology, Rama's magic circle around Sita, and the forces of an uninsured evil swirling beyond the blue line. An attendant marches across the line to meet us: bald with sharp facial hair, glasses, angry at his age, at his job, at the absence of sunlight and fresh air in this windowless hull of a warehouse. He barks orders, patronises. Pala fills in a work sheet, then his log, puts in a 6 p.m. checkout. It's 3:30 p.m. now.

'We won't get you done for 6 p.m.'

The attendant snaps it fast. Pala looks confused, understands him only at the second, repeated snapping. We walk back to the truck. Pala mumbles:

'Maybe he will go slow to work after 6 p.m., so that he paid overtime.'

'Really?'

Pala nods despondently, 'Maybe, maybe not. Many places like this.'

And I smile to think of the wages: driven so low to satisfy bosses, shareholders and politicians on the lookout for financial efficiency, but simultaneously pushing people into a poverty where they will create the genuine inefficiency of working slowly, in order to earn a decent wage. I consider Pala's logbook, with every moment falsified to stay inside his regulated hours. To think that his broker expects this falsification, and so too the government and the state troopers – all of them knowing full well that, done by the book, Ohio to Arizona takes four days and not two and a half. With the workers working slowly to receive overtime, and the drivers pretending to drive fast to stay inside the law, you have to question for whose benefit it has all been falsified.

Pala mutters angrily, 'This time I think he is telling truth, but you cannot always know. First time I remember I wait hours at warehouse in Arizona, then second time other driver tells me to give money: I pay twenty-dollar bribe to union lumpers in warehouse.' He laughs, 'Was six-hour wait and suddenly only twenty minutes! This is how world works everywhere, Emre. In Punjab! In America! Everywhere!'

Lexington, OH

Pala sits in the cab of his truck, watching Punjabi television on his phone, interrupted now and then to speak via video to a friend from India who lives in Glasgow. He passes the phone to me, and I see the compressed face of a man reclined in a sofa, his neck doubling under his chin. A Punjabi man speaks English to me in a Glaswegian accent.

'Where are you from in Britain?'

'London.'

'What part?' I sense interrogation, concern for his friend.

'North-east. I've been there most of seven years now. How long have you been in Glasgow?'

He lifts up, moving, his face turning into squares and fudged pixels of brown against the white paint of the walls and a blue settee. The image refocuses and he crackles back through in broad Glaswegian: 'Long enough to sound like this.'

An icon comes up on the screen: green receiver. Pala takes back the phone and says something to the man, vanishing to be replaced by a woman: Pala's wife back in the Punjabi town of Kukar Pind. I give them space, some privacy inside the cab. I walk out into cold air of Appalachia where the incinerators roar heartily and the smell of molten plastic goes up into the night. I wander back inside the hull of the warehouse, my feet following the blue line, painted for safe passage through the crates and pallets and turrets formed by rolls of plastic assembled high above me. The staff are still riding their fork-lifts, all of them in boots and denim, twenty-first century broncos on industrial rodeo. They race through stacks of plastic shrinkwrap kept on rolls, the forklift batteries squealing, humming. With two wheels at the front and one at the rear, the things spin, turning on a dime with whoops from their riders. The cowboys set about racing one another with goading calls at slower loaders, jokes against the manliness of their colleagues as they disappear into the dark holds of the trucks. Orange lights roll round over the long walls of the trailers, before forklifts crash back over the drawbridge ramps that span the gap from the vehicle into the white glow of the warehouse.

Through a small window I watch a man smoking outside. He leans on a wall: all in denim, one knee raised, the sole of his boot pressed behind him in the pose a Marlboro advert once taught society. A truck, longer than all the others, takes its turn at approaching the loading bay, so that the empty rubber of the airlock tunnel reaches towards its rear doors still bolted shut. I watch the rig, the best part of thirty metres long, with a driver peering over his shoulder and out the window to ease the rear two of those eighteen wheels down into the concrete gully where the hatch will dock with his truck. He turns the wheel some four times to move the truck imperceptibly to the left, somehow bringing the vehicle into line as it keeps rolling backwards without losing momentum and scuppering the direction of the approach. A high wind blows through, rocking the trailer, so that he hits on the brakes and gives a further heave at the steering. I watch this labourer at work: so precisely reversing eighteen wheels and thirty metres on to a berth and an airlock aligned perfectly with the trailer. For a moment I think of the economy, the executive bonus and the shareholder dividend that rest thanklessly on the minutely refined skills of this driver, and I wonder if the CEO could reverse this eighteen-wheeler, or make much of a salary if this guy could not.

At one in the morning, Pala takes his turn in performing the same manoeuvre. Just under an hour later, loaded, his engine fires up and, at last, here we go. With the cold air slouched cruel around us, sticking to skin and deep inside bones that sat so many motionless hours in the cab, we are moving, we are gone.

Pala mutters determinedly to the road, 'We must make Indiana tonight or big problem making miles tomorrow. We try to get to I-70 and then we stop for night.'

The two of us hunch forward, as if doing so will bring us closer to

I-70, closer to Arizona and then me to California. Pala sits with only his left arm in his jacket's sleeve, trying to keep it warm against the midnight air that leaks through a hole where the panelling has fallen from his door. Our breath breaks to the blackness in front of our faces, sailing ships of white vapours float out to meet the chill, turning frightened upon themselves before sinking down into cold. The head-lamps on the woodland roads shine white, we gain on a car in front as red taillights blink from the blackness some way ahead, turning in and out of view with the twists of the highway between the trees. Not a word is spoken as Pala concentrates on an idea of Indiana and then Arizona to make one more payment on his truck, and I concentrate on an idea of San Francisco for a purpose that I hope will one day make itself known to me. The car ahead draws closer, our own bright lights joining with it so that together we stick upon that same course through the woods. From nowhere it comes. Deer in headlights. One-two-*three* of them break the trees and leap to asphalt: white tails and spots are caught glowing in headlamps as two of the animals dash clear to the far side of the road and the third fails to make it – gets punched, punched hard by car. Fist. Red fountain blows. Gasket. The rump falls, body turns elastic, slips fast from the front of the bonnet before the white tail vanishes into the dark and the rails of the road keep us moving forward. Reaching over my shoulder, I lean round into a pocket of my bag and pull out my knife. Pala follows the move-ment, looks at the knife and keeps on looking at it so that I realise that whatever the bonhomie, we are not yet comfortable and that I am still a stranger. I lean back to the bag and silently explain the knife by pulling out an apple bought at the last truck stop.

I gesture his way. 'You want some?'

He turns back at the road, considers, nods. I cut a slice. Carefully, I lift out the core on the blade's edge and hand it over. Pala takes it, crunches.

'You British love apples too much.' Pala crunches, jaw rolling. 'What is saying I hear? *An apple a day keep doctor away?*'

Springfield, OH – November 19

Eyes open slowly to the box I'm shut inside. A grey, carpeted roof less than a foot above my nose. Where am I? Why am I moving? Ah yes, the truck. We're already under way, the rocking of a sharp turn into position. Daylight down and Pala in the seat, engine humming. You feel the movement of the whole thing, like a vessel, a ship. You are part of a bigger beast turning slowly with you stowed as cargo on board. Kicking back into my jeans, I jump down. Throughout our days together, despite his protestations that I sleep as much as I want, something will always lead me to feel bad about being driven, chauffeured as Pala works. Every moment of the road, I sit up front, useless but well intentioned. Pala laughs as, clambering down, my foot misses the rung of a ladder and slips into the bin of plastic trays and milk cartons. The nooks and crannies of this place, not to mention the dishevelled panelling and levers, all take some getting used to.

We leave the rest area of last night's sleep, a nothing highway area no more than a toilet and vending machine. A truck comes to a halt in a parking bay as Pala begins to pull out. The outline of a man in the opposite cab twitches curtains and makes ready to sleep, now that dawn has brought drivers less dogged than he back to crowd the roads for morning. Pala gives an upwards nod, points to the sky-blue trailer, darkened with road dust and the word written there: 'Lakhani.'

'What does it mean?'

'It is family. *Lakhani* is very common family name.' Pala looks at me knowingly, 'A Gujarati family.'

'Are there lots of Gujarati drivers on the roads?'

'So, so many Gujarati, but many not driving.' He turns to me, stops to give way to the Interstate junction. 'Gujarati community very strong. They very help new people come here from Gujarat.' Pala watches without hurry for an opening in traffic. 'Punjabi community, they help, but Gujarati community, when a new family member come, all his cousins must give ten thousand dollars.' And Pala points a finger, one by one, to the imaginary Gujarati family lined up in the cab between us. '*Cousin-cousin-cousin-cousin.* Everybody have to give ten thousand dollars because that is what everyone gets when they arrive and big problem with family if you don't give. As soon as you arrive you saving little-little every month for next person to come. Punjabi community hard-working, but Gujarati community so, *so* strong. Gujaratis come here with fifty thousand dollars to start … Gujarati people own all truck stops now,' Pala throws his arms up in resignation at the hierarchy, invisible to all those outside his profession and Indian origin. 'Punjabi people just drive trucks.'

Slowly landscape shifts and I sense one of those precious moments between US geographies: the spaces before the die is cast and you don't see another change in rock or fauna for the next ten hours. The folds of Appalachia are spreading out, East Coast moving further distant so that clouds are more seldom trapped between rock, rains fall less to earth and trees shorten to brush and then to grass. Everything here is thinning towards the plain, humble tabletop of the Midwest. Out the window, the woodlands are first cut open for the pylons that march on the cities, and then the tree height drops away altogether, fading from a heavy, black-painted line along the horizon to only thin, pencil grey as Ohio breaks into Indiana and the forests are over. Trucks jostle all around, swarm into formation: a pack drafting one another close behind to save fuel inside the slipstreams of the leading vehicle. They move together, right-angles of industry flooding as if one organism in a petrol ecosystem where eighteen, thirty-six and then fifty-four wheels go ripping over tarmac … rig-to-rig punching through the air in almost seventy metres of uninterrupted truck.

At the highway edge come the reminders of human life. Evangelists reach out to the Interstate souls driving quickly by. *Jesus is Real!* stands in such big letters that it seems this roadside billboard doth protest too much. Bursts of starlings tear above fields of corn chaff, cut close to the earth where wooden barns wait, timber falling from their walls. Through the land appear muddy rivers, stirring beneath the bright white antlers of a lone ash, its trunk surrounded by the pretty dress of red leaves that lies fallen at its feet. With passing time, agricultural land begins rearing up with more persistence. Industrial countryside gets under way so that here, acre after acre, comes corn subsidy – lands where you grow as much corn as you can, with more taxpayer dollars the more you plant. That's how America ended up with corn syrup in its bread. You simply have to find somewhere to put all the by-product from so many acres of subsidised corn. Throughout the fields go radio masts and wires, each pulling into the distance above combine harvesters eating, gulping corn: thrashing, spewing chaff as silos and hoppers wait in air thick with corn dust. Car transporters line beside us on Interstate and then at the roadside, asphalt suddenly stops and turns to railroad track: the sidings set with carriages, lined up in the toy train set of a yard. A railroad yard. *Shit.* My god but I want to ride a freight train.

Beyond the tracks lie drifts and geometries of construction site: yellow-black plant machinery with ploughs and metal teeth and spindly, conveyor-belt spines. Road-shaped outlines wait, demarked by ropes and the tripods of surveyors, all of it sketched in orange sand against brown earth waiting for humans to one day drive along … new roads to fill with cars and then bring the need for still more roads. The lands run entirely flat, a place so large and unchanging it is almost as if none of the rigs is moving at all. At a stationary scream we press ahead, float silently through a parallel dimension, stuck in a loop of time with all those same trucks that will make this same journey next week and those that made it once the week before. A slow crying goes up from land set with lines of fence, barbed enclosures beside where pampas grasses grow sharp and rough in culverts and from brackish ditches.

At my side, Pala winds his window slightly down to replace the still air with a new one: crisp and scented with the outside. I watch the pane of glass start to reverberate fast, shaking in its frame. I watch Pala, born of the Punjab, but in the image over his shoulder I see the eighteen-wheel rig and the domed, polished metal of the wing mirror bending the reflection of his Khalsa face. The US recedes behind us, flooding away in a fog of roads with trains rumbling alongside, the sleepers pulling in all sound as a thousand tiny hammers go tapping at the sky. Wetting dry lips, I swallow an hour of silence:

'Do you like things about it, this life on the road?'

Pala turns with a smile. 'I see so many beautiful things. America is so beautiful, my friend. I see Washington and Oregon, with snow cover all hills, the green and the white where it melts, very beautiful. Ocean. *Ohmygoodness,* the ocean is so beautiful. So, so beautiful. Very pretty. Nebraska and Kansas is flat, no hills, no turning. Wyoming, my friend,' Pala throws hands left-right with a look of distress, 'Wyoming wind is too strong, is too windy. My truck go side-to-side. I am scared and so I stop. I like when snow starts to fall – so pretty – but after one hour it is dangerous, with very much black ice and so I am afraid. Some things good and some things bad, my friend,' Pala waves a palm of hard, cracked skin, 'like everything.'

In my head I hear a folk voice and the simple-strummed guitar of 'This land is your land, this land is my land', so that I listen to a Sikh trucker meeting Woody Guthrie out on the highways of a new century. I watch his classic profile, set with the solemn gravity of those faces from the five rivers of the Punjab: a face so exactly and only Sikh. From the side, his profile comprises three ridged contours: the curled, clipped tail of his beard never cut, fastened below his chin in a small clasp. The lump in the bridge of a proud nose. The bump of a bun of hair tied beneath the cloth of the turban and under the formless woolly hat. His steel kara on his wrist rests on and off of the wheel, and now and then I will look at him and see the scar on his forehead, which eventually I will ask about, and Pala will laugh as he explains it was acquired in an agricultural accident with a threshing machine when he was eight.

Looking at Pala, somehow I can't help but think of the Sikh army and his ancestors, lined up to drive Sir Hugh Gough and the British from the north of India, the sound of Khalsa drums pounding the air to terrify their enemy. And now, two centuries later, across his profile I see the plains and hills of the Midwest. I see the old high-top barns, a Greyhound bus and constant billboards. Traffic lights flicker from concrete overpasses, lanterns hanging, dancing fandango from steel cables as prairie winds pick them up and push them back and forth. Over Pala's shoulder, the two giant mirrors of his cab reflect his rig, the lower of the two with a curvature that tilts up at blue sky with clouds upon it. Another eighteen-wheeler looms up behind: a radiator grille, set with teeth, stares at the mirror beside my vision of Pala. That image of Pala in his turban, framed against the flank of his eighteen-wheeler and Interstate, is as true an image of America as one could find.

'America it is very beautiful but trucking life, *ohmygoodness*, is so hard to make money.'

'But you still do it. It must be OK?'

Pala looks in his mirror, checks the truck beside us. 'When I first arrive and I hear I can earn six hundred dollars for driving across California,' he turns to me, '*ohmygoodness,* I am so happy.' Pala puts fingers to his eyes and waves them open to show sparkles. 'My eyes like this and I think I am rich man. I think that with only two year of work I can buy whole village in Kukar Pind, but after five years, you realise after you pay costs every month there is nothing left! Maybe a few hundred dollars if everything works OK with truck.'

'It's that bad?'

'Sixteen hundred dollars per month to pay bank for cab. Thirteen hundred per month to pay for trailer. A thousand dollars for insurance. Four more years like this, my friend, and that is if no change in law!'

'What laws could change?'

Pala nods, wide-eyed, as if it must be such bliss to lead a life so naïve.

'Many things change, all the time, to make life harder. For example, California change law on engine emission in 2010, so I have to buy new truck. My old truck was not bad and money OK, but because I now have new truck I have debt, so I have to spend all my life on the road going cross-country.'

'But the changes were good for the environment?'

Pala looks startled, as if I've said something astoundingly stupid. 'The environment? *No, no.* Change is only to stop state bankrupt and sell new trucks. In California is all about money.'

'But don't you have an advantage over drivers who can't work in California because they have old trucks?'

'Yes. But I have to pay four thousand dollars a month for advantage!' It's as if I just don't get it. 'This is *no* advantage. If my truck is free then is advantage, but not like this because I had to sell old truck and take big debt. Broker take 5 per cent of what I get, for this job that is one hundred fifty dollars. It takes two and half days and I get three thousand dollars for Ohio–Arizona, but I have to pay my fuel. My trailer has two hundred-gallon tanks, so that is thousand litres. To fill tank is maybe three hundred ninety dollars.'

Pala gives a cunning wave of his smartphone. 'I use phone to find which state petrol is cheapest. Indiana has low tax and cheap petrol. Oklahoma and Missouri too. I always only drive sixty-five miles per hour, to save petrol, but in my logbook I put time for speed limit at seventy-five.' He looks at me, 'You remember?'

I nod, beginning to think in Pala-English. 'It sounds like you have very big pressure all the time.'

'Big, *big* pressure. I all the time have big pressure on me,' he points to his shoulders. 'This is why I never break law or take risks.

If I lose my licence, I am in trouble, if I lose licence my cousin in trouble. Too big responsibility, my friend!'

A panic seems to enter his voice at the very thought of it. I look at him: the beard that grows right up to his lips in a tight ring, the creases that run parallel to his nose and up to the tops of each cheekbone. Dark rings of skin – looking older than thirty-eight – wrinkle around his eyes, deep brown and fearful. There is a hard intensity to even his resting features, but look beyond that and you see only a man reduced to another labour input, a working human commodity.

'Definitely worst state is Arizona. State troopers in Arizona pull you over for anything. One time, my mud flap has funny angle. State trooper pulls me over, asks me questions, checks my logbook. He takes my wallet and calls the oil change station to check the time in my logbook is correct and I am telling the truth. If he finds I am lying then he give me fine. Truck drivers are very scared of Arizona. So, so scared. Highway patrol there all want to give tickets. So unkind, all just collecting money for the state. Only in Arizona is it like this. Five years ago, people on weigh stations were retired truckers. They understand us, but now it is just young boys with computer. These people don't understand truckers!' Pala pretends to inject his thigh. 'We are not animals. I drive ten hours a day, do not break law, but some days I can drive thirteen hours and I am still awake. Some days I can only drive seven, some days two. I am only allowed to work total fourteen hours a day: say three hours for waiting, fuel, eating, loading and unloading. If loading take six hours, then I am only allowed eight hours driving even though I have not moved anywhere and I don't need to rest.'

Pala takes both hands off the wheel, lifts them as he asks a final question, 'If I don't make delivery on time, my broker not give me job. Then what? State trooper doesn't care about my truck debt, doesn't care about my cousin sign for debt. Then what?'

I-70, Indiana

We pull to the outskirts of a town with no right side to its tracks, a satellite of sprawling Indianapolis. Roads and rails orbit the place with everything stuck fast inside the middle. I sit with thakka dhal and rice in the first of the Gujarati truck stops Pala spoke of. I drink from one of the glasses of water filled for us, slide it away. Pala looks up. 'No good?' I shake my head. Tastes of pipes, of metal, corrosion. He takes a sip, looks at me sternly – 'lead in pipes' – then leans round and orders bottled water from the Gujarati man at the till. Impatiently, he gives Pala a nod to acknowledge that he has heard, but is busy.

Two women are beside us, occasionally and indiscreetly fussing at faces a shade of methamphetamine grey: their blood vessels constricted by the drug, skin bruised by the nervous tic of their fingers, so that all note of colour is long faded. Four glassy eyes are lined with dark eyeliner, one woman rubbing the nose off her face and both of them gurning, sucking mouths in all directions, up and down, lips pulled ear-to-ear as they chew the inside of cheeks. As we arrived in the yard, Pala had told me this stop was always full of prostitutes, said prices started at twenty dollars.

Outside the window a coal power station fumes. Smoke stacks rise from a single concrete shoot, straight up. The two women go outside and I watch them shining with the sunlight reflecting back from their faces, the light looking so golden soft and optimistic from inside the restaurant. We eat our dhal, breaking two large rotis as the women drink down their cigarettes. Across from me is the television. I've been here long enough, should have learned my lesson by now. If you're from Europe, believe in social values and can't help but watch a TV screen placed in front of you, then when in the US be sure you always sit with your back to the TV. The final advert of a commercial break grabs me. Medical product recall: *Has your teenage son developed breast-like swellings on his chest? Risperdal ... out of court settlements have been won, all you need to do is call.*

As if it were not bad enough that teenage boys are developing breasts on account of an unregulated, out-of-control medical establishment, still worse is that here in the US you only hear about it, not as a health warning, but because a lawyer is about to make a buck out of the catastrophe.

After the commercial break, the television show resumes. It starts back with a banner straight up across the screen: *Have I been fathering another man's son?* An overweight man paces the stage like some caged beast in front of an audience, while a man with a suit and an air of authority commands a microphone and stands centre. The man paces, eyelids shine silver in stage lights, bleary eyes ... 'he has to be my son ... he has to be.' In a fit of theatrical emotion, the man storms off stage. For five seconds. Before he storms back ... turns out agony is less bearable away from a camera. An unfaithful woman watches guiltily and meanwhile it is announced that god incarnate, the white man in the suit, has commissioned a paternity test. Suspense builds. More pacing. Man with microphone takes up his pedestal. Audience waits: a hundred of them left hanging. The envelope is opened ... Bated. Breath. I watch, clueless as to how the country wound up here, but with lead in the drinking water and two methamphetamine-addicted prostitutes out front by way of answer.

On the counter is a bright blue charity collection box for some Christian church: *Need help? Drug, alcohol, sexual addiction? Domestic violence, codependency, abuse.* A whole catalogue of disaster that the good Lord can help with, if only he shows up in Indianapolis before it's too late. I look around. 'Too late' looks like it has already been and gone. The whole scene looks like rock-solid, ecumenical evidence for God's non-existence, only you have to hope people go on believing, for without brazen, spiritualist irrationality I've no idea how anyone would ever entertain making some positive difference in such a sorry place as this.

Pala and I return to the truck, where a woman is seated – door open – in the cab next to us. She rises to her feet, to stand on a step while stuffing fat, pale breasts back into a scarlet bra, forcing pink nipples under the wire frame and into their cushion. She looks up, suddenly hard and accusing. Black-painted nails are on the end of two fingers she immediately sticks up at us, tongue licks over lips and then slides out from between the V of her fingers, rattling the air. She hoists up her jeans from the tops of her thighs and, with sallow flesh squeezing out of denim, tugs them back up to her waist. Pala and I keep our heads down, say nothing, climb into our truck as she moves towards us and disappears below the height of the door. Then, looking across at Pala and his regular profile, up come fingers, a hand, groping, palm against the glass and its skin pressed yellow-white like a raw chicken fillet against the window. She keeps her hand there, pumps it at the glass. In and out. In and out. And then trailing downwards as the engine shakes life into the cab. We pull away and into the release of brakes I breathe relief and turn to Pala:

'Did you see that? What was that place?'

Pala looks at me, then allows himself a small laugh. 'My friend, there is worse.'

Now I can say it. Out of earshot I can state the obvious: we have an underclass problem. My god but we have an Underclass Problem. I do not say it in snobbery but more a sort of honest despair, for nothing will improve with only the comfortable myth that society's down-and-outs are all a noble, virtuous poor who deserve better. That those people deserve better cannot be disputed, but nor can the fact that many of them have fallen to ebbs that don't seem so deserving or worthy as it would be nice to believe. We are all blighted by their condition, for their existence mars our own even where it is invisible, and if this is the language of the nineteenth century then perhaps that's just because the scale of the problems to which we're returning belonged in the nineteenth century and ought rightly to have been left there.

We entered, I don't know when, an age too minimal in emotion and reserved in expression for people to deploy the energy our social problems came to demand. Nobody wants to speak out of turn, the idea of causes or campaigns grow unfashionable, and no notion of social justice can be made to seem as desirable as the safe, aesthetically pleasing lifestyles we are presented with so consistently that we now know nothing else to aspire to. The problem with your average twenty-first century, Western bourgeois is that it's just too big a knock to the self-esteem to fully and comprehensively grasp, without the comfort of humour for things not exactly funny, just how our societies have been demolished. We'd sooner lie to ourselves and argue the world fair than admit we have been cast into an age of terminal irreverence, where no loss of human life or potential is so profound that it cannot simply be put down to collateral damage. Where does that leave us, with so many in need of change but everyone afraid of any alternative on offer? Side by side, Pala and I drive away, bumping over the crumbling highway, the truck stop floating into the distance beside ruined and abandoned garages, all of it under the shadow of the chimney stack's single, concrete shaft, its torrent of smoke blowing ceaseless into the sky.

St Louis, Missouri

SMS: 'I think I could make it to California, maybe Yosemite.'

The road changes again, treeline floats down to floor. Indiana gone, Illinois corn receding, it's Missouri's turn to fill the corners of our windscreen. God Belt is coming. Religion rises at the roadside the further south you turn. The billboards, once content to probe at the curiosity of doubtful drivers, become more forthright: *Where will you spend eternity? Jesus Christ has the answer!* We cross a wide, stagnant culvert that plunges under the road as the air above goes hovering with translucent wings and long abdomens, floating in a tight knot of insects that breaks at the push of glass. Deer carcass litter the highway. A headless, red stump at the end of an empty neck: white tail still up and limbs folded inwards on themselves. Evidence appears for the fact that humans occasionally get taken down too: the low-wage labour or inmate work gangs that collect up debris or repair old, iron Armco barriers. We pass a signpost: *Hit a worker – $10,000 fine and lose your licence.* There is no mention of life, only cars and cash. You hit 'em where it hurts.

The chaotic cocktail of religion, casinos and sex shops appears to light up their wares. All over the world, the closest friend of God is always Vice, and just as religion becomes more apparent, so too does the market for satisfying the frustrations of those attempting in vain to live by it. Casinos rise, hands of neon cards flutter in and out of light. Beyond them – the lettering more discreet, large but utilitarian – are signs for sex shops and adult movie theatres. The truck and landscape take it in turns to move across one another, so that sometimes we and the truck move forwards, while other times we stop in our tracks as the world gives the engine a break and instead rolls past to help us on our way. Coming out of the last of the Appalachian range, the bright line of the road pulls ahead, and in the distance stand final mountains, where lights skirt across lower reaches of the hills and then abruptly stop, tracing an electric version of the snow line to mark the point at which humans lose appetite for inhabiting the barren slopes above.

From the dark night a fitness centre pulls alongside us, an island of commoditised health in this emerging wasteland of obese gluttony. Expanding guts will be one further feature that marks the drop south. Across the Interstate a two-storey gym looks out on evening where, from the second floor, a silhouette labours at a cross-country skiing machine bathed in fluorescence. A man comes at us, stationary, but skiing out from the horizon: his arms and legs reaching and swinging, reaching and swinging, above the overpasses and ornamental trees of a lifeless car park.

Time rushes by, forever comes quick. The hours go slowly and then go fast and then stop altogether: a single consistent feature the immediacy we keep motoring through. At the side of Interstate, green signs mark the miles we put away and your only hope is that you can cease paying attention to them, remove them from your vision or else enter into a tyranny of nothing more fulfilling than three-hour counting sessions that destroy all capacity for thought beyond 3245, 3246, 3247. Now and then, I will realise I must have successfully shut down, stopped counting, because suddenly it is 3295 and then 3296. Labouring against weariness, I look round to Pala.

'How many miles to Oklahoma?'

Pala laughs back, just as he'll always laugh at my innocent questions.

'Miles? You ask me miles and I never know.' He picks up and flaps a notepad he has positioned deliberately to conceal the dials on his dashboard. 'If I look at miles I go crazy. I think in hours.'

In front of us, to the right-hand side, is a flicker in the twin shafts of light our truck presses into night. Suddenly, only the centre of the road is illuminated ahead of Pala, while the hard shoulder and grass fading from the road immediately in front of me has dimmed. Pala clips his tongue on his teeth in annoyance.

'Light problem. Always that light. We must stop and repair. State trooper can pull us over and give ticket.'

At a small gasoline stop, little more than pumps and a hut offering snacks and drinks, Pala and I stand in the gravel on the edge of a forecourt. The hood of the truck engine is up, exposing conchs, pipes and a fan concealed behind a grille. Lifting away the cover fitted over his headlamp, Pala reaches in and unscrews the bulb. He holds it up to the lights of the station, inspecting the filament a moment before deducing that it is still intact. From the pocket of his jacket he pulls a small, blue-yellow canister, a red straw in its nozzle that Pala, reaching forward, directs down the long, metallic tunnel from the bottom of which he unscrewed the bulb. He gives two short, sparing presses to the nozzle of the canister, so that oil shoots with a hiss over the sound of wind and the rumbling of another truck engine.

'You tell me if works,' says Pala, screwing the bulb back in, before turning to the steps to the cab.

In the dark I stand as he climbs up, sits back to his seat with a bounce, and turns on the lights: one comes on, the one in front of him, illuminating half my body. I lift a thumbs-down and see Pala slump. The lights go off to leave me dark again. A moment passes before lights hit me full in the face, soak across my clothes to turn them sheer white. From out of the bright, Pala is looking hopefully down at me. I lift a thumbs-up and see an uncertain smile from him. He swings from the cab and jumps back down.

'It will be OK for Yuma. I repair properly in Fresno.'

Pala looks over, better spirits on him as he pulls a paper bag from his pocket and withdraws two large, square muslin bags that he hands my way.

'You like masala chai?'

I give a laugh at the idea of masala chai in Missouri, nod as I take the bags from him.

'I do logbook. You go in cab, small kettle near my bed. Make hot water to make us chai,' Pala opens his palm, draws a medium-sized circle in it with a finger. 'This much sugar right amount for me.'

St Louis comes up. Road points south. In my head I see our journey as if made on a map, traced along the contorting red arteries, their numbers inside balls of pale blue. From each road sign and utterance, reliably, every place name hits me twice. Altamont, Greenville, Troy … just as America is smitten by some romantic perception of aristocratic British refinement … so do I feel myself falling as guilty to my own fantasies, whereby the most backwater of US places can seduce by name alone, tickling at the European calm that comes from ten centuries of mistakes, religious war, famine and ensuing pessimism. The muggy history of Indians and of pioneers, of the European colonialists and then American-sized doses of twentieth-century Dream – all of it, ranging from fabricated to rotten to illusory, invokes such senses of adventure that even if the frontiers have long since been settled, and even if the great excitement that once was America has been shockingly mismanaged, still it all sticks fast in place names that to an American must sound no more exciting than Portsmouth, Ryegate or Rotherham to a Brit. Rationally I know all this, but inside me it persists all the same.

Hands cupped around the warmth of the chai in the cold of the cab, memories of home coax at me, woven from dark blue clouds on the glowing horizon, above where the river keeps flowing muddy at our side. But listen to me, talking of the river as if it were only some large stream … This river we follow is the Mississippi. In the night it moves beneath us, and Pala, the river and I are all of us watched over by the enormous steel arc that marks St Louis a hundred metres into the night sky. A band of metal shines with the city lights to crown a monument that you are compelled to look upon, perplexed as to whether you find the thing stupendously captivating or only utterly pointless.

The city slips. William Burroughs' town envelops us and we enter with the cab swaying under Punjabi folk music. Pala and I drink from plastic cups of sweet masala chai. He searches through a glove box, finds a cassette tape among the paperwork, and strings, recorders and drums start to rattle a rhythm. Women sing and saris swirl inside the cab as the St Louis night opens, hands clapping time while horns go blaring beyond the confines of Pala's rig. Before us loom the locking triangles of a truss bridge powerfully large on the skyline. Piers of stone paddle in the waters of the Mississippi, beneath double-decker girders spread like dark, iron rainbows from bank to distant bank. Between the girders of the bridge I watch the freight go clattering across, exchanging west for east and lights reflecting in the water as a series of yellow engines shunts slowly forward, pulling three miles of cargo behind the words *Union Pacific* and – damn – I grit my teeth … but I wanna ride a freight train.

Lights sprawl. Floodlit cement works burp beneath high turrets of still more old industrial bridges over the Mississippi. Coal trains line the rails, patient and haggard, assembled all the way to the edge of sight in both directions. Into the whirlpool of concrete and overpass we fall, drifting underground, spiralling down between vehicles far below the water. A family holds pace beside us, shut within the car: children sleeping on the back seat, tiny scenes of love boxed inside glass and steel and motoring hard to get through these badlands, these places they call Flyover Country because there is nowhere here to reach, no destinations, only land to travel through on the way to somewhere else. The Missouri countryside regroups from out of the onslaught of the city, roads rise up over hills and mountainsides cut purposefully open to make a flatter path for our journey. Pala sits, his hand drumming the wheel, occasional rain falling on the windows, and music from the far side of the world sliding up the glass to meet with the wind of the South. From the higher hills you see the lights of America split to segregated neighbourhoods either side of the road. A colony, a lifeform spreads from the single red-white illuminated line of Interstate. Glowing logos float like buoys upon the night. Hotels and drugstores wait, breathing slow life through automatic doors as they stay ever open to satisfy this country and its timeless, all-hours need for the possibility of commerce. Pala points out of the window, speaks above the roar of traffic on this thrashing section of the highway.

'Very many sign makers for Interstate now go out of business,' and he moves his hand, points to his phone. 'Everyone just see place on map now, check rating. Having sign taller than trees not important any more.'

We drive on past floodlit crosses, under the coattails of a lightning storm far away, the breaking white forks trying desperately to reach earth through the gathering black of the horizon. We drive under the ragged, thin-stretched skirt of cloud, from which rain starts to drop heavy on the windscreen. Wipers wave fast for but a brief thirty seconds, after which we burst from under the edge of the cloud and the drum of falling water. Pala turns to me, hits the edge of the wheel and points enthusiastically to the cab.

'You drive the rig some time. Very easy.'

In both wonder and fear my eyes swell. 'You're sure?' and then I add what seems a prudent truth: 'I don't have a licence.'

Pala leans in, curious. 'No licence at all?'

I shake my head, watch Pala still pondering his initial proposition. 'OK. Maybe not good idea.'

Oklahoma City, Oklahoma – November 20

A truck stop. The sun is up and has replaced the night, so that it must be another day, although there is little on which to base that thought, and certainly no real amount of sleep inside the truck. Interstate time and its endurance driving has the tendency to grey to a single moment, identical in its repetition and a sense of monotony improved by few things other than considering the countless times Pala and thousands like him have made the same journey. The windscreen from which you watch all the world comes gradually to take the properties of a television set from which you cannot avert your eyes. A hiss of brakes bites us to a stop, and a part of me struggles to believe we're not simply arriving again and again at the same place. This latest one lies apparently somewhere outside Oklahoma City, though there is scant difference between it and the one that we passed at Indianapolis.

A small mobile trailer leans beside a metal hull with tyres stacked and the veins of air lines moving from it. Paratha are served, paper plates slid down to us: hot flour, ghee melting into a brown-spotted surface, spinach slipped among a dough spiced with garam masala. At the centre of the table is a bright yellow pickle, the colour of turmeric and made with chilli and cauliflower. It sits beside a bowl of yoghurt that we ladle out with pieces of paratha torn in hungry hands. I eat paratha and look at a landscape of prairie. A man brings more food: a Sikh dressed in a Levi's shirt and a cap that reads *God Bless America*. Another plate is laid down. Pala insists I take a second paratha, refuses more for himself. He smiles, puts palms to belly.

'Soon you will be walking again. I still be sitting in truck. No more food for me.'

At the far side of the trailer an old, all-American trucker, with a silver moustache and 'Hell' tattooed on his forearm, ladles dhal on to a plate. He turns to the opening of a door where a black man in a denim jacket appears. The newcomer tips the peak of a baseball cap as he addresses the room, direct but courteous: 'How the meals here?' Then he speaks as if to himself, 'I do normally like Indian food.'

One of the Punjabi men lifts his plate a little off of the table in offering.

'Would you like to try some of my meal?'

They sit together, the newcomer starting to talk excitedly, and I listen as a black man and a Punjabi man sit in Oklahoma talking about Jews, gentiles and the FBI, moving swiftly to Jack Ruby and the assassination of JFK in a conversation of supremely assimilated conspiracy, that stuff so integral to this nation and its existence almost as pure as physics. People mostly expect the world to be rational, and so when they have to comprehend the irrationalities of inequality, poverty, sick people on the streets ... they expect to find a rational answer to why things are that way. Conspiracy theories are people trying to impose rationality on the irrational. They have to make it a plan, a predetermined and sinister agenda because reality is harder to get your head around.

The second of my paratha disappears to crumbs as I watch Pala's eyes discreetly on three Sikh men gathered on stools in the corner, hands planted on knees spread wide, sharing earnest conversation. Now and then a voice is raised angrily, met with lavish nodding of heads so that despite their irritation, everyone in this highway parley seems to be in something resembling agreement.

In the kitchen a woman peers out from under a headscarf. In her hand a pair of tongs turn a chapati fast from side to side, the white flour swelling on top of the blue flame until a bubble flicks with sparks of burning flour and then bursts in a charred ring. The owner fills a jug of water and walks towards us, placing it on the table, just as in the Indianapolis restaurant with the corroding pipes, only a day but the better part of a thousand miles ago. Pala points at the jug of water, chin low to the table. With a playful smile he looks at the jug and then at me. 'You drink first.'

Back in the truck, a toothpick hangs from Pala's mouth. He leans over his logbook, trying to calculate how many hours he needs to claim he has stopped in order to fit within the law. He mumbles to me, words sliding down the length of the toothpick:

'Always so funny, community. Everyone meet, and complain about everyone else, and then they carry on, and feel better.' Pala shakes his head with a smile, muttering to himself while rummaging under his seat. 'Funny, funny, funny.'

'What were they arguing about?'

'No argue. Only complain. Something about religion and gurd-wara. All too stupid.'

'You don't take religion strictly, do you?'

Pala puts down his logbook and toothpick, hand to chest in indication that he is about to explain something precise.

'For me religion is personal thing. My father is very strict Sikh. He is why I no drink or smoke, but strict religion is no good. Religion is supposed to make happy. Strict religion is not religion, it is just strict! When we were children, our father make all of us pray every morning and every night. With my father there, was always big burden on our head.' Pala looks firmly at me, a hand on his head. 'Every day I feel it! With burden on your head you cannot be happy. And all religion comes down to same principle. My cousin's daughter ...' Pala points back in time to Cincinnati. 'She seven years old, she come home and say, "All religion come down to same principle".'

The sun is warm, bright through the windscreen of the cab. Outside a hosepipe is left on, spilling gulps of water from the barrel over which it rests, so that dark puddles move in tendril-like shapes cut from the white concrete and running towards a drain. A man washes the cab of a nearby truck, a high arc of water spreading from the hose, droplets lifting with the wind where a faint shadow of colour splits from the spray and picks – pink-through-green – out the spectrum. The scene prints on to a blue sky, where trucks go thundering on the road beyond us.

'Why aren't you strict Sikh now, if your father was?'

'We all would be, my brothers and sisters too, but in my family big trouble when I was twelve, when I was thirteen. My brother make big problem for family.'

I wait as Pala for the first time takes off the cloth that covers his hair, leaving the large, tight bun of shining black revealed on his forehead.

'My brother was a terrorist. But not a *terrorist* … he fights for free state in Punjab, against India, because Indian politicians take everything from Punjab.'

Pala talks fast, his voice accelerating as if in some urgency to be believed, or perhaps to quickly clarify the detail in such complex truths.

'The police come to our house. They beat us all, beat my whole family. They beat me twice, and always they ask "Where your brother?", even though I don't know. My brother he put us in very big danger, so one day my mother sends me to go and live with friends in new village where police cannot find me.

'I go to live with my friends, and there I am not strict Sikh. If I did not go to live with them I would still be strict Sikh now, would not come to America, would be priest in Punjab.'

Clouds pass quick outside, and sun turns shadow turns sun. Pala reties his turban and I watch, imagining this man before he had age in him. I think of how the gentleness of his spirit could have been of no concern to police officers intent on his beating and the information it was supposed to bring.

'Where is your brother now?'

'In California. There he has,' Pala snaps his fingers and thinks, 'I don't know word in English. He has …'

'*Asylum*,' I offer. Pala snaps his fingers again.

'He has asylum but cannot travel. He is restricted in UK, in Canada, because he still works for Punjabi free state and India say he is a terrorist. Britain and India still very close friends, so he must stay in US. He still collect money, he has meetings here.

'I used to give money, because I also believe in free state. Our politicians they look Punjabi, but they are not Sikh. They all educated in America, do not care for our people, only for money. I believe in Punjabi independence, but not in violence.' He gives a short laugh, 'Problem is … without fighting, nobody give you anything.'

I look at Pala, speaking to me in English, his thoughts always so simple, tender but straightforward, always with the innocence of a younger man than he, his spirit untarnished. And this man, who now I have spent the last fifty hours sitting together with, I wonder who he is when he is not in English? I wonder if he is more stern, his nature in any way less pure, if he loses his temper faster, has some assured self-importance or makes fewer jokes. I wonder who Pala is, when he is in Punjabi.

Clinton, OK

Horn fires urgent. Pala moves to overtake the car in front, just as a truck rears up in the outside lane. A second too late he sees it in his mirrors, utters fast from his mouth, 'Ohmygoodness … OK, sorry about that!' Pala pulls sharply back in with an apologetic wave of the hand, the other driver steaming alongside us scowling. Pala looks round at me, opens his eyes wide in an imitation of fear.

'Driving in America is very easy, no like India. In America nobody is driving on wrong side of road.'

Oklahoma goes by outside. The land is flat, green, unremarkable: a covering of baize as far as the eye reaches in any direction.

'Did you drive trucks in the Punjab?'

Head shakes. 'Not big rigs, mostly farm machinery, not big difference.'

'Your family are all farmers?'

'Some. Punjabi people are always, through all history, very good at farming. Gujarati people work smart, but Punjabi people work very hard.'

Pala cocks a thumb out at the green nothing that is Oklahoma. 'Give Oklahoma to Punjabi people and twenty years will be very good farmland. Now is only ranch and empty.'

A smile spreads over my mouth as I consider this annexation of Oklahoma by the Punjab.

'What would you grow?'

'Many crops. Oklahoma could grow many vegetable.' Pala straightens, raises his finger as he always does when drawing my attention to a point of particular value, 'Best farming in America is almonds! You buy one hundred acres in California and plant almond trees. This is good life, my friend! Many Punjabi truck drivers now doing this. One acre of almond trees is one thousand dollars of almond a year. One hundred acres is one hundred thousand dollars for very little work.'

'Almond trees won't grow in Oklahoma?'

Pala shakes his head firmly, 'Wrong soil, wrong weather.'

'What do you grow in the Punjab?'

'Everything grows in the Punjab: food for eat, for animals, grow cotton, many farm opium too. Opium good money.'

'For medicine?'

'Sometimes for legal drugs, but if farmer has permit for two fields then he grows four and sells two fields on black market.'

He turns to me with excitement, 'If you have money, Brazilian land very cheap and fertile, because of rainforest. Very good for growing crops. You buy land in rainforest, make big profit.'

I laugh, startling Pala as I shake my head, consider what chance exists for those millions of years of trees.

'What funny? I mean it. Good soil.'

'Of course, Pala, it's a rainforest!' I laugh. 'What about the environment?'

Pala looks at me uncomprehending.

'What you mean "the environment"?'

I'm smiling. 'The trees! Breathing in the carbon dioxide and breathing out the oxygen. Millions of different animals and plants. You know … *the environment!*'

Pala turns the corners of his mouth downwards in light contemplation, then gives a little grin, the rig pressing forwards as another sign flashes at the roadside, placing us on the road for Amarillo and the Texas state line at only a few hundred miles' distance. We look over at one another, each with a smile for the other's complete difference of concern.

I-40, Elk City, OK

Tyres through water noisy as hell, Interstate torn apart and sinking. Great plumes of spray jet from each truck wheel ploughing forward alongside us, like the boughs of galleons smashing against waves, the roar of rubber amplified by rainfall pooled upon asphalt. Grey cloud is scraped in a comb-over for the blue sky, holes inside it opening fast to let through the sun as it goes exploding in quickly appearing and disappearing bursts of light.

The horn of another rig hits loud, crashes from four large klaxons above the cab, the horizon twisting wide in the curved metal. Brake lights flare like nosebleeds running down the droplets of our windscreen, sun comes back again and the wheels of cars under us turn in constant, heaving calm. Their small shapes bounce as bowling balls between the lanes as white skittles of cloud stack upwards where Interstate meets sky. From above, I watch another muted argument rage in the front seat of a family car, heading west with New York plates.

We keep going, Pala drumming his hand to a sound I never heard. We keep going. And then there's a howl, and at last, finally, it is here. We've arrived, we're underneath it and all movement stops: a watch face, a well shaft, a stone falling fast upon us. Big Sky comes down. A palm outstretched, a meteor strike, a Navajo Chief, Custer's last stand, Big Sky crashes on a land suddenly so small, freezes everything in the last movement of its final motion. It's ended, it's over. Each of us becomes only some breathing fossil of our old life. All trifling of humankind waits: the laminate for the courgettes, the family feud from the family holiday, it petrifies and then bursts, splits into only shards of sunlight through cloud breaking over such splendid, rotten Big Sky. First the thing makes you larger than life before kindly, so gently, proceeding to show you your own death, and then suddenly, beneath the closing jaws of a vice it is all simply so terrifyingly flat. Vertigo sets in and then we are squashed and then we are flying and then all I can see is sky. The clouds make up forests, nothing but flat, the land lies down, exhausted, not a crease to its face. We fly into the flat, yellow grass scorched now and then by old fire. The sky is titanic, is crushing us. The trees have gone. I see sand and rock beginning to peer out. A rumbling comes momentarily from the surface of grooved road below, comes just after the sign *Bridge Ices Before Road* where Pala and I shoot off over the plains and into the space above a wide creek. Beneath Big Sky we turn invisible, are all nothing, as if the land has shrunk into a footprint visible only by magnifying glass. The wind is all that moves, so strong you can see it across a land of prairie, flooding grasses set as waves around where horses graze and a fantasy of buffalo roams wild. Then, after a while, it becomes routine. Euphoria wears thin, we move on, driving away from the short-lived romance, the memory of Pala's playful chuckle and prescient words: 'I don't know why you think Oklahoma so special. You wait seven hours and then I ask.'

The state draws west ahead of the rig. Grass shortens, first it pales and then grey-brown patches of thicket peer as if a rash spreading among it. In the harsh geography rising there come the first signs of industrial livestock, stepping slowly forward to replace the industrial crops. The shapes of cattle range across a land emptying of life and then, gradually, black cows and bulls in turn change form and merge instead to become the outlines of hoists and swinging pulleys as the scenery of oil country begins. Pump-jacks start to creak, but also at the roadside comes that familiar old and discontinued machinery, the remnants of rusting pipes, drills and arms. Grass thins still more sparse towards mud, dirty brooks widen and fields ever less kept shoot with only a sporadic growth of cypress trees. Another landscape appears behind Pala's still unchanging face. Old, dead pines lean at the ground: white, split and wizened where the bark has fallen, or else charred black by lightning strike fires, so that the trees are now all naked – disgraced, exposed – branches contorting desperately back in at the trunk to conceal a little of their lost majesty. Black-yellow oil tankers bisect Interstate, looking fell as they roll over the rails towards Texas, pulling to halt and change crews at towns where water towers are the one thing still growing above the horizon's middle. The bales of hay that once waited beside the Interstate are gone.

At the roadside, in charming forms, the upkeep of human society comes to an end in shacks and settlements no longer worth the investment of time and miles it takes to reach the nearest populations. Gradually, the natural world begins to go about its own business, reclaiming those structures left to it by humans, painting them with thick dust now and then etched into by old rainfall. A caravan lies abandoned on deflated tyres, the last post before finally even nature gives up on growth, turns scrub, and I see America's first wind turbines, spinning electricity back towards places where people still live.

At truck stops, stepping from the cab, air lands cold on the skin, but its chill does not penetrate as it once did, and keeps kindly out of the bones. For the first time, Pala begins to leave the cab without the protection of a jacket. The people grow larger, rounder, then faces turn Mexican, Hispanic. Cowboy hats appear, rims pulled up either side of the head. Tastes change. The truck stops cease to serve black tea that is anything other than iced and with lemon.

Beside the drinks stand, the faulty vending machine drips hot water into a quickly filling basin. One more large, cardboard sign shows a Greyhound bus and bargain-price rides to casino destinations behind us in Oklahoma and further west in Nevada. More bus journeys that lead to great, green handfuls of cash, feathered out and held strong in a well-manicured palm. Only in America do you realise the least glamorous, most important and all-round unsung institution of functioning democracy is perhaps nothing more remarkable than advertising standards.

I-40, Exit 131, Texas

'Emre, is correct sentence: "On Interstate is only old people"?'

I turn to Pala, 'Not sure. What do you mean?'

'Look.' Pala points to a passing car with two patches of grey hair in the windscreen. 'On Interstate you only see old people. All young people are in cities and all old people in countryside. And all old people all love past and all young people love future.'

'Perhaps say, "On *the* Interstate, you only *see* old people".'

He mulls over the difference between his attempt and my suggestion, waves a hand as if in dismissal of the English language and its unreasonable hair-splitting. He can make do. My tired head rolls and I watch the landscape pass another giant three-dimensional cross of Christ, appearing at some distance and then falling away to be replaced by a sparse scattering of pump-jacks emptying lonely wells. A dusty honeycomb of dry rainfall marks the windscreen, sunlight picking through to land warm on the face. Trucks drive towards us, the walls of white trailers reflecting a sunset so that barges of gold ingots come floating our way from the last blue sky. Pala straightens with purpose. The stints of driving have become longer, our conversations replaced by the sounds of the truck through the landscape.

'In few miles we stop. Very special place.' Pala smiles, always so happy to share his delights of the roadside. '*Soso* quiet. This is rest area, but also … underground, tornado shelter. My favourite place in Texas. You see why.'

We pull in as a Punjabi trucker walks back to his cab, a Fresno address printed on the door, plates registered California. Pala taps me twice at the knee. His face doesn't move, his neck doesn't turn as the man, dressed in a turban and with a kara at wrist, walks past us.

'Look,' Pala gestures with his head, 'another Muslim.'

Legs returning to motion, the normal sighs come from us both as we open the doors and jump down. The air is warm, but under a breeze, and this the first stop since we left the cab briefly in Oklahoma.

'This very nice weather,' says Pala, as we amble towards a low wall. I stretch bare arms, dressed in only a T-shirt for the first time in days.

'T-shirt weather.'

Pala smiles. '*Noooo*, not T-shirt, not for me.' He feigns a shudder. 'Only in India.'

We stand together, next to a sign warning *Rattlesnakes! – do not stand on rocks*. Pala is beside me in his turban and jogging bottoms. Side by side we look out on land and silence big enough to see. Miles in either direction, and all the way to the horizon, is only scrub. The feathered tail of a windmill turns, twitching with slight changes in the wind. Pala leans to look out of a viewing telescope, into wilderness, rotating its barrel with a rusty whistle. He steps back, excited.

'Look! People! Out there!'

He ushers me to the telescope and there, at the centre of the black circle, is a tiny ranch and a barn the size of a doll's house.

'How they live out here?'

The spindle of the telescope squeaks as I rotate through almost 180 degrees, see the house of a neighbour, another tiny ranch, miles away.

'They have neighbours,' and I return the telescope to Pala, who bends to peer in, gives a nod. We stand together beside the telescope and nothing but silence,

silence,

silence hangs all about. I reach down, touch toes, crack my neck. All of it amplified so that the only noises are those pockets of air squeezed from cartilage. Pala does the same. I look at us both, making time for stretches, eating our diet of vegetables and lentils.

'We must be the healthiest people in any cab, in any truck, on any Interstate in the country.'

Pala shakes his head.

'I have a cousin, also Punjabi trucker, vegetarian. Every morning in his cab he does yoga for half an hour. He very healthy.'

From the left-hand side of where we stand silent, a moth flutters over the space between us, rising and falling sharply as it climbs and drops between currents of air. Pala smiles at me, says it almost in a happy, mystified confusion.

'Here ... it is so quiet.'

And we stand there. Me and Pala, and Texas.

Amarillo, TX

My eyes loll, and I almost sleep a few more dreams of Interstate and mile counters. The bottom of the clouds turn pink, the world glowing in a last light. Silhouettes of trees are sketched in charcoal, and the yellow beech leaves flutter down towards a few wisps of cotton left behind on the tough, harvested shaft of picked plants. Gateposts stand at the end of driveways so long the houses cannot be seen: gateposts without gates, because a gate would suggest the need for some sort of fence and this land would require many millions of miles of fence if ever it were to be enclosed. The fields behind each nominal opening are marked by only a few tin feeding troughs and watering points. Trees grow short, dogged and hardy, until eventually disappearing inside bursts of black gorse. Dots of earth appear, the textures of occasional grass, growing green-yellow among a ground marbled red-black with iron and dark, igneous rock.

With the hardening terrain and loss of forest, the deer carcass have long since disappeared, and the roadkill has become dog. Wild, stray hounds and jackals lie with old fur pulled into felt by hard rubber, all stretched on the loom of the road where broken bones lie ivory-white. Telegraph poles flank the Interstate, grey gorse and black grasses weave to mark the path of dry rivers where once water must have run. A thought of peace comes back to me, for I always loved the deserts most of all. I fell in love the first time I met one, in Kazakhstan, where the wind tore every day and uninterrupted towards the sun as it slipped for the horizon. I still love the way a desert will kill anything that refuses to respect its hardships, that doesn't heed the lack of water and strength of heat. It makes me sad that energy helped humans defy and disrespect these rules, that pumping water and cooling air opened these places to us, even if only temporarily. I've got faith, nature's patient, plays the long game. One day we will be kicked back out.

Across the growing sands and earth, pipes stretch in long rectangles to carry water over the wastes and towards ranchland. I blink, breathe, gag as Pala announces that something is coming: 'Very sad here, so sad'. And then red desert turns to a solid patchwork of black-white for the cow farm, the abattoir: where the entire land starts stinking with the heavy smell of pre-dead beef so that United States can eat burgers every night of the week. Even as we drive at sixty-five miles an hour, still the cows keep coming, with dust hanging behind cattle as if in a moody premonition of their fate. Feed towers line up, and then a geography of beef begins: acres of it, a blur of bulls, incessant cow, the land moving black-white. A pod of them fatten at a trough, beneath a metal building where smoke stacks climb like bagpipes. Above them stands one small, ominous incinerator chimney, a thin trail of smoke leaning away as commodities feed in the shadows.

Eventually you realise that in sights such as these, you see America simplified. The politically disempowered people I meet, so many of them so vaguely furious but in return given rights to: 1. Meat, 2. Petrol and 3. Guns, in order to ease the loss and make them feel big again. Excessive meat, excessive automobile and – the ultimate token Power to be wielded by the powerless – recourse to firearms. The costs of all three are externalised, so that they are easily absorbed into a trillion-dollar economy, or else exported overseas. The emissions from the petrol are borne by the voiceless environment, a few million subjugated in the Middle East, and the far-off places that will be first to sink under the world's rising seas. So too the meat: its costs are felt in the deforested lands that grow the feed, and the world's poor, priced out of grain so that Americans can fatten their livestock with it. The costs of the guns are the only ones that are truly borne domestically, and even then they are a non-monetary cost: a few dozen daily shootings, a toddler accident here and there, a mass shooting every so often and the following tears of some parents, lovers, friends and siblings. Meat, Petrol and Guns are the rights Americans are now given or will gladly trade in exchange for all that might once have constituted freedom. The occasional mass shooting by a snapping sociopath … a man altogether haywire and yet more sane than any European would dare realise … is only the cost of the American Way.

Pala shakes his head as we watch the animals flow through and away. Gradually, they pass behind in the ever-cold judge of the curved wing mirror. The windscreen reveals clouds breaking above the horizon, pulled delicately apart as flocks of birds fly through golden levels of light. A closed-down filling station, grasses streaming blond and long from all around its pumps, grabs at the corner of my eye and then is gone just like everything else. Train yards of Amarillo wane: the old boxcars left to rust on forgotten rails as only the splintering canvasses of graffiti artists. The discontinued carts hold large and colourful flames, monsters, names, numbers, angels, octopi and harps, all painted in bright, human colours against indifferent desert. Kept at a distance are intermodal flat-loaders with their ocean-shipping containers that see so much of this world. And I consider whether the old boxcars are jealous, or were exhausted and ready to retire anyway.

Pala starts as he remembers something. He says it slow but excited, points at what will be another gift of his roadside, another curiosity in store for me.

'Watch now on left. Fun thing. We stop and take photo if you want?'

I shake my head, 'We don't need to stop. What is it?'

And Pala just nods that I should wait and watch. It appears as if the menhir of Stonehenge but newer – newer and automotive. In a line, watched closely and captured by a line of photographer-tourists, are a series of cars, bumper down, planted on their heads in the desert earth. Perhaps a dozen of them stand so, parallel to the road: automobile statues stuck in the ground, axles and wheels baring their backsides to the setting sun.

The mood has changed to one of purpose. Pala is an athlete preparing himself for a last performance that will seal his fate on this delivery, complete another petrol Odyssey to pay one further instalment on this cab. He has a concentrated composure, as if it's the final of the field hockey tournament back in Kukar Pind and all expectation rests on his proud shoulders. After this we drive all night, Pala on the verge of recouping the last of that time dropped waiting for the load in Ohio so far away.

'There must be another six hundred miles?'

Pala waves a hand in dismissal, same reply as always. He takes a bite out of thin air, imitates a chewing sound and says, 'I eat miles.'

We amble from the cab to the truck stop glowing pink, green and blue, where the two of us sit across from one another, eating quesadillas, our refried beans and cheese squeezing out into a plastic tray with the thin shreds of lettuce. Between us are a small pile of sachets, torn across the top, and spots of chilli sauce dotting the table of this, our last supper.

Pala pulls his hand down his moustache and into his beard, dislodges a piece of lettuce. 'Do I have food in my beard?'

I shake my head. 'Do I?'

Pala shakes his head, scrapes back his chair. 'No. Now we go?'

I give a nod and we rise from the table, walking back across the polished floor of the truck stop. Pala looks round at me, 'This is our last stop. We take a photo.' And he turns away, towards a tall man in a basketball vest, walking out of a burger bar. Pala approaches him, his phone held forwards.

'Excuse me, sir. Can you take photo of me and my friend?'

The man startles at the stranger, then makes a mock protest and throws up his arms, voices brashly, 'How much you gonna pay me to?'

And he laughs, but somehow not enough, because it seems too close to the truth that so little in this land is untainted by thoughts of money. He takes the phone, points it at us quickly for the photo. We all pause. And then he hands it back to Pala, walking away with languid steps, pulling his jeans back up. Something in Pala's nature stops him being agitated by moments like this. They roll off his back, and with a smile he turns the small screen towards me. There we stand together: the white lights of drinks refrigerators over our shoulders and displaying a neon bell beside us. Pala in his turban and beard, with me held under his arm, the two of us shifting into large, hazy pixels by the movement in the camera as the photo shot. Pala gives a hit to my shoulder, and we move towards the exit, past the large, brand new Peterbilt truck cab that waits, illuminated with its polished exhaust stacks, shining black tyres, revolving slowly on its turntable inside the entrance.

Pala stops in order to look up at it, casts his arm as if it were a painting. '*Soso beautiful*, and so much more comfortable to drive in.' I watch him standing in his tracksuit bottoms and jacket, a slight smile of aspiration and America on his face. I watch, remove some centuries of history, and behold the way Pala's great-grandfather in the Punjab must have looked at a new plough or a fine ox.

'Next time we drive together, I have one of these for us.'

The cities of New Mexico wait ahead in order to fall behind us, to join the history of the journey as its future gets smaller. Pala's face is calm, quiet in the shadow of a darkness. The highway lights scroll again and again from his lips over his bearded cheek and then disappear across his turban, returning him to dark in a moment that is then replaced again with light.

Waves of Interstate circle one another, gliding concrete crescents with cars cresting at their edges. The highway has been set down as a nest of frantic light, stretched into an electric tangle with Albuquerque throbbing at the centre. A purpose takes hold of it all, an intent gathers in which everything is moving on rails and the glow of the city. A giant circuitry stands illuminated beside us, bright trails making their way home as parcels of human code shift across the motherboard. Heaviness settles in the cab, I can feel a sadness is coming, growing inside me. I know I'm about to leave, to lose my friend, leave Pala for good and probably never see him again. This time tomorrow I'll be alone again.

From far away, out of nowhere, lights drift inexplicable among the black as cars head down minor, unlit roads towards Interstate. Flagstaff, a city built at 2,000 metres, will take me in the morning, and if ever you have been to Arizona then you will know the one place you go to after Flagstaff: that hole in the ground into which we pour all of our superlatives. Pala and I sit beside one another, looking into highway, leaning forward into our destination still 500 miles of night away. Two trucks appear behind, looming large in the mirror, each illuminated like houses at Christmas. Bulbs dance all across their radiators, around windscreens, up and down the trailer and the underside bars that stop things falling between the wheels as the two matching, glistening trucks roll beside and then ahead.

'You like them?'

'The lights?'

He nods. I shrug, 'You?'

'Strange people. I not understand these truckers. If one light out, all lights go out. More money, more complication and more likely state trooper can stop you. For what?' Pala laughs his gentle confusion. 'To show people you have a truck with many lights?'

I smile at his straightforward spirit, without need for consumerism and immune to advertising and show, because there is no ego in Pala's understanding of what a success in life might be. I think of the children he will one day have, once his wife has moved to California from Kukar Pind. I imagine how his second generation will be, not knowing the hardships Pala experienced so that they did not have to, nor the humble life he knew and left in order to provide for those who came after him. I see Pala's second generation: I see large, new trainers, I see a gleam inside the stone of an artificial diamond ear stud, I see large pickups with lights across them. And then I look once more, and see only Pala, dressed in the shapeless puff of his jacket and the hat over the top of his turban. He looks round.

'Emre, You never say why you come here in first place?'

'To America?'

'Yes. Or California?'

'I came to America for a job, and when that was cancelled, I decided to come to California, and to San Francisco.'

'Have you seen San Francisco before?'

I nod, 'Once, maybe five years ago, but only for a night, and after dark.'

'First time I saw San Francisco is when I feel I am in America. The skyscrapers and the bay, the bridges. I think for the first time I am in a real city.'

'Why California?'

'My cousin here. Makes easier.'

'And why America?'

Pala shrugs. 'Different places for different people. For me, America is OK. My mother's sister in Ontario, Canada. My friend has a restaurant in Frankfurt, cousin is a pilot in Luton, England. I have another cousin in Leicester. I know one man who flew to Guatemala, he live there two months then bus to Mexico, there one month, then he pays the donkeys,' Pala clarifies, 'traffickers … to smuggle him across border. Now he in America twenty years without papers. Each time they turn down his application for status, he appeal. Eighteen years he appeals. Sometime the Americans make an action to send him home but they need all of us here illegally, for the farms, the services. They very need the Mexicans for the economy, the low wages.'

Impassioned, Pala continues, 'I want to help my sister come here. But solicitor tells me waiting list is fifteen years for family visa. Very long waiting list for India people, for China, Nepal too. Many Indians go to UK on student visa but not to study, only to work. My sister want to come to US so that her children have opportunities here.'

'You think they will have opportunities?'

Pala waves a hand, gestures that there is no way of knowing. 'Money in America is only for educated people,' he hits the dash-board firmly. 'Not trucks. I want family here, and my children can have education. Not trucks for them.'

How to phrase it: 'And it's worth the *sacrifices* you make?'

'Sacrifices' doesn't hit home, Pala doesn't get the word and so I go again. 'You're happy to have such a hard life, to make things better for your relatives?'

'When we first come to US, to England, we live five person in a room and we send money home to help family buy land. Now we have a room for all of us, we helped our families buy the land back home already. We cannot keep sending money.' Pala drops his tone to a sense of almost sad finality: 'And so now we make lives for our-selves here.'

He draws a loop with his finger. 'It all go in circles. US politicians complain when we send money to India, but then our children grow up in America, they say, "I don't care about family land in India" and they sell all to pay for house in America. All money come back to America plus more because Indian rupee is now much stronger.' Pala arches his shoulders, points his two hands towards the oncoming Interstate, palms facing inwards: 'Immigration is a very long-term thing, is everywhere, is never stopping.'

Winslow, Arizona

To the sound of the Indian subcontinent I awake. A reciting of prayer ripples round the cab, Pala sitting at the wheel of his truck with his eyes closed and hands out in front of him. His phone is on the dashboard, rattling slightly with the sound of a chanting that fills the cab. As I sit up on my bunk, Pala looks over with a smile, rain trickling down the windscreen behind him as he says simply, 'I pray,' and he points to the phone. 'It come live from Punjab.'

A laugh escapes me at this sight in Arizona, as rubbing my eyes I ask, 'What you pray for?'

'I pray for no state trooper and make delivery on time.'

Rain lancing, charging at us as Flagstaff and 2,000 metres nears. It's cold outside. Out of the purple dawn, the early morning light brings Cholla Power station. Drifts of black coal are piled high outside as if tumours growing on the lungs of the land. A steaming lake of hot water surrounds cooling towers, turning mounds of white mist in the cool morning, as the cloud goes piling upwards and, ghostlike, a power plant sails eerily towards us, steam squeezing fast from the chimneys.

Out front is a sign where someone has seen fit to make a tourist attraction of a working coal plant. This country is in love with coal. They can't shake the idea that progress should contain an element of a dirty, black fuel that had its day two centuries ago. The secret is that the future to which we all stumble has in it no rationality, only emotions and aesthetics. In an age so full of information and statistics, anything that can conjure a little feeling of the heart becomes a thing more precious than information, no matter its accuracy. In the twenty-first century, knowledge is vulgar in its abundance and feelings come to possess great beauty, if only for their scarcity. Coal is an aesthetic of industry and industry an aesthetic of progress that can resist all argument.

At the next stop Pala disappears for the bathrooms, growing progressively more concerned and distracted by the delivery deadline. On the runway outside is a small chapel made from the trailer of a rig, with steps going up to a door cut from one of its walls. A sign invokes God as an antidote to loneliness, one trucker milling uncertainly as I pass into the stop, stretching my legs and watching a candle in a jam jar beside a cardboard sign. The flame breathes up and down the glass, lighting the dark skin of a forehead and cheekbones, leaving pools of shadow inside the sockets of his eyes. He is tall and broad, clean shaven. He turns his head to one side so that the truck stop lights catch lucid eyes with focus and thought still in them. This one's still on planet earth, no space cadet. He blusters into his speech: says he's leaving Los Angeles, the place is too busy for him, he knows lots of people, it's hard to start again and get free of trouble. New Mexico, New Mexico is the land he wants, knows people he can work for in cities across the state.

The sign reads: *Vietnam Vet – Going to Albuquerque.* He looks a bit young for Vietnam, but to be honest, I now suspect that in the US 'Vietnam Veteran' describes as much a state of mind as the particulars of any military career. The role can be played by almost anyone. If you can't think straight, if you hear a ringing in your ears, if you can't abide the institution of a family, home or workplace, and so take to living on the road with your life on your back, you're only ever a short hop from being a 'Vietnam Veteran'. In a nation so full of storytelling, where white lies and dreams rub shoulders with every fact, none begrudge a down-and-out their own bit of fairy tale. Give anyone thirty years in this country, living off of Interstate, and soon enough you'll have bred a brand new Vietnam Veteran. Those guys will go on existing long after the last of them have died … Whatever story helps most in the hustle. I watch a man walk up to him, with a dollar bill folded to a V and proffered downwards. The beggar reaches for it and then, in just an instant, the man pulls it back from his outstretched fingers and laughs. My eyes gape at what

I have just witnessed, but then something worse takes place, for the comic Samaritan puts the bill back out and I half-hear and half-read his lips: 'I'm just kidding ya.' I watch as the veteran laughs along at the gag of which he is the butt: a man either so broken, or else so accepting of his lowly rank, that receiving this currency pays for any of the dignity he might have expected.

Like cheerful friends, the driver and veteran part company, and quickly, like headlights on a signpost, the veteran and I make an eye contact so direct that now I cannot just walk past him. We're both humans, and I at least need to explain why we cannot help: that we passed Albuquerque last night, are now going the opposite way. We talk road, talk war, he lifts up an apathetic hand, a *this is my lot* wave of it, his fate cradled in the palm. A tentative judgement comes out of me, a reference to the war machine.

'It's a shame the politicians didn't learn their lessons, went and sent a load more young men and women off to Iraq, killing a load more innocent people while they were at it.'

He speaks a slow lament, 'That's right … suppose we never asked to go in and keep the rest of the world safe, but we was the only ones could do it.'

'Keep the rest of the world *safe*? But don't you think the world became more dangerous *because* you invaded Iraq? And there were never any weapons of mass destruction to cause danger to anyone anyway.'

He sighs with wasted life, moves effortless and without scrutiny to the government's second line of reasoning. 'That's true, but then, regime like that, where Saddam had palaces and some of his people couldn't even afford to eat … we had to end that.'

The poor guy, it feels so harsh to say it but, my word, what an idiot. Seamless, with the memory of a goldfish he moves, just as the politicians did, from one justification into the next, as soon as the first falls down. It was about weapons and international security, or maybe it was about liberating Iraqi people. He doesn't care what it is, so long as something explains why the injustice was not an injustice, especially now his own life has fallen victim to it. Beyond that though, still more surreal, serene in its irony, is the veteran in a US truck stop, busily criticising the injustice of Iraqi wealth inequality, as he sits next to a cardboard sign and begs the money for his next meal.

'Well,' I speak as bright as I can, as if it is only a curious, casual observation, 'you're in a very rich country, richer than Iraq, with lots of billionaires living in luxury, and there are people everywhere here asking money for food.'

He barely pauses for the response, sees my point and from out of a deep sigh, eloquence comes.

'You right, ain't no country got exclusive rights on poverty.'

*

Like all the rest, it came to an end. They all do, they all have to, that was the deal all along. To share so much, then have the person drive away from you at a roadside that meant as little to you as the one where they pick you up. It can be hard to believe that perhaps you just made a friend. We leant in towards the centre of the cab, above the gear shift. We hugged. 'I really don't feel like you are a stranger. I feel now I really know you and you know me!' Pala smiled it at me, and then we both just nodded our agreement with the sentiment as I stepped down and he prepared to head south for Yuma.

We parted at a junction outside Flagstaff, he left me to climb an Interstate bank and head into the town. Snow was on the ground, and I shook out my legs, jelly, as I stepped from the cab and pulled back into the straps of my backpack for the first time in a half-week. I pointed to my legs as I stepped away from the truck, exaggerated the way they buckled underneath me, danced a jig and, with Pala looking down from the window, we both laughed. He was there in the windscreen, with an empty space where my own outline had recently been. He smiled and together we waved as the hiss of brakes sounded farewell and the red cab pulled away. It seems only a detail, but for the last four days, since we first met, I had not spent a cent of my own money. Pala refused so devoutly, time and time again. He wouldn't hear of it, nor accept even a dollar. That man from the Punjab seemed to have in him every warm characteristic of humanity, that many others seemed to have lost. I wondered often if Pala was rare, or if everyone was a Pala, only sometimes too shy, scared or wounded by life to show it.

PART IV

WEST

Flagstaff – San Francisco

DOW JONES: 15927.05 (-0036.22)

Flagstaff, AZ – November 22

Storms have landed from the Pacific: tropical currents forced high by desert mountains, turning cold and flashing downwards. The rain halts, the clouds are light grey and air brisk. Snow is ready to fall on Arizona and its desert. A first few flakes come down as I walk towards Flagstaff and they grow heavier, blowing frenzied circles on the wind. Hitchhikers, a brace of them, are gathered with their belongings at a reservation in the middle of the junction. Snow falls. At a distance, a woman works the traffic, approaching windows while a man waits with their belongings. The two of them are dressed in heavy, winter coats: toggles and large buttons, a few frayed holes. He stands with a cardboard sign, she carrying an old-style rucksack, military green. A car stops at the traffic lights beside her: the window goes down, I see an arm appear, snaking out with a couple of dollar bills, folded in half and pointing straight at her. The woman leans forwards, mutters something into the car. I catch 'god bless you'. The window rises. Together they stand between me and Flagstaff and whatever difference waits in our futures, still manners oblige me to say hello to someone with the same immediate purpose as mine, another member of the same, rare highway species.

While she moves over to another car, he shuffles my way. On top of his head is a woollen hat, light blond hair coming out either side, thin stubble. His smile of greeting reveals no front teeth. Black-blue roots. Crack-cocaine, class A-drug front teeth. He smiles at me, the tunnel of his missing teeth gaping large, the eyes sparking with erratic gleam. In me a resentment rises: in part because he has in him an air not to be trusted, but more because I know that all those passing by us, and who have already passed me by, feel that he and I are the same.

His mouth moves, chill air whistling at the tunnel through his teeth. '*Friend!* Where you headed?'

'Up to Canyon. You moving somewhere warm?'

'Sure am. California!' He speaks so light, breezy, no breaks between words as he goes on, 'On our way back from Texas, went there to bury my mother last week. She died.'

I look at him. The casualness of his words offends me, the familiarity of telling me such a thing, and telling it as if only to report a bag forgotten in their previous ride. I'd rather he were lying than telling the truth in such a way.

'We got a good ride last night, all the way from Gallup. Four hours.'

From a blanket at his feet comes a sudden, twisting movement. The blanket winds, contorts and then white teeth rise up from a golden coat as it barks. A dog appears: long fur and a wet, black nose. The man looks down, snaps suddenly:

'Shut up, Little Shit!' He looks back to me, 'That's my dog. I called him Little Shit.'

The dog recoils back to blanket. I look across at the man, flat, right through him and the hole in his teeth. I've gotta go.

Down on Flagstaff, overnight it snowed. Snowed properly. The weather has subverted Arizona's desert. Trees and rooftops are white, Grand Canyon at winter: curtains of dripping water skirt perfectly at each building as the snow melts from the rooftops, dropping into the white below and thawing pools of black road where it lands. It's cold. I follow the highway, daunted by the monsoon season in the making. I don't rate my chances of staying dry. Clouds alternate a constant white-to-grey, the mountains come in and out of view. Flagstaff streets stand with snow washed clear, lines of black rails where tyres break the white and pull water off tarmac. Slush and slurry form in the gutters and the shops, saloons and cafés of the town stand in perfect, two-dimensional order as if a theatre set. The mountains above stay white.

On a level crossing, the bell rings and barriers lower with their warning stripes and red sirens. A large, bright headlamp comes up ahead: rolling discs of metal, four orange engines and then freight train. Slowly it rolls by, intermodals and each one asking me, daring me get on, coaxing and goading as they ascertain if I really mean it or if all of my train fantasy really is just the stuff of dreams. I feel the weight of my bag straps at my shoulder, they weigh with doubts of a stumble and a missing hand, a twisted ankle. We're alone at the roadside, nobody to see my jump, but still my feet stay rooted. The opportunity rumbles on in front of me, still coming and I figure out how to time my run: what would I reach for to grab on and haul up, what direction would the train take me? Train keeps coming, going strong, keeps coming as I consider my options, deliberate whether or not – and it's gone. The last carriage disappears and in my vision, a train is replaced once more by a town.

Cameron, AZ – November 23

The floor of the creek is covered with thin, yellow acacia leaves. The jeep points down at an angle of forty-five degrees, though it feels like more: my body is falling forwards, held fast against the seat belt. There's a clearing up ahead, the rain's still coming, the snow's still melting to reveal red. The water's muddy brown, filling up slowly in a pool at the foot of the rockface. Streams come cascading over the sides. I'm not sure I've ever ridden in an off-road vehicle when it was actually being driven off-road. The trail that got us down here is loose, gravel and shards of stone, large boulders either side.

'Why not? Sure, I'll come take a look at the spring the Navajo showed you the other year.' I said those words less than five minutes ago. I open my mouth again, looking out the window at the diagonal land. 'Can't believe you're going to drive this thing back out of here.' I think I say it in impressed rather than sceptical tones as the jeep points down. The guy's from Los Angeles: baseball cap, California suntan, well built, shoulder muscles pressing at the leather of his jacket, a fleece collar, a ready-for-anything cut to him. His girlfriend dozed most of the last hour in the passenger seat, the two of them perhaps thirty years old, hers a made-up face with eyeliner and foundation applied for the drive to Colorado. He takes issue with my doubt, jeep rocks east and west as gravity rolls us down to the spring he wants to show us, buried in the rock with 'the cleanest water I've ever tasted!' He turns to me: 'Of course it'll get back out.' He bounces throughout the vehicle, bounding. The guy's a puppy, nothing but energy and enthusiasm: 'This is an off-road vehicle, man … It's four-wheel drive, dude!'

Out through the windscreen there's a slope bigger than all the rest. The slight pause opens and pulls the girlfriend from her sleep.

She looks up, she's going to say something. Right in front of us is a pool of brown, muddy water. Maybe half or a whole metre but either way it looks deep. You can't see the bottom. Driver swings the steering wheel round, floors the accelerator, and sticks it straight in, nails the engine. High revs. We displace a great wave of muddy water, it flies out as we fly in, carrying all of our momentum up to. Thud. Turns out it was a whole metre. Three heads jerk right forwards, the jeep's pointing down, straight down. Silence. No engine hum. We're not moving. The bonnet is half under water, steam winding out from under it. The girl's head falls backwards in the passenger seat in front of me, she shakes, shakes hair out of her face as her head resettles and she looks at him. Silent fuming. He ignores her, he's concentrating, not even looking her way. 'It's OK, baby, it's OK.' I spectate. He turns the ignition. It revs to nothing. Revs to nothing, nothing. She looks round at him, then down at his feet. 'Ohmygod … ohmygodohmygodohmygod … there's water coming in!' And she's not wrong either. He revs the engine. It starts, it fires, sucks in the last water as it does so. It stops. It splutters. He tries the ignition. Starter is silent, resting peacefully. Water still coming in. He pauses, a second, then two. He lifts up like a silverback, broad shoulders, elbows out wide and one fist hits the wheel, he hammers … two fists, pounds it hard … *one-two-one-two* … *'Oh man!* I fucked it up! I did what I wasn't supposed to do. My parents are gonna kill me. There goes the fucking trip, man. That's the moment. Right there! There it goes. Right fucking there! I'm sorry, baby. *I'm sorry, baby!'*

The girl is composed, admirable, holds it furiously together as brown water pools around the handbrake. I can't help but ask, 'How long have you guys been together?'

She stares, unflinching, out of the window.

'Four months. July. Fucking July.'

*

The local Navajo pulled us out. Three of them marched down the hill, all in jeans and boots and yellow rubber rain jackets, not a horse nor shaman in sight, just a long length of heavy chain slung over one shoulder, a winch across the chests of two others. We tied chains around a tree trunk, found the tow bar submerged beneath the rising water, and gradually we hauled the jeep out. Two hours we took it in turns to pump at the winch, tiring one after another as we lifted the lever perpendicular and then flattened it back to earth, the metal cracking over sprockets as the chain rattled impossibly taut and we prayed the links didn't split. From the muddy water, rain falling and with rocks under each wheel to stop it slipping back in, chains rattling, the jeep returned to us one inch at a time.

With the Navajo, I returned to one of their cabins to refill my water. One of the three, who appeared the youngest, his dark hair falling wet over his face, drank from a bottle of bourbon. Having upturned the bottle, holding it vertical a moment to wait on the last drop, he pulled it from his lips and threw it to the land. It lifted in an arc and smashed to splinters on the hard earth.

With the sound of the chains clinking, draped across shoulders, we walked in silence back to the reserve. In the centre of a handful of cabins, metal chimneys smoking, was a ceremonial tipi of wooden timbers without any opening. Rusting cars, much of their bodywork stripped and upholstery missing, were parked around the expanse of land. With few words, the men went their separate ways, the man who had thrown the empty bottle moving towards a simple house made from breeze blocks under a tin roof. The man who had given instructions as we retrieved the jeep, turned to me as I waited hesitantly at the door step.

'Come inside,' he instructed plainly, looking down from the step, his bowl of charcoal hair pulled across his face by the wind, dark eyes shining against smooth brown skin. Inside the cabin's timber-clad walls, a wood burner filled the room with warmth, an orange glow from the small window in its door. The man took my canteen to his sink, refilled it from a tap, then rinsed a large plastic bottle on the table, and started talking as it filled.

'You should take extra water if you're going to walk all of the Canyon.'

On the wall opposite me were photos, almost all in black and white and stern faces looking out of the glass. Images of braves lined the room with the strong, angular features of America's only true natives. Some of them wore plain sweaters, others waistcoats with embroidered patterns down their fronts, others had feathered head-dresses and long lengths of hollowed wood hanging from their necks.

'Your whole family lived here?' I asked, gesturing to the wall as he returned with the water, gave a nod of confirmation.

'All of them. On this land.'

'How's life here?'

'Life's good.' He paused, blinked. 'Some people leave, but they always come back.'

He put down my canteen and his large bottle on the wide surface of the cluttered table

'And you, where are you going after Watchtower?'

'California.'

'You camp out tonight?' I nodded. 'You got stuff for a fire?'

I shook my head. 'Do you think I'll find any wood on the road to Watchtower?'

'Some. But it'll be wet with the snow. Cut into the bark to get the dry wood. That works.' He pointed at my feet. 'You got spare socks?'

I nodded.

'If you won't miss a pair, use the elastic from them. Cut it out. That burns. That gets a fire going.'

'Thank you.' I took the bottle of water from the table, fastened first it and then the canteen to a strap of my bag, hoisting it back to my shoulders.

We shook hands. 'You just come back, if you need a place.' His gaze settled on me a moment as I smiled thanks, saw a worry briefly in his eye.

'Aren't you afraid?'

Highway 64, AZ

No, I am not afraid, for how could I be afraid when the worst thing has already happened? Out here there are only endings, every last one of them and only endings. His death was in every word of mine ever printed on a page, along with the knowledge that he would never get to read it. And after that, I became invincible, for suddenly the world was only skies and rain and rocks and sunsets, a place where no human indifference or malevolence could ever hope to touch me.

Up above, the dawn breaks blue and then to a dim brightness as I walk the first of fifteen miles west, continuing on foot towards the Canyon's south ridge. I was always unsure about coming to this place, sitting out in Arizona like a landfill site for our absolute proclamations of the world's marvels: the *stunning*, the *most beautiful*, the *breathtaking*, the *one place to see*. Even Bob Dylan said that a sundown view of the thing was the meaning of life. To be honest, from its reputation, and against all of my intuitions, a small part of me wants to believe that this might be the last place on earth that can move me again. And as a result, I'm not sure I even want to see it. I'd rather believe in incomprehensible wonders than see the realities and discover that it's only geology and rock. My feet pull me on as I look down at the road. Passing below, in the roadside gravel are a pair of nail clippers and a fridge magnet snapped in half, separating pink letters and illustrated asteroids: 'Gr– Cany–'.

Every last eyeful of this scorched and reddened land is detailed in a full colour edged with snow, and all that keeps me going is that the beauties of this world still stick as fast as the sorrows. From the desolate, deserted road out to Canyon, where none see me, where my company are all ghosts and there are none in front of whom to feel self-conscious, from in me comes a sadness that won't stop welling. The highway leans up and down great, slouching bends, beside which tussles of black brush, short and stunted, slice up the wind and whisper ambivalent questions of whether the stranger's face is crying or simply beaten by rain.

I walk on as the landscape screams, all cut in half and waiting to be pulled apart. In life we have in us so many different voices, with most so moderate, but out here, rising from a snow-capped desert there ushers a language written in acid and in blood. Stone dead, I write a fire that the twenty-first century will never know again, and that come the twenty-second none shall ever even believe existed anyway. This world, so inhibited and concocted, where a thing inoffensive to many comes to be of more value than that which is loved deeply by a few. In this there is no grandeur, and even quite the opposite, for I am hardly even here. Nothing but a bystander, my brain is burdock: rows of tiny hooks so that I am just a scrapbook and the entire universe snares itself upon me. For just a few pages, let me write for only myself. From inside, years waiting, it bursts and finally on the road to Watchtower, he comes back to me.

Cleaved in two, gaping wide and stumbling, a crevasse of my own opens so much emptier than any other canyon in Arizona. Rain trickles over my eyes and into my face, and my heart beats close at my ribs. Life, the centre of my consciousness, has been living in my chest for so long already, but here it seems to come stronger. Here is my father, locked in this landscape with spirits that dwell inside long fissures, and which fire up at you when you realise the words of splendour people spoke of this place were only that, words, and you will find no solace in the rock to ease your pain. The colours have all gone, the sounds only drone, death is riddled through everything and I am so heartbroken for this place. My father taught me the meaning of death before I had learned how to live my own life, gave me that gift as special as it is painful. For all the confusion and sorrow that weighed on my brain, at least I learned then why the world is as it is, why adults become so afraid of hope, sceptical of changes for the better. It's because they are hurt, wounded to the last. Life hurt them, took their spirit and instead gave them fear. In his dying, this world, and most without having ever known of it to begin with, lost the most beautiful presence, so that I was obliged to try and remake things in his image or else know his beauty was gone forever.

My boots walk, they hurry, as if the road were my emotions and with enough haste we might yet reach the end of them. A pock in the asphalt scuffs at my toe, pulls me down with a small whimper snatched out of my control. A piece of me died when he did: at least half, for we were one and the same, and if he were truly no longer living then either it must be that he had never been larger than life at all, or else life was a thing so much smaller than I'd believed. It took years just to comprehend the simple fact that he was dead and I wasn't, that his heart had stopped beating and mine had not, and that therefore, strangely, we'd been separate people all along. In him there was magic, and without him, magic could not exist: we were all just flesh, for I lived for him, and the endless task of making him proud was my only real meaning, wrong as that might be. I still thank him for that tendency, because it made me realise that impossible feats are the best of companions in this finite life, for they are the only things that will remain constant and stay with you forever.

The first weeks in particular, I waited for my own death. I wouldn't lock the bathroom door in case I died in there and nobody could get me. I waited to see which one of the chest pains would really twist in my arterioles and finish me off as they had done him. Sometimes I would have to stop, sit down on a park bench, feeling so sure I was about to die and that if that were so then I should at least, for the sake of comfort, be seated when it happened. Then there came those dreams, where I would see him as if he were alive. Those dreams were so precious, treasures of memory brought back to life, and my subconscious, though knowing it was only dreaming, would still so desperately try to stay sleeping, in order that he need not stop as he had done in the real world. Slowly he would fade and I would wake, leaving me part proud and part ashamed at the very thought that I could one day survive and cope without him. It was madness, I know, but for so long that was how each day passed. Death was always so close, was everywhere, and the world felt entirely upside down. I know it's something everyone says, but it was inescapable. That all the sky were earth, the leaves and branches roots, and that the roots were trunks and branches stretching into a sky of soil. The seat of human consciousness was in our feet, and we walked on our heads along a great floor of atmosphere. I promise all that sounded so much more plausible than the idea that he was over and never again would I hear his voice.

That's still the hardest part. His face ... I can still see his face, can still see it clearly in both memory and photographs. It is his voice that fades and gradually leaves me. Such a baritone he had, so strong and calm, the voice of an oak, now gone forever with no recording of it left in this world, save some vague remnants I can sometimes raise from the depths of my ear. My heart is still so broken that now all I want is to break everyone else's heart, and afterwards we can love one another as we should have done all along. We are all of us grieving or else only waiting to grieve. The one important thing, that which simultaneously cripples you and yet armours against everything else, is to have a love for someone so great that their beauty and joy could eclipse the rest of the world. If it can be possible for such love to exist, then there can be no heartless stupidity or plain deceit that cannot also be undone and cured. If you love someone like that, and then live by that love with others too, then all will be well. Let it humiliate those who derive their purpose from power, from riches or rank. Let it make every last one of them ashamed to feel anything but love for all the wretched of this sad and often wayward land.

The Navajo man said I was alone, but all around, locked in a landscape of burnt red caskets, beneath the ephemera of roadside litter and white bones of snow, I sense there are stored the souls of both our ancestors. Walking into the cold wind, columns of rock stand black and grey on the horizon, turning red as they near and then lean over me. As the miles pass, silent but for my footsteps, the hard face of the rock becomes such comfort, offering no judgement of solitude and no response to grief, so that eventually, faced with only indifference, all human emotion subsides and stills. A calm resettles, or perhaps it is only nothingness, but by either road it brings with it that sense of peace that was all I could have asked for. I walk long hours, and as the afternoon light fails, my thoughts they rest. Out of this journey, dragged purposeless over North America, let me write a story to provide meaning for ten billion different souls, spread all across the world and still waiting to be born. And that will be politics, and that will be love.

*

Grey clouds appeared in a monochrome sky. With dusk descending, rainfall turned to drizzle on a land with only the thin branches and needles of small pines for shelter. The concrete pipe of an irrigation channel ran under the highway, and I climbed down into its cover. At the opening lay the half-bare carcass of a wild horse, its chest scavenged and pulled open, ribs lined up like the keys on a broken piano. The remains of a coat of hair, preserved by the drying of sun and then cold frost, hung with the flesh beneath it all gone, the empty leather stretched across the frame of the skeleton. A long face, teeth gripping jawbone, grinned at me as snow went on falling and I gave a gentle kick to the hide, hard and pulled taut, so that the sound of my boot boomed out, slipping into the tunnel and off into the hills. I gathered old branches of dead pine, did as the Navajo had said, and with my knife cut beneath bark to where the wood was still dry. As a small pile of kindling took the flame, larger sticks drying at the perimeter of the fire, I watched the white snow on the ground melt and then retreat, draining down into cold earth growing warm. Under the branch of a tree beside the tunnel of the road, I sat on a rock and watched the night play with the shapes of distant rocks. A corona of light lifted from the fire into a sky, where stars gradually poked holes and shone down at my resting place beside the upturned ribcage of the dead horse.

Hours passed in the gathering of wood and the watching of flames, their shapes shifting upwards and burning in an eerie mist. Snowfall resumed, each flake scalding fast, evaporating in puffs of steam from those that blew too close to the fire. Finally I crawled beneath the road into the cold, concrete crib of the irrigation channel. From the mouth of the tunnel, the fire died from red to orange, and then a shade of grey marked by the ruby red of its last embers.

Sleep began to take me, and then was snatched away again with a noise beyond the tunnel, fidgeting beside the carcass and setting a sound of tugging, of shredding, through the quiet night. Reaching for my torch, I shone a light towards the noise, the sight returning to me only the image of two, steady green eyes. Turning off the torch, I reached out to throw a handful of gravel in the direction of the eyes. Waiting a moment, a sound of claws on rock seemed to retreat, and again I reached for the torch. Two green eyes, still steady, still set, waited at the end of the shaft of light. Staring towards the dead horse, I wondered if the owner of those same eyes was perhaps responsible for turning the horse to carcass.

Canyon, AZ – November 24

They're sitting at the table next to me, one with glasses, both grey-haired, in heavy wax jackets, boots. Dressed for the weather, a moustache that runs perfect, uninterrupted from the right-hand side of one face to the left-hand side of his friend's. Two cups of coffee. Two checked shirts. The only movement is from table height to mouth: they don't let go the handle of the coffee cup, keep holding the thing down on the table, as if it might escape. They drink together. One of them has a small chainsaw beneath him on the floor. They both talk in steady, flat tones, abjectly unexcited in conversation about the snow, the storm, the next week's work. Their voices hang with the patience of men who have seen a lot of weeks come and go, discuss recent strangers that never hung around but are not yet forgotten. The door of the small café opens from time to time, on each occasion with the same squeak of hinges that serves as notification of a new person, a momentary potential for a changed life. Each man's head turns, each time, straight to the sound of the opening door and the new message it might bring with it. No matter how quiet and sleepy the valley they live in, they speak like men who have seen enough, and as if for a long time all change has felt unwelcome. They discuss chainsaws and falling trees, lubricants and engines: the pitch of their voices is constant, as if there's no excitement nor disappointment left to register. Life's happened already. I watch them quietly over the top of the fried bread, chilli and jalapenos piled upon the Navajo taco that'll walk me the next twenty-eight miles of Canyon.

'You see Doug's new truck?'

'Not yet. I ain't been over that way in a while.'

'Me neither. I saw it on the computer, on that website.'

For the first time, one of their faces moves. He's disappointed, surprised, slightly affronted, his mouth puckered up with hurt. He combs his hand over his grey head, with a little breath of emotion. The corners of his eyes wrinkle and this old, life-hardened man gives a small, wounded gulp.

'I told him I wanted to see those photos.'

'You can. He's always putting new ones up. You can see them too, but first you got to add him. You got to add him as a friend.'

*

The view of the Canyon from its southern ridge is breathtaking: the most perfect sight you ever saw, a poetry beyond words. They've thrown eulogies at it all down the ages, they'll go on doing so, but not one of them, either then or now or ever again will get close to doing it justice. Because the hot desert air, lifting out of the Grand Canyon, has collided with the cold front of the storm that found me in Flagstaff. The two have collided at the Canyon's southern ridge, and there, spilling out and over the land, is nothing but a dense mist that claims all but the five metres in front of your nose. And so I stare at the most serene sight America has given me to date.

A dozen Chinese faces are looking right past me, into where Grand Canyon was supposed to be. They're crestfallen, woebegone and this image of opaque white is not a bit like in the brochure. A couple of ladies start to shiver, each one of them looking miserable. All I can see are frowns: perfect heartbreak as the developing world starts getting their hands on first world problems. Fog in Grand Canyon, Nature refusing to perform, Grand Canyon is faulty.

Valiantly, one of them pulls out a camera, removes a lens cap and takes a shot. Captures mist. Perfect mist. After half of a brave, disappointed hour, they turn away. They regain their bus, which starts its engine and pulls off with a slurry of snow. As they disappear, for a slight second, only the briefest of moments, the cloud slips, its fingers part, and for the shortest time I'm given a quick glimpse of that famous red rock torn apart, an eyeful of Canyon with the Colorado River shining thin and brown at its foot. And it is beautiful, and it is magnificent, and your mouth does open, or at the very least it smiles, before the clouds fold back, and the Canyon is gone again.

'The drum has to keep moving, even when it's empty, otherwise it can damage the bearings when you drive over an impact. They're Japanese steel in there. The best, precision parts. Real strong, but still.'

We stand together, under the cement-mixer, blue and white paintwork shining under a thin coat of road dust. 'This one's brand new. I'm just delivering her.'

'Where to?'

'Driving down to Los Angeles, from Minnesota. Two thousand miles nearly.'

He leans on the platform, the bed that holds the rig. The sun cuts through his face, leaves one half of the thick moustache dark grey while showing the other half as white. Above the moustache, sunlight burns in his spectacles, hits one lens, glowing solid and orange-red. He removes the glasses, polishes with a sleeve. Tiny eyes. Short stature. His shirt is tucked over a round stomach, navy-white checks, buttons pulling slightly apart. He's wearing trainers, hands clean but dark with a shadow of labour that never washes away. Bristles of black hair are turning grey on the knuckles. He's oh-so-softly spoken, down-to-earth written all over him.

'They make these in Minnesota?' I go on, half-curious, half-looking to strengthen our relationship, ready for The Ask. He stands beside the tyre, head height, industrial rubber only just below his hairline. An exhaust stack is over him: hard metal next to rosy cheeks.

'Chassis from the East Coast, parts from somewhere else, maybe some from Asia, I guess. But yeah, they assemble it all in Minnesota.'

We pause, cement-mixer small talk winds down. 'I just stopped here to rest my legs.' He sticks his hands deeper into his pockets, his feet flex inside his shoes, toes lift as if to prove that, yeah, here he is, just stretching his legs. He asks, half-peering at my cardboard sign, 'Where you headed?'

'West. Kingman first, I suppose.' I know what's coming.

'I'd love to give nice guy like you a ride, but,' I'm already nodding my understanding, 'company policy.'

I smile out some more nods, don't like to make anyone feel bad. 'It's OK. I don't want you to get in trouble.'

He lifts up his shoulders, smiles, thanks me. We're drawing to a close. Even with my genuine cement-mixer interest, there's not much left to say. Then he straightens – he's clearly just hit on an idea – I sense hope. His body lifts up full, inflates with this new thought, so that the shadow-sunlight line moves down across his neck.

'Say,' he goes to a back pocket, 'if you're ever up in those parts, up in Minnesota,' he hands me a leaflet, the front of it showing a cross and a forest clearing, 'my family, we started a place, and out there we decided to start telling the stories of Jesus. You should come, brother.'

Ash Fork, AZ

Chicken thighs marinated in olives and pimiento, straight out of a plastic freezer bag. It disappears into my mouth, the first thing since my meals with Pala that tastes subtle, seasoned and not too sweet. He throws a packet of crisps my way, combs the long hair away from his face, smiling excitedly beneath black-rimmed spectacles that he pushes higher up a long, thin nose. He's my own age, happy at the company. I've got grease up to my palm, lick fingers with an oily tongue. They won't stop shining, dusted with fried potato debris. Desert shoots by: blue sky, yellow sand. Road. The towns are nothing but boxes that either sell burgers or house people, telephone poles the highest points on the horizon, rocks around their base to stop the sand blowing away as the wind excavates a cavity for the pole to lean into. The car is full of blankets, water containers and air mattresses. Ryan is moving back from his sister's house.

'Right, so I just figured cooking was my real love. Back then I was JP Morgan Chase. I was making, what, a hundred thousand. I mean, it looked after me ... a hundred K a year! And then it all collapsed. The market went. I lost ten years and four hundred K in a week.'

I don't ask why or how. He's a good guy for sure, but bankers burned by banking crises figure low in my heartache index.

'So I started thinking about how that whole system worked,' – good of him to do so, at that stage – 'and I just realised it was all ... so wrong.'

Desert passes us by. A cluster of space observatories line the horizon, telescopes peering through the domed roofs of concrete bunkers. Having told me the world according to him, Ryan falls silent. Cacti pass, abandoned cars. Highway 66 tourist towns move by us: that old east-west route kept on life support by diners, kitsch and nostalgia. I hear him sigh a little, like he's become only my chauffeur. I check back in.

'Why you going to Seligman?'

'I'm heading to the post office there. Arizona just legalised medical marijuana. I gotta go get my permit.' He looks round at me: 'I smoke.' He rubs the small of his back: 'Helps with a pain I get down here.'

I laugh, the second time I've heard this story today. 'Seems a lot of people suffering with pain since they legalised it.'

He smiles, 'Colorado made a hundred million bucks of taxes from fully legalising it, but here they make getting the permit so damn difficult. Just the bureaucracy is painful enough in this country!'

'Really?'

'Yeah! I mean, they don't even give me a name. My permit is in the post office there, and I have a number with me here, and when I go, and if my number matches the number on their permit, then they'll give it to me. You don't even get to be a person in this system. The last two times I drove out here, they didn't have my paperwork, and couldn't find my number.'

'Sounds inefficient.'

'Damn right it is,' Ryan leans his arm on the door, window down. He lifts his hand, spreads his fingers to float with the passing current of air. 'Organising anything here is deliberately made Byzantine, so that everyone hates it, so that people have no faith in bureaucracy or systems, and so when a corporation wants to dodge a tax or a regulation, people relate to it like it was their own lives, like it was an easy mistake to make.'

The desert presses on outside, hills becoming more pronounced.

'Does it make it harder, being so isolated out here, when you're so far from towns?'

Ryan rocks his head between his shoulders like he's weighing up my question.

'I mean, it's annoying to have to drive further to the post office, but there's always people.'

He gives a kind of grin that makes me think something is left unsaid.

'Before, it was quite hard, but the internet helps a lot. I've always had problems with girls, face to face.' Sheesh, he really is getting to the chase. 'But I'm an OK guy, and it's easier to have that come across after a few days of sending messages.' I nod, feel I'm listening to the future again. 'There's a new app which even tells me about new girls signing up in the location. I can find out how far away they are, and I can even figure out where to drive to.' He smiles, 'Then I just put that into a route generator and I can optimise the journey and sometimes meet more than one girl in a day.'

With a hint of disbelief at the logistics of mass desert romance, I smile, witness technology allowing the strategic thinking of an awkward ex-banker to enhance his dating prowess and keep his code in the gene pool.

'Doesn't that sometimes cause problems?'

'Well, sometimes girls can be in completely different directions, and you have to travel a lot of miles.'

Mileage hadn't been the sort of problem I'd envisaged.

'Sometimes the sort of girl you can meet out here is different.'

He sounds almost apologetic, as if something that he's not talked about before is weighing on his chest.

'Sometimes they're not so assertive.' Ryan pauses, then lurches, 'Sex is sometimes a problem.' I wonder what he means. 'Especially with younger girls.'

The tone has turned unsavoury, but I'm intrigued. Ryan clocks the disapproving nature of my look.

'Not *that* young. I mean girls in their early, mid-twenties, girls who grew up with the internet, raised watching porn. I guess they're kinda educated with it just like I guess boys that age are.'

'They have different expectations?'

'Kinda. The sex is always kinda a bit brutal, impersonal. Like they expect you to want it to be really rough, a bit, like, obscene.'

I don't know what to say, I've no reaction to give any more. The road leans in front of us just the same as ever: its unbroken yellow lines straight down the centre, perfect desert either side and the two of us next to one another and heading into a never-nearing distance. The rattle of the engine presses along with the sound of a passenger window that will not wind shut. Ryan mutters something to himself.

'Sometimes, when it's like that, it can be really, like *really* hard, to find some intimacy.'

Seligman, AZ

SMS: 'Someone told me you're in the US. Are you coming to SF? – H.'

Mike was born in Arizona, another moustache: those things worn here with blue denim jeans and blue denim shirt so that altogether they form a state uniform. His fair hair is stolen by advancing middle age, he's smoking his way through a pack of Camel in his breast pocket. He's drinking Budweiser and on the feet that press the pedals are cowboy boots of brown hide. He hits the steering wheel, the two orbiting hoops of a logo from Nagoya.

'This is my eighth Japanese pickup. I'll only drive Japanese models now.'

My window is down, letting out the smoke of Mike's cigarette. I watch Mike quietly. Mike's lonely. You sense the need for communication, expectation ripe in all the pauses, but on first impression his loneliness is incurable and I'm only palliative care. He's driving a hundred miles, to Kingman: a good ride. I can tell he wants conversation, but I can hardly manage it. I can't remember my last good sleep. We're in his pickup, though he's a trucker proper, big rigs: driving home from Flagstaff where he's been repairing his engine. He talks slowly, laboriously, like each string of words are boxes that need lifting.

'I drive Arizona–New Mexico every day.' A sigh follows. 'Drive from Flagstaff with a coloured stone, called cinder, and I drive back from New Mexico with corn, milled corn for the dog food factory in Flagstaff.'

Mike's drunk. He opens his second beer, although less than a quarter of an hour has passed the clock face since I got in. His words are slow, his face red. He leans towards me as he talks. I smell beer. I look at the face, leaning over to me. His buck teeth are spaced wide apart. His moustache is thin, whiskery. The guy reminds me of a walrus dressed in denim. The Aquarius Mountains split either side of us, the sun falling sleepily on my face as the mountains move so beautiful slow. Ahead, the road goes pendulum, goes ribbon, the mountains back-and-forth on a lullaby highway in late afternoon.

His drink-driving rests just a moment in my mind. Mike's pickup is military, armoured, and there isn't a school or child in sight. I suspect the truck would hold together even if it crashed, and we won't meet any person for him to mow down. Besides, I get the feeling he's well practised in driving under the influence. Let him drink. He finishes a cigarette, a cough rattles up with loud mucus as a hot cherry of ash falls from the cigarette to Mike's lap. I watch it drop to his oily jeans: a trail of smoke follows it, sinks down, returns as a slightly broader trail rising up. I watch as, it seems, Mike really is about to set himself on fire. I thought this only happened in cartoons, and look for the words in my mouth, but the question 'Are your trousers burning?' is somehow too strange to voice.

'Whatthe?!' Mike brushes, yelps, beats, he smoulders on. 'Shit!!' He opens his legs, finds the ember, brushes it off and turns to me. Small eyes and a closed-mouth smile. 'That one almost got me.'

He resumes coughing, words ricocheting out through catarrh, phlegm, tar.

'Want some pot?' He coughs, pointing at a small pipe beside us. I wave a hand, decline. He goes on coughing. You can hear the cancer, the deep cough, the air running through narrow corridors, slamming doors. Mike picks up the pipe, holds it between fingers, goes into the glove box and takes out a tube of red plastic. He shakes it so that a metal ball rattles, then puts it to his mouth, presses its silver button: it gives a puff, a high blast, a *toot!* Mike eases, stops coughing, removes the inhaler and replaces it again with the pipe for his pot. He takes a lighter, the pot *cr-crackles*, milk on to cereal crackles.

'I didn't smoke pot for twenty-five years.' He draws deep on the pipe, breathes out with the memory, slow. 'Then I got a toothache, really bad, in one tooth.' He points a thick finger, bitten nail, to one side of his face, rests a cheek on it, stares blankly. 'No! Wait a minute!' Realisation dawns, verve in him, 'I got it both sides!' He points to the other cheek, then looks at me. 'Toothache's all gone now.' He gives a giggle, looks over with a smile. 'Thought I'd carry on with the pot all the same.'

We drive on into silence, windscreen whiting out in sunset. Mike tries to dodge sun behind visor. 'Can't see shit,' he mutters to himself, leaning forward to open another beer, as if to help the visibility. The Aquarius gape before us. Scrub, yellow with bursts of green bush and grey rock. We're deep in silence, just the hum of tyres. Mike looks across at me now and then, expectantly. I should say something, should pay for my fare.

'Think you'll always be a trucker?'

'Nope.' Mike pauses, surprises me, what's he got up his sleeve. 'I'll stop when I have a heart attack, give it up when I die.'

He looks with a smile, like it's a well-rehearsed joke that is normally received better than this.

'I'm fifty now,' he tells me, looking twenty years on that. We round mountainside and the horizon opens a moment: purple mountains break to reveal dry desert and the right-angled growth that is Kingman.

'Think you'll stay in Kingman?'

'No use moving. Everyone else in all the other places they're already dead. Sometimes on the road, I stay in a motel.' He chuckles, looks over, 'Somewhere clean, TV. No use going back to Kingman really, ain't many alive there but me either. My sister died ten years back, she was forty-five.' He drives, unmoved, 'We weren't close anyway.' He pauses, reflects, 'I can be alone at a motel just the same as in Kingman.'

I soak him up. Mike's unstoppable. The guy makes me look full of beans. I've never found such a plain-spoken acceptance of death, the inevitability, and yet at the same time not stirred even a little by as much, no desire to seize any of what life might offer in the meantime. In Mike you see the human face of that statistic, the rising morbidity of white-skinned, blue-collar America: men in particular who no longer see any worthwhile living reason not to either intoxicate and numb their senses or simply check out of this world. From prescription drugs and alcohol, from the illegal drugs they take once the prescription drugs are no longer enough. Mike is the all-American man in a country where he no longer recognises himself in the stories he was raised on, and has been given nothing real to replace them with.

'You still like driving the truck?'

Mike shrugs, lets his head move side-to-side as he makes a noise of uncertainty.

'How about the other truckers?'

He lifts, snaps bolt upright. I've got him. He's awakened, has found something worth saying.

'*Assholes!*' I suppose that was predictable. 'They don't know how to drive, these new drivers. Don't use hazards when they're slowing down, they don't use the lanes right. Old boys like me, we're the minority now. Time was when if you were pulled over at the road-side, every truck driving by would be coming through on the radio, over the shortwave, asking if you were OK. But these new drivers,' a finger goes up, 'they have no decency.' A second finger, 'And they have no courtesy.'

Mike's started looking at me rather than the road, leaning over, hand on thigh, steaming drunk, eyes shot red.

'Back then and everyone would check on the other guys, we was all always on the radio. And now there's not even a radio no more in most trucks, because they've all got their own cell phones nowadays, and nobody talks no more.'

He breathes a moment, a short cough. 'One time, in my last pickup, I had a CB radio, and this road we're on now was closed for an accident. I came in over the radio,' nostalgia is up in Mike's face, rivalling the booze, his eyes lighten, 'I got on the radio, said I was a local boy. "Come in, drivers, come in, drivers. Follow me! Follow me! I know a back route …" that's what I said.' Mike laughs. 'And me with a whole line of trucks, we went winding over the hills, through the back roads to avoid the incident, to keep on moving. It was all of us together.'

Mike looks at me. I look at Mike. A moment of connection, because he's just told me his Glory Day and we both know it.

'You still have a radio in your truck?'

'*Abso-lutely!*' He leans in, clenched fist, road and automobile and seventy miles an hour have now been completely forgotten. 'Sure I've got a radio, *and it's always on too! Always!* But there ain't nobody to talk to no more.' He points to an empty tray, some black and red wires, above us in the roof of the pickup.

'I could put a CB radio in there even, in this very pickup. And you can be sure I would too, but it's no use. There ain't nobody out there. Ain't nobody left to talk to.'

Kingman, AZ

In the shadows beneath the white light of a billboard, a large area lies covered with shards of demolished concrete, lengths of rusting rebar protruding from it and the land as if overgrown by some invasive, industrial shrub. A car is parked up outside a pizza restaurant, the smell of sweetened baking on the air as I crouch to retie a straggling lace. From the restaurant's illuminated sign, yellow against the violet of the night, there is a crackling of escaping electricity and as it hisses, beside the leather of my boot I see a pale, tiny white shape. With scorpions it is said that the smallest are the most poisonous, and that is one small sting that arches upwards next to my nose. Its feet recalibrate position, and two claws snap tentatively as the scorpion backs away, only a few centimetres from death by boot, the power for now all mine, but with the possibility for an enormous revenge of karma when I later lie sleeping on its desert floor. I stand back as a freight train horn fires shrill off to one side, and a motel sign nearby advertises: *We've got the Elvis Suite – $44* in straight letters stuck to a white backlight. The Chamber of Commerce instead offer: *Kingman: great place to raise a family, start a business, or just take a holiday*' I pick my way towards the pizza restaurant, across the edge of the acres of concrete rubble. A shard of manmade rock goes falling and rattles between collapsed platforms, so that a rabbit hears my approach and its white tail goes thumping fast back to the desert.

Inside the restaurant the light is low, with two older men the only other diners, sitting at a table by the door. They stroke their chins, each runs finger and thumb across his own shapely pitchfork of a moustache. In American facial hair, it has become my general rule that conservatives have moustaches while liberals grow beards, they just let the thing go. The men face one another, relaxed in front of two pizzas: one with cubes of pink and pineapple, the other covered in balls of squashed meat. Between the two pizzas there shines a flash of silver, catching the light, and I hear words spoken between mouthfuls, 'What I really like about the .38 is its feel in your hand.' One man passes the gun to the other, who cradles it delicately in his palm.

Standing at the counter, I look at photos of the meals on offer as a man in a thin white T-shirt, his dark chest hair pushing through the cotton, appears from a room behind a slatted partition. I give a smile, which he hands back to me in a scowl. I take in the appearance of his double chin, lengthy stubble, ponytail, standing tall above me. He doesn't ask my order, just lifts his head upwards, like I should get on with it. My finger traces down through the menu, I remark about the field of concrete that blocks his establishment.

'Looks like they demolished something quite big out there.'

He's firm, challenges unflinching, 'Who's asking? We own it now and that's all you need to know.'

Sun sets. Blue. Orange. Black. The desert sky goes through its regular colours as I walk towards downtown. I near vehicles in parking lots, hoping to perhaps ask directions to a bar, but I am left to watch as cars edge away with their windows winding up. There's nothing personal that I have against Kingman, but it's hard to find endearing. All America's desert towns are built on two principles: endless petrol and endless land. They spread. The streets are all motorways, and as a result you see no people because they are all shut away in cars. Few opportunities for chance encounter interrupt people in their managed journeys through these places, and so the realities depicted in news and films become harder to dislodge. When I need directions I no longer approach female drivers going to or from their cars. I'd rather save us both the aggravation.

I walk towards a car with a male driver shut inside his glass and steel. He sees me, door stays closed and window up. Muffled from within he looks up, innocently, 'Is there anything I can help you with?'

'Am I headed downtown,' I point, mouth through the glass, 'I saw a poster for a brewery with a bar.'

He hears the accent, seems amusingly reassured by the fact that the stranger is not American, and so for some reason more trustworthy. He opens the door, looks down from the truck, warming to me as if, just maybe, it turns out humans are OK after all. He has got a short goatee, the green-yellow of a John Deere baseball cap and a face that I'd guess was born long but has started to grow round and collect weight at the cheeks.

I mention the bar again and he smiles, 'Sure, it's here somewhere. I'm actually going there myself, my wife's already there.' He points to the enormous, twin-exhaust, off-road vehicle beside his own. 'That's her truck, so it must be close.' He sticks out a hand. 'Chris. Good to meet you.'

Together we step over the threshold where a large, refrigerated chest of beers with taps coming out of it watches the entrance. Three brewing cylinders stand at the far end of an empty space, and three televisions hang above the bar to guarantee freedom of sporting choice. Football, ice hockey, basketball. I'm introduced casually to Chris's friends, his wife, and then Will: a big guy with another goatee, glasses, a wide silver hoop pierced through each ear and tattoos down to his forearms. Chris introduces himself as a railroad engineer, drives a train, a nice guy but the meeting feels like a gathering of old friends, and so I sit down at a separate table just beside them, make my apologies as Chris smiles and puts his hands respectfully up. 'Of course, of course. You just relax.'

After a while, coinciding with a break in one of the games he's watching, Will arches his back, spreads his shoulders and one of his large, labourer's hands pulls up a barstool beside him. He turns to me.

'Sit down,' he announces as Chris laughs. 'No way you're sitting alone without us buying you a beer.'

I don't know what I expected. Maybe nothing, or at least not much more than Arizona Republican. I expected to know what was in front of me, as if I'm now qualified to predict the way America thinks and behaves and what is up ahead. In short, sitting down in Kingman, I think I know the world, its characters and its ways. In short, I've become an adult. In short, I have become complacent, presumptuous, stupid, precisely because I'm so sure I've accumulated some sort of knowledge of the world. Where once I would have listened to the experiences of any stranger as a life full of lessons, nowadays, exhausted with my own lot, just about bearing up, I've slaked my thirst. The hunger to pull every thought and experience from the people life presents us with has abated. My child, curiosity, spirit has quietened and I've contracted adulthood at last, become a prick. 'To burn always with this hard, gemlike flame, to maintain this ecstasy, is success in life.' They were the words of Walter Pater. Oscar Wilde lived by them, and a friend once passed them to me as his talisman for hard times.

Down in Kingman, Will orders another beer for me, slides it my way along the bar. 'Enjoy … Welcome to Arizona!' he bellows, and four faces look at me before he goes on.

'You travelling through?'

I nod, drink. 'Heading to San Francisco.' And for the first time, happily, I realise California has grown close and is no longer so specific an answer.

'Where you start?'

'New York?'

Everyone opens up with an amazed sort of laughter, thighs are slapped. 'That's amazing', 'awesome' ripples over them. If everyone who thought hitchhiking across the US was awesome actually picked up a hitchhiker once in a while, then the whole thing would be a lot easier. I shrug it off, not sure how to deal with the awe. The football game resumes, so that suddenly I'm less interesting, awesomeness limited to the halftime break.

'Where you sleeping?' asks Chris, still paying attention, and I gesture to my pack.

'I've got camping gear.'

Will's head swings round, he pipes up and lays his hands down on the bar.

'It's gonna get cold tonight. Hell are you sleeping straight out. You're staying at mine!'

Four nights in a truck cab, a few more in the snow and I can handle having a roof forced on me tonight. Together with Will and Chris, I raise my glass and we drink to the plan. Will, with my sleeping arrangements safeguarded, returns to his game on the television. When the football comes to an end, he rotates his stool a half-turn and points it more directly to face the screen showing ice hockey. Chris remains turned to me, interested, gives the collar of his shirt a quick pull and begins a conversation of the road.

'When I was a younger man I went hiking around Mexico for three months.' He gives a self-conscious laugh, patting at an emerging belly as if to indicate that it hadn't been there at the time.

For Chris to have gone travelling around a foreign country already places him in a vanishingly small portion of the American population. For him not be talking about Mexico as a shithole puts him in a minority smaller still.

'The people there, that's what I really remember. My god.' He shakes his head in a happy bewilderment. 'Here people have everything and they won't give you a thing when you're in need.' He still smiles, but his face turns red and he leans forwards, so that I don't mistake him. 'There, there they've got nothing and they'll give you the shirt right off their backs. Here and someone gives you the shirt off their back,' he plucks an imaginary wad of cash from his pocket, fans it at me, 'they want to know how much you'll give them for it.'

There's nothing I can say to that, and I turn the conversation to his job, the railroad, and ask what line will run me to San Francisco. He breathes in deep, looks away from me with a pulled face, as if we're doing something sinister just talking about it.

'Bakersfield. You want Bakersfield. But just be careful. I don't want to be hearing about no hitchhiker who's lost an arm. Other than that, just get on and enjoy the ride. It'll take you right in to San Francisco.'

I'm heartened by the advice: 'Get on and enjoy the ride' isn't quite the reputation the bulls have preceding them.

'You sound like you enjoy the trains.'

'I've got a good union job. I'm paid well and they can't move my job to China. I was lucky when I got it fifteen years ago, and I worked at it ever since cos that's the way I was raised. But after a while, you know, like anything,' he shrugs and smiles, 'it's just a job, it pays a salary.'

The crowd at the bar erupt and then subside, hands grip frantically behind heads at a near-miss on the screen. Chris and I continue:

'Back home we just hear about Arizona as really conservative and pretty Republican,' I look apologetically at him. 'You don't seem like that.'

Chris rolls his eyes, like the question of party politics is uninteresting to him, just as it has been to everyone else I've asked. 'I voted Republican last time, but I've voted Democrat before. I'm not a Republican or a Democrat.' He smiles, 'I'd vote for whoever seems least bad.'

'But the Republicans don't seem to care about unions, or even workers?'

'Right. And on that, we're different. Because I think people should be paid a good wage, and a worker should have rights, otherwise you won't get good workers. And even without that, it's just the right thing to do.'

'So what do you agree with the Republicans on?'

The rest of the crowd stay stuck, watching the game. Chris sighs.

'I think we have too many people not working, living off the state. That's why I vote Republican.'

'But like you just said, all the jobs have been moved to China.'

Chris lifts a finger to remonstrate, 'Even with that though, before I was on the railroad, I had an office job. We'd have people walk in, straight out of bed, not had a wash, ask for a job. And when you tell them you don't have a job – because, looking like that, you don't – they give you the paper to sign so that they can keep on claiming benefits. Some people just don't try.'

I can't argue with that, am not about to tell him his experiences are not what he says they are, do not mean what he thinks they mean.

'But you say you got yourself a good job, paid well, doing something you quite like.' Chris nods as I go on: 'Do you think the economy is still creating those jobs?'

'Absolutely.'

'A job where you can earn good money, buy a house, get a pension, send your kids to college and live comfortably?'

And at that once-simple wish, Chris chuckles a pipedream laugh, like I've told a good one. 'Oh no, not like that. That stuff's history.'

'So where's the incentive then? It makes sense to work hard if you know your life will improve for doing so. But why would anyone work a mindless job for forty years, only to stay where they started?'

Will, half-turning to listen in on us, seems to watch our

conversation for a moment: his hands are still placed firmly on the bar, the silver hoop hanging from an ear tilted our way, a small froth of beer is in the black stubble of his goatee moustache. As the silence settles, he turns back to the screens. Chris isn't about to challenge back, nods as if in an agreement that he won't quite voice. We both drink beer, reach for our glasses together, as if it were the only sane response to this conundrum of population, labour and scarcity. I consider Chris, just as Aaron before him on the New Jersey highway so long ago. The average American seems far less hostile to unions than American news has led me to believe. It's almost as if large media corporations were demonising workers' rights in ways not representative of everyday attitudes on the street. Meanwhile, those same corporations have likewise demonised welfare recipients, in so doing driving a wedge between the jobless poor and the hard-working not-quite-poor. And it's almost as if multibillion-dollar corporations might have something to gain from fostering such a divisive climate of mutual mistrust. Chris interrupts my thought, backtracks, lest he's been construed unduly severe in his worldview: 'It's not like I don't agree that there should be support for people out of work.'

The ice hockey has taken a commercial break, so that we now have a line of heads back in on us, nodding agreement.

Chris goes on, 'Everyone should work as hard as they're able to. Different people will be better at different things. But everyone should have a right to decent work, a home, supporting their family.'

I give a sort of nod in response to Chris's last remark, both of us drinking our beers, and with a warm glow for the thought that such a thing could still be possible.

With each game of sport finished, side by side we drive through the Kingman night, high in the front of Will's pickup, and heading for a fast-food restaurant.

'I need to grab some dinner for my son.'

Will sends a message from his phone, asks his son's order as Kingman passes us, car lights catching the scratches in the windshield.

'How old is he?'

'Eighteen. About to finish school. Been just me and him since he was three.' Will looks round, glasses reflect traffic lights, his goatee long and pointed, the man built like a wrestler but evidently as gentle as they come. 'His mum fell in with the wrong crowd. Really the wrong crowd. She started taking meth. I didn't think it was right for Matthew to be around it.'

I listen, the guy so devout in his humble opinion of himself, so unassertive in his views. He makes the point as if there could still be an alternative perspective, that he'd be open to a second opinion on whether toddlers and meth might have worked out all right. We roll into a drive-thru. Ramp lowers, crackling speaker opens up. 'Large Coke and a super combo with fries.'

Will turns to me: 'You want anything?'

We drive back to the house, dinner wafting a scent of fried flour and sugar from the seats behind. 'I don't know why she got into drugs. I guess for me I was always happy.' A petrol station stands illuminated, a chemical plant, silos. 'It was enough of a high to go out driving in the woods, take some beers, or go hunting and just be with myself.' He looks over at me, 'I think I did an OK job with Matthew.' He says it, waits on some approval, but my heart almost hurts at his humility. 'Seeing him to the end of his education. Sure others could've done better, but on my own all this time, I'm just glad I got him through school.'

A lump is rising in my throat. A man who labours all his life to stay in the same place and do only the decent thing. I'm pained by the gulf between the dignity of this man and his lack of assurance at his own value.

'What does Matthew want to do after school?'

Will looks straight ahead, has a passive voice as we drive by an empty warehouse, hangar doors open. 'He wants to join the military.'

Fuck. I sink. Eighteen years single parenting and the kid's going to put himself up for cannon fodder. Gonna wind up dead because Washington politicians in thrall to the arms industry will pack him off with a shot of flag and a mouthful of country to go invade the neighbourhood of some poor Arab who's also worrying what his kid will do after school.

'What do you think about that?'

Will lifts an *I-don't-know* hand open as we pull into the drive, beside a smaller pickup truck for the eighteen-year-old. 'I've told him I'll support him, whatever his decision. I just want to be a good parent.'

Wrong answer, dammit ... Will has the wrong answer.

Will leads me down the corridor towards the house. In the hallway are a couple of taxidermied heads from his hunts. He passes a stag, ducks below an antler and stops beside the bristling snout of what looks like a dead boar. 'This one's a javelina. It's a pig we have round Arizona.' Its glazed eyes look out at me, solid, the tusks lifting to sickle-like points. Will stands proudly beside it. 'Shot that one with my bow.' He lifts his spectacles up his nose, puts a finger to the tip of the tusk and lets it prick the thing. 'Look at that!' and he gives a happy, gleeful laugh.

Together we walk to the end of a corridor. The house smells slightly of old dust, of two men living alone. I follow Will as he calls, 'Matthew, dinner's up, we got company.' The door opens to the front room: I see a skinny kid, a bowl cut of hair, legs crossed up on the chair, white socks on his feet, pulled all the way up his lower leg. He's pale, freckled, doesn't say a word as he takes the brown paper bag of his fast-food dinner. He looks quickly to me, his hands holding the controls of a computer game, which he then uses to resume dropping a ring of power into an erupting volcano on the television screen opposite. On his thin arm is a single tribal tattoo and as his game finishes he turns. 'Nice to meet you,' he says, a voice breaking with puberty, an uninterested hand lifting in a quick wave as his gaze falls back to the screen.

Vegas, Nevada – November 27

A woman looks up from her business card on the pavement: the strap of a thong halfway up her back as she pushes breasts together and shows me the deep red of her nipples, licking her lips beside the large, printed digits of a phone number. The image is signed off with a promise that the reality is every bit as good as the photo.

On a bench nearby sit a group of Mexicans. I watched them arrive on bicycles with panniers bearing the tools and costumes of their trade. Some carry cleaning products, ready to move through windscreens in stopped traffic. Two wear T-shirts with the large words 'hotass girls!' and a pole-dancing silhouette across the belly, and the workers snap and flutter a deck of business cards at passers-by. Another man stands rigidly upright, his legs clad with the metal wires, pistons and silver panelling of a giant robot suit to entertain the crowd. His friend lifts the cold face of a transformer over the brown skin and black moustache of his head, where thin hair falls into tired eyes. Beside them is a green-yellow diplodocus, or at least the body, tail and feet of a diplodocus. His soft, cuddly head smiles at me from the bench where a Mexican head, sweat on its features, drinks deep on a cigarette as his diplodocus chest begins to cough.

In front of where I sit is one of the hotels that all the people around me have seen in a film, which means that as a result they themselves are now tantalisingly close to being in that film. Music, *The Entertainer*, starts up from the front of the hotel: a large pond where water shoots and sprays on gyros set against white light. The fountains begin to turn, sway, spin and pirouette water in time with the music, so that the water is dancing for us. The show finishes and crowd shuffles along. On the ground, behind the row of screens, a homeless man wakes up and props his head on to his elbow as if he were in his own bed. He has a long face, threads of thin saliva hang from a yawning mouth, dribbling on to his pavement pillow.

*

Alone with just my shadow, I walk the street they call The Strip. In the strong, artificial light, my shape is cut clear on the pavement: my home on my back, a sleeping bag hanging from it, the solid outline of my water canteen. I see my boots: high over my ankles, jeans bunched above them, and right now my shadow is everything I'd ever want it to be. I'm so proud and so content to be so simple, as the brash madness of Vegas swarms around. All of a sudden comes the loud, stuck-pig squeal of electricity as a microphone jack is plugged in. I look up to see a boy with fair hair and blue, religious eyes, soft skin and a gaze that now sees nothing but the words of a book and the words of a minister. He stands beneath a black-yellow sign, opens his act with the words there written: *Jesus died for us all. We have all sinned.* He passes in the human flood as I walk by, and yet, truth be told, by now I'm with the religious loons, would throw in my lot with them rather than go down with the rest of Vegas. I don't have sense of humour enough for this place, it's not my mess.

On another corner stands a man in a leather jacket, his mouth wide open in excitement at the sign he's been given to wave: half his own size, the sign advertises foot-long sandwiches. He lunges side to side like he's mounted on a spring, waving the sign for all he is worth, thrusting the inflatable sandwich sign at the crowd to impart his own divine message. I hear languages pass me by: Arabs, Italians, Turks, black, white, brown, yellow, disabled, obese and white. Everyone on earth, irrespective of skin colour, creed or impairment, is equal in the greedy quest for one further entertainment, a little make-believe at what it might mean to be rich.

The pointing finger of an inflatable hand leads me through the entrance to a casino, curious to see what might be waiting inside.

They say that the casinos pump oxygen inside to make the gamblers feel good, swell the confidence of the gullible. In truth, I think this is a myth, for all I sense inside is the stale smell of cigarettes in the only place of the US where smoking indoors is still permitted. The must of it comes back to me, reminds me of the school bus that always made me sick as a child on that half-hour drive to the swimming baths. Inside a casino and everywhere is failure. I've never seen a sight less glamorous. Obese men sit, legs spread with a slot machine between them: enormous, fat, bollocks are pressing at the inseam of over-tight slacks. An old woman hangs on a lever: she pulls, she pulls, her spare hand leans on a cane and a shrivelled face on top of a gaunt neck turns with the fruit machine into a cactus, a bomb, a basket of fruit. Coins drop into the gut of another fat woman: she picks them out greedily, like sweeties, and shovels them back into a mouth where the machine gobbles them down. It's unclear where the machine ends and human starts. A family are gathered to one side, as heartily as some Thanksgiving dinner table with huge cheers that draw me to them. A man with dice stands in tracksuit and shades, he high-fives a brother in long shorts, hugs a woman, the whole family in it together, heartwarming: working to make it in America the only way they know how and gambling probably no more fruitless than waiting for social mobility. At least gambling provides a little fun along the way.

Another game of dice rolls by next door: a long table with chips set down and padded walls around the sides of the baize. I stand facing the man, placing down his coins like some pilgrim peasant on his lifetime visit to this secular Lourdes. The table lies between us: me in my backpack, he the two-metre table away from me. The croupier moves chips. The gambler throws dice far, assured. He throws them like he knows the length of this table, he's played before. He's good, he's confident, chest out like a barrel full of self-belief. The dice come towards me: large, red with white spots, two huge dice, right at my face and then they fall, bounce the table, bounce the walls. Stop. Six.

Two. Clenched fist. *YES!* He's a winner. He rolls again. One. One. Loser. Again. *Loser.* I watch this man age before me. His proud chest punctures, deflates and falls in a little. The muscles of his arms and torso relax, softening into skin, to the beginnings of breasts. His eyes get smaller, pucker as he keeps on losing, but still he can't stop himself because he remembers so keenly what it was to win.

Heading back to the night, in the entrance lobby a woman has started dancing on a raised runway. Cleavage forces out of bra, pants disappear up arse, buttocks out. She has long thin, blond hair falling over her shoulders, stomach and jaw. She has strong, gym-membership definition: the muscles that she works out are gripped by a suspender belt on the thighs, lights splash all over her. People drink around the bar beneath. The music tries to force energy but few are watching. I wonder how the woman feels, having not even been turned into an object of desire, because nobody here desires, and so she is only an object – a prop, unasked for and uninterest-ing compared to the prospect of money. She radiates calm, patient misery. She looks so sad, like some ghost of the lives she might have led. I look around the room at all the men with daughters and mothers. I look at all the women who share the anatomy of the dancing girl striding the runway aimlessly in her boots, hooking the cleft of a knee around the metal of the pole. A green light plays in her blond hair, turning blue, turning green.

The rest of The Strip rolls under my boots. The lights fade behind me and the night comes back. A desert hare runs out into the sand and the rock, the casinos reflecting off its long white ears. Police cars are all pulled in with iron bars over headlights, black/white bodywork and red sirens. Mean. A pod of cops guard the city limits. I walk for hours. A couple of times I stick out my cardboard sign: *West – I-15 – Barstow.* Or else my thumb. But I don't mean it, I know nobody will pick me up. I only do it to play my role properly, my hitchhik-ing character. I leave the city, return to my post-apocalypse world in which everyone else is dead and it's just me and the machines. The wide streets carry the occasional jeep as alone I walk wide pavements: a pedestrian, a pervert, petrol deviance and a rare freak without a licence, no plate and no two thousand kilos of attendant metal and combustion. Just me and two feet which, to everyone else, makes me the most absurd creature in this whole city.

Flyovers lift above, underpasses sink into a warren and perfect concrete crescents cut the night sky in arcs as if Vegas were a gift, tied up in bows. I look up: a streetlight, bright on my face before I scale a concrete balustrade and my shadow hauls up, clambers one link over next and with a cymbal crash from the chain link fence. I throw my bag over: it falls into the high escarpment of stones that hold the freeway in place. I descend, red cubes of rock snapping and tumbling under my boots like those dice still rolling behind me. I pass into the shadow of the flyover: two chains of traffic – one lit white and nearing, the other red receding – glide purposefully perfect in a chiaroscuro so eternal and divine. Each car drives at the night, presenting an image of destiny with such determination in those twin cascades of light. I wait for a break in the traffic, dash across asphalt. Flesh on the freeway. A violation. My tiny limbs scarper as a car appears, a horn sounds. I climb the opposite bank, with more red rocks clattering as I flee from sight.

*

Two hours walking. The asphalt is hard and the miles register gradually in my shins. I break from the city limits: the pavements turn to dusty, dry imprints in the mud. Suburban dogs bark at me from behind gates, and each time I am alerted to them by the laughter of a chain rattled by a thrashing neck. Eventually, after another hour, I strike gold. The oasis, glowing on the sky: *TA – Truck Stop*. A whole truck stop, just for me. I climb over concrete pipes, move through the crooked, broken and curling wires of an old ripped fence. I sniff,

sniff night, sniff tanks still being filled. I smell petrol, gasoline. My nose twitches like a rodent's, a mile scavenger once again.

A line of engines leads towards pumps where two trucks are filling up. A Mexican is cleaning his windscreen to one side. To the other, a driver strides back to his cab, engine rumbling. He's wearing a leather jacket, white shirt: clean cut, chino trousers, not too over-weight, blond hair, a well-kept trucker, engine-oil-advert look to him. I near him at an oblique angle, not straight at him: the guy is six-foot broad, surely knows how to take care of himself, but he's still an American and these guys they scare easy. I angle in, walk up, back into the Kingdom of Fear. 'Excuse me.' He changes course, doesn't break stride or acknowledge that I exist. I repeat. 'Excuse me?' Turn and walk after him, still some self-respect. I'll be rejected all day long, that's his right and his prerogative, I've all but no pride left, but all I can demand is manners, some acknowledgment that I exist. 'Excuse me!' He turns, snarls, barks like I'm one more suburban dog. 'Beat it!'

They say America's socially flat, a classless society. And you know what, I couldn't agree more. They are dead right: Americans have no class, none at all, no style or gravity either, they lack the modesty that class demands. As for the idea that Americans have no social preju-dices, no *class* system, that idea could not be more wrong. Day in, day out and homeless people are being treated like dirt all across these fifty states, just most of them don't turn up writing about it. In America, when a person appears wholly down and out, there exists a suspen-sion of manners inconceivable in Europe. Where class is concerned, the Americans are not so subtle in their snobbery as the British: don't worry about knowing your Rembrandt from your Caravaggio, your types of cheese, preferences of bread, favourite radio programmes or fondness for seafood. Americans don't split social hairs so much on a basis of refinement or culture, but money. Money those guys understand. Money makes the perfect ranking system, it's class done metric. Bigger numbers equate to respect, lower ones to a lack of it.

If someone is truly poor, in America you can talk to them like an animal, like a mutt, do your worst. If you think they have no money or property to their name, then you owe no manners. That is not to say everybody exercises this right, far from it, only that it exists and sometimes takes the form of a contempt unimaginable elsewhere.

This time I'm burnt by it, scalded. I keep after this trucker, this prick. I demand some manners out of him. He turns on me, stops and shouts, arms out: 'You want to fuck with me?' I keep on, can tell he's all talk. That's another thing you soon learn here, people know just how to show front – guys in particular – they give it *all that*, they're raised John Wayne. But I'm wise to it, I'm in his face, shout back.

'No, I don't want to fuck with you. I just need a ride. All you do is say "no". It's not that difficult.'

He turns, he marches on, quickens his step so that I'm back alone. All around the refrigerator units are humming, their reverberation amplified from that nook where they sit between cab and trailer: carrying meat, carrying orange juice, carrying the ground-up, boiled bones that turn to dog food. A pair of drivers pass me: a driving team on the way back to their cab, one of them half-catching my eye as they pass. After a few steps, he turns on his heel, comes back to me with a tug of conscience that reveals they too think I'm homeless, only these guys still have souls, have that warm generosity and spirit that means despite all of the uglinesses, you are never entirely able to give up on this damn country. He's thin, wiry, glasses and yellow teeth.

'I'm sorry, man, I wish we could do more to help,' his voice fills with regret, 'but we could lose our jobs.' He takes out a roll of dollar bills. 'Here, let me give you some cash for some food.'

I gulp, 'It's good, man … I'm good for cash. If you're going inside anyway, then maybe get me an apple.' He looks at me, confused at such a modest request. I look back, shaking my head, 'In fact, don't worry about it. It's good, man. But thank you.'

He puts a hand on my shoulder: a road hillbilly with a heart of gold. He wouldn't understand the truth of what I'm doing here, I scarcely know it myself. We look at one another, a strengthening sort of look where you know the other person cares about you, is feeling something of the same humanity. Whatever my history, wherever I've come from, right now he's right: I'm homeless and need a place to sleep. He puts a hand on my shoulder. We embrace, and then he's gone.

Walking through the rigs, the curtains are all drawn: everyone is either asleep or simply keeping to themselves. There's an irrigation channel around the perimeter of the forecourt, dry stones form a little rampart. Beyond that, a fence with a ditch beneath the wire. I crawl under into a storage park for highway barricades and concrete storm pipes piled high. I size it up: feel an excitement rising and this place a veritable hobo palace. Quiet. Secluded. Sheltered. Fenced-off. This is a homestay all right, my own apartment bunk, tucked inside a large pipe. And then I catch myself: take a reality-check of America, where such a brilliant shelter is actually a terrible shelter, the worst going. Nose twitch, I smell others: my senses are heightening, my hobo radar bleeps. America is three hundred million and the destitute among them need places to hide out. This place is like a hotel: either I'm the first to ever come here or else all the rooms will be taken. I pass an old mattress: blankets, words scrawled in marker pen on the concrete pipe above. This is someone else's bedroom: the scene of a heartbreak just like the rest of ours, only these ones happen without roofs or emails. *'Please ... I'm sorry darlin ... take me back ... I miss ya.'* My feet sleepwalk on, one of those slight fears that make us go further and ask for more. I walk slowly along the concrete alley, reach the far end. Movement hits me fast. Another mattress unfolds. A face looks up and out. A head. Eyes. Eyes and soot. Jungle. He's more scared of me than I am him. But still. I'm gone.

Across the road, a strip mall offers a better option: open and exposed, but right now open is all I want, I want to be seen by the upstanding rather than joining the hidden, I'm not one of them yet. The time must be 2 a.m. I step through the car park and roll out my sleeping bag among the ornamental shrubs below a supermarket sign still glowing. I put my head down. Here'll do. I sleep a light sleep. Movement in the bushes is coming at me. Awake. I lift up but too late, he sees me: a baseball cap and baggy jeans, a young guy, perhaps a little drunk, a shortcut on the way home. He sees me. Starts. Frightens, turns immediate on his heel as I rise. I hear his voice, fading, sheepish as he beats the same retreat I just did with the man in the storm pipe. 'Oh shit, I'm sorry, bro, my bad.'

And then I realise: tonight I'm this guy's hobo.

Enterprise, NV – November 28

Young guy, approximately my age, a little junior. He is the youngest, most fresh-faced and innocent hitchhiker I've seen yet, still looks untainted by road, speaks kinda coherent. Perhaps he's having as much fun as I am. We're out front the petrol station, his sign's beside a sleeping bag, he's going to Los Angeles, rubs his face as he talks.

'I slept here last night. About a week ago I started out in Oregon.'

He sounds like he hasn't talked a while, the mouth and tongue remembering the shape of words. I feel bad, a pre-emptive guilt for the fact that we're about to be rivals. Last night there was one trucker, a Brazilian, said he was sleeping nearby, going west today. Only had one seat. If that guy comes back round, there'll be no time for sentiment. I'll drop this kid like a hot potato. Meanwhile, I take up responsibilities as an elder, feel I've got more years and more miles behind me.

'How you finding it?'

He's got bright green eyes, pale skin and freckles, a hooded sweater, big trainers, takes out a phone with a cracked screen. The phone is another sign of some belonging: a sign that he is a part of the consumer economy and that there are other people elsewhere in this boy's life.

'Sometimes it's good. Up in Oregon it was easy finding rides, but round here it's tough. Sometimes folk are so mean.'

Poor kid. I smile, nod. 'That's it, man. In America, it seems to me like when people think you've no money, some don't feel you're entitled to any manners.'

'*Yeah!* That's it, y'know.' His face opens right up, like I've just explained something to him. 'I think that's exactly it.'

'If I were you, I'd keep your phone visible. If people think you've money for a phone, they'll be nicer.' He nods a little. Vague, uncertain thanks come my way. I ask, 'Why you going to Los Angeles?'

He lifts up the phone, slides fingers over its cracked pane. 'I got no work up in Oregon. Used to do removals. Last woman I helped move house, she couldn't pay me. It was only a hundred bucks, but she didn't have it, said I could take this instead.'

He turns the screen my way, shows me something Asian-looking: ornate, ornamental, stone hands praying, Buddha with packaging, Buddha sitting on a pallet with polystyrene bubbles caught in his robes.

'What is it?'

'It's a statue. They sell for up to ten thousand bucks.'

I look at the kid: his freckles, big teeth, excited smile. His green eyes, all hope. Can't be much more than twenty. European and he'd stand a forty-sixty chance of being on his autumn break from university. American and he's off to LA, trying to sell a fucking Buddha to make pay on his last job. The vitality drains out of me. Damn, these guys are doomed, every last one of them. Thank god he doesn't even realise it, round here idiocy is mercy.

'The woman in Oregon, she had a contact, a buyer. A woman in LA who'd bought from her before. She gave me the woman's address, but I didn't have money to drive there. So this, *this* is my journey, for the Buddha.'

I smile, there's nothing more to say. Either I become a lunatic like the rest of them or else keep stumm. They're on a different frequency to mine and it's dangerous up there. Should I ask why he's travelling without the statue, how he'll get it there? I should offer to buy him some food? At least that way I don't have to say anything plausible in respo– *Toot-toot!* A high pitched horn sounds, not so shrill, almost like a vintage car.

'*Emre!*' The Brazilian shouts over, 'You coming or not? I've gotta get going!'

Oh boy! *Ohboyohboyohboy!* He's hanging out the cab, leaning on the wing mirror. I'm about to get shot of Vegas, I'll be in California! The truck's a mess, white turning brown with mud, insects, rust, panelling hangs off the door. The truck is short in length but tall, the blue canvas at the back looks loose, torn a little in places, but who cares. The Brazilian's come through for me! I wave, I grab my bag, I take my little madman by the hand, shake it. 'Good luck! Good luck with Buddha, with your journey!' I look hopefully back into his face, I speak his language, talk American English, talk Big. 'It will all be great. *I know it!*' and I'm turning on my heel, running, clenching a fist, a fist full of solidarity and never-see-you-again.

I-15, Baker, California

His name's Albino. I know in an instant that Albino is a good guy. Stout build, glasses, warm and open-hearted. I make my judgements quickly. He's first generation, the country's yet to take hold. He pulls the handle above his head, lets off rounds on the horn as motocross bikes bounce over the sands, race courses cut out of the desert beside the Interstate, riders flying up above the plumes of dust beneath them, leaping against the clouds and landing back on bouncing suspensions and coiling springs. A big smile over his face, Albino looks over. 'Fantastic, no?! In Sao Paolo I race them. Fantastic!'

He leans round, a cupboard beneath, comes back out with a cardboard box: oats, muesli. He shakes it, gestures to a drinks holder with a bottle of organic milk in it. 'Want breakfast? Or bread?' The bread is wholemeal. Albino is offering me muesli or wholemeal bread. I've found another.

We drive away from Vegas, out into desert, where a settlement of tin panels and tyres appears at the roadside, shrouded in scrub and cactus, built out of a hill in the shadows of grey rock. Abandoned cars rust slowly, preserved in hot dry air that fades the paint gradually silver-red-brown. Long industrial pipes and old car exhausts hang as wind chimes from a tree, and goats pick through the debris of automobile parts and sparse fauna. The cab is cool, with wind blowing in from a hole in the metal, somewhere out of sight. I take the muesli and the milk. Albino reaches to a cupboard and hands me a large mug.

'Sorry. Normally I have proper bowls, so as not to throw away the plastic, but,' Albino points behind us, a bunk, covered in documents and newspapers and blankets and water bottles, 'I lost one, so I have to use the mug.'

I laugh. 'Most people here don't worry about that sort of thing.'

Albino looks at me, ever smiling, but with a certain alarm. 'You have to! Because it all ends up in the ground somewhere! I always gave money to Greenpeace. Every month.'

I laugh disbelief, a Greenpeace member driving I-40. 'You still do?'

'Of course I still do! And when I see Greenpeace people, what do they call them, the Arctic 30, protesting against drilling in the Arctic, when I see them in jail in Russia, and I know my money helped pay for lawyers, that makes me really happy.'

I laugh more, civil society is actually thriving, right here in a messy truck cab spattered with crane flies and the remains of a hundred other bugs. I pour milk as Albino leans out towards a rattling from above the driver's side window. The door panelling is falling away, so that Albino stands up and half-climbs out of the window. He takes a section of plastic fairing, presses it back into position. With a snap, it fits back down. I gesture behind and he bounces back into his seat.

'What's in the truck?'

'We're taking cars, classic cars. There are three behind me, we're going to LA to get number four, then I drive back to Florida to a dealer there. This is a closed transporter, so it keeps the cars clean, no damage. There aren't many of these trucks around, so there is always a lot of work. This truck belongs to a friend. '

Albino leans forward and reaches round to the small of his back. 'I drove for FedEx, my own truck, but I had a crash and they fired me. Because they didn't employ me any more, they said they didn't have to pay insurance for my physiotherapy,' Albino shrugs an American shrug, his voice still cheerful, 'I have some pain, but it's OK.'

He plays a tune on his steering wheel as I eat cereal, ask, 'How come you came here from Brazil?'

'Money, I suppose.' Albino takes his hands off the wheel, plays a guitar in front of him, looks like a bass guitar. 'I was in a band, we played music all over Sao Paolo and Brazil. And we were good! Latin rock and samba. But we had an agent, who took all our money – 70 per cent! I mean, sure he has to take something, but not 70 per cent! So eventually we stopped. But I still love music. I *love* music! How about you?'

'Yeah, I like music.' And I ponder whether anyone ever answered that question any different. I go on, 'You still have family there, in Sao Paolo?'

Albino beams proud, as the truck's canvas howls with the hot wind tugging against it. 'My daughters! My two beautiful daughters!'

'You see each other often?'

'We talk all the time, on the phone. They are twenty and twenty-two now, just starting jobs after university. I send money back to help, so that they won't have to work like me. And now I think Brazil has changed so much since I was there. Last month, I was talking to my daughter on the phone, and she went into the metro station to catch a train to work, and I heard the loudspeaker bleeping and announcing things. And I started to say goodbye, and she laughed at me and said, "It's OK, papa. We have the internet on the subway now."'

Albino straightens, a knock-me-down-with-a-feather sort of smile, cheery disbelief at Brazil's progress as meanwhile America's twentieth-century Interstate project goes on crumbling beneath us. 'It makes me really proud of my country, that we are developing.'

I hear his words, they strike me, because I've heard so many

Americans talk of a pride in their country, and yet this is the first time I've heard a national pride I can smile with, for it comes at the expense of nobody else's perceived inferiority, nor in connection with some vision of nationalist superiority. Albino sits there, smiling at only an innocent idea of a nation that has provided something new and useful for its people. Ahead of us the highway keeps on, a single sand dune rises and falls. My head rests with sleep on the headrest of the seat as a lonely cloud moves over the sun and the axles thump and pound beneath us.

Yermo, CA – November 29

A petrol station, a warehouse, a junction. A car pulls into the road-side, stopping for some reason that isn't me, dust lifting from the rear tyres as I near and it pulls away. Around the town, if you can call it a town, I see no more buildings than I can count on one hand. The buildings just landed on desert: parachuted in, small imprints in the earth around them. One pickup truck is pulled over, the only difference between me and nothing. The truck waits on the opposite side of the road, the town in the near distance. He's not going my way, but it's been hours since Albino set me down, and sometimes it's good just to be reminded other people exist.

He's sitting on the lowered tailgate of the pickup, a flash of light going from lap to mouth, a baseball cap keeping his eyes in shade. I near, the silhouette gains detail: he's drinking from a Thermos, sun catching metal. Denim shirt. Denim jeans. Boots. I put up my hand, open palm, mean-no-harm. His knee is up, one hand resting on it at the wrist. He lifts up the fingers in hello.

'Where you heading?'

His voice is young, younger than his face. The voice doesn't drawl, doesn't sound like it's from round here. He's got the American accent, the one you never hear on TV, an accent that is slow and considered and storytells without the slightest effort. He has fair hair, a short beard, a dot of white hair growing in the stubble at his jaw and under one ear. His face is open, I can see trust in his face.

'Barstow.'

He laughs, 'What you going to Barstow for?'

'I'm hitchhiking, heading for San Francisco.'

'That makes more sense.'

I stand, realise I'm now standing on the wrong side of the road for Barstow, we both know as much, and there's nowhere to take this conversation.

'Well, I'm going the other way. I'm sorry.'

I nod that I know, smile.

'You from England?'

'Yeah, London.'

'Want some coffee?'

I shrug a shoulder, 'Why not. Thanks.'

The thread of the Thermos whispers as it unscrews. The desert is silent, each small noise roars. The pickup is dark green where the rust hasn't opened up the metal to show the rubble of the desert from through the other side of it. The smell of coffee lifts: steam catches sun, waves away as he hands the lid to me. I nod thanks. He's got scars branded on the side of his wrists, caught by hot metal. He has labourer's hands, large and blackened, the weave of his skin and fingers engrained deep down black. He nods back, our eyes meet: his pure blue, with age sketched either side.

'I don't think I've seen many people with a Thermos recently. You guys normally just seem to throw away cups.'

'That's us.' His face seems ready to say more, and then he just laughs.

'You don't seem like you're from around here either?'

He rubs a hand through the beard, the desert breathes a sound of stubble on hardened skin.

'I've moved around a lot. Born in Michigan, a small town, left in my twenties. That's a long time ago now.' He looks around the desert. 'I worked in Seattle a while, worked in a kitchen there for a few years and now I work out here, over in Nevada.'

'How come you moved down here?'

'I like the desert, even though my politics is more like Seattle. You come out here with a college education and the guys out here they give you a rough time to start with. After you've learned how to suck out your own rattlesnake bite, they loosen up, and they're genuine, often a lot more than the liberals on the coast.'

'You must be the only Democrat in Nevada.'

'I live over this side, near Bishop, California. Culturally it's more Nevada than California, but this state's changing. They say it's turned blue for good, and it certainly won Obama his re-election.'

'Really? What changed?'

'Vegas. Vegas, really. The gambling, you can drink on the streets, which is unheard of in America, legal prostitution. It's a very socially liberal place. It's hard to contain that influence, over the last five years it's changed the politics of Nevada.'

'And what are you doing here now?'

He points over his shoulders, up towards the line of black mountains on blue sky. I see a pickaxe: the sun catches a steel toe cap with the leather of the boot worn back. 'I'm working in a gold mine, exploratory stuff.'

'They don't have machinery for that?'

'Some of it, not all. Not yet.' He smiles calmly. 'The guys I work with are more worried about immigrants for now.'

'And you're not?'

'Things figure themselves out. Main difference is that I don't blame the Mexicans for coming here.'

'Most do?'

'No, they all think it makes sense, but they don't look at the policy that caused it. Not many of the guys I work with will talk about something like NAFTA, the free trade agreement back in the nineties. NAFTA let all the US corporations into Mexico, which killed off all their agricultural jobs, so the Mexicans now have to come here looking for work.'

He goes on, 'You think anyone wants to leave their home and family and swim the Rio Grande at night to try and get a decent wage? The Mexicans come over to California to labour for the grape harvest late summer, then they move up towards Michigan and the Midwest, and they pick berries in the autumn harvest there.'

I listen as the guy relieves himself of what sounds like years of conversation. 'Last year, because the way the climate's changed, because it's warmer, the flowers on the cherries in Michigan blossomed before the last frost, and so the harvest failed because the frosts killed off the flowers. Mexicans hear there's no work up in Michigan, word spreads, and so they don't make the journey north. The farmers in Michigan, they start complaining there's no cheap labour!' He laughs, 'But they'll spend the rest of the year complaining about immigration.'

My lid of coffee is empty. 'Want another?'

I nod, sit down beside him on the tailgate, let the straps of the bag fall off my shoulders as the hinges creak with our combined weight. A truck rushes by, throwing out hot air and gusts of tumbling wind. Our faces contort away a moment, pucker, our hair sits back down out of the dirty air. He refills the lid, coffee churns, yellow bubbles on top of the black and under the sleeve of his shirt I notice his forearm with the rough letters of tattooed names: Hemingway, Whitman, Kerouac. We sit there, arms down, our hands on the tailgate, leaning forwards.

'You seem to know a lot, but not be too concerned by it. You don't sound as dispirited as your opinions.'

He laughs, 'I guess I've been around long enough to realise how hard it is, changing people's heads. You can be sure I tried.'

Silence settles. Desert and mountain and the two men on the rusty tailgate of an old pickup in Nevada.

'You like America?'

Silence settles. Desert and mountain. A few cholla. Broken shards of black rock in the sand and rubble. A car tears through, the rattle of a broken exhaust, metal on asphalt, a flash of white catching sunlight and throwing spark.

'It's hard to, especially when it's hard to see how things could get better. We need to be making more people better off. We need more people with incomes and quality of life, so that they can educate themselves, and inform themselves, and so that we can stand a chance at trying to make change. But that's just not happening.'

'You think it gets worse?'

'I'm not sure I think like that any more, not sure anything surprises me. Republican senators in Ohio tried to suppress the Democrat vote by passing laws to limit polling hours in black areas. They even talk openly about it at their conventions. You've got the whole country buying their schoolbooks from Texas, because Texas has a lot of schools and so the business makes sense – economies of scale and so on – but that means that kids nationwide are getting a Texan education that's Christian and conservative and doesn't teach evolution or slavery or the Vietnam War as it happened.'

From somewhere, I think I feel my hope buckling at last. He goes on talking calmly, but you can tell it hurts him. 'And our elderly, dying people receive more spending on them in the final two days of life than in their last twenty years. At the end of their life an American gets every injection, scan, surgeon visit. Bodies are like blank cheques from insurance companies to hospitals that need to make money. Makes good business sense to go through a load of procedures rather than just leave someone to die peacefully.

'Man! And none of that even begins to account for the jails. You got these diesel inmates, driven constantly between penitentiaries so that they can't make relationships with other inmates. In jail those guys are working to stamp licence plates or weave body armour, prison labour is the cheapest workforce in America, so we've got a profit incentive in locking people up. The guys running the jails take back most of those wages by fining the inmates for small transgressions on the inside. One in a hundred Americans are living in jail, I mean, can you believe that?'

My mouth opens to say something. And then it just closes. His fingers release, relax their grip on the tailgate as we sit on the back of the truck. Something in the air hangs like an understanding. Silence. A crow moves along the white branch of a dead tree.

'And the Republicans can't speak sense because the Tea Party is holding them to ransom on the right.'

'Yeah, I heard. But we have that in the UK too.'

'You do?' He sounds heartened.

'Yeah. We've got a party more right than the Conservatives, and the Conservatives don't have the vision to look for votes anywhere else.'

'Not sure that makes me feel better or worse,' he laughs. 'Always nice to believe there are places that have got it right. A lot of people they'll say this country's been ruined, people always like to say it, and they say it without knowing how or why or what they even mean.'

I listen to the guy, not quite understanding something.

'How can you know so much, and feel so strongly, but just work in a mine?'

He turns a little to me, defensive. 'I'll write letters now and then, that sort of thing, and there's nothing better than hitting rocks with a pick where these kind of thoughts are concerned.' I smile, something between us, as if we both sense that a joke didn't cut it, doesn't explain it.

'Life's long, I guess. You're young and you see all the injustices, you're enraged, and then you get older. People you love get sick, they die, and suddenly your own mortality starts to feel more important than politics. It'll stay unjust forever, don't worry about that, and life's such a bitch that even the winners feel hard done by.'

I laugh, disarmed, this guy should be writing scripts, speeches, and here he is with a rusty pickup and a pickaxe, on his way to work in a Nevada gold mine. I wonder how old he is, wonder if he has family and if someone loves him as he should be loved.

'Do you think you'll head back to somewhere like Seattle one day, or anywhere more,' I can't find the word, 'you know, where people have the same politics as you?'

He looks distant from the question, as if it doesn't make sense, as if it is outside the terms in which he thinks.

'I'm happy with the desert. Seattle's changed a lot. The city's full of tech employees nowadays. I'm sure it's still a good place, I've good memories of it.' He lets out a large, youthful smile. 'Reciting the last pages of *Dubliners* at a Halloween party, shining a torch on my face. Or the old Chinese man who ran a tea shop and baked his own pastries, he used to ask me to watch the place when he went outside for a cigarette every fifteen minutes. I often think about if those places are still there. There was a chef, a head chef in the brasserie where I worked, Ray La France was his name, never been to France but proud to be French all the same.' The man bursts suddenly to laughter. He keeps on laughing, his face turns red, and he pinches at his eyes, keeps laughing, laughing with his eyes shining at the beginning of tears.

'And when we invaded Iraq, and the French refused to join the coalition, all of America started renaming French fries as freedom fries.' The guy is laughing so hard he's tearing up, and I realise why he's OK, why he hasn't despaired, and it's because he's got the humour, that humour which is all that can nurse a brain through all this madness. 'And they told Ray La France to change the name from French fries to freedom fries, and Ray just shrugged his arms and said, "*Non*" – just like that: "*Non*". Said he'd walk out the door. Telling Ray La France that he couldn't call them French fries, oh boy, that one was brilliant.'

Barstow Junction, CA – November 30

Nobody is watching. We're alone. All their backs are turned as one more comes whistling in. Desert and blinding daylight. Whistling, it calls me over, the tracks singing choir all the way to the horizon. I've waited. Damn, but I've waited. I been patient and no good it's done me. Car after uninterested car. A Mexican teenager stands in the pool of shade beneath an umbrella, selling plastic pots of mixed fruit. Mango, cucumber, pineapple and orange with lemon juice squeezed over and salt and chilli flakes poured in. It feels so long since last I got a ride and meanwhile the freight trains at the Barstow Junction are whistling, can't stop themselves playing out my fantasies right over my shoulder. They've been doing it all day, freight trains singing: calling me over as one motorist after another drove right on by. Closely watched trains: I've studied each one, its direction, where the rails seem to switch course and where the fence is lowest.

One more comes in, whistling a tune, and this time I'm through with it. My brain has no idea what's happened, but my soul spoke to my boots and suddenly I'm done with asphalt and I want only those rails. Suddenly. This wasn't planned. This wasn't planned, but boy I gotta. Suddenly I'm running, I'm making a break for fence as a line of empty cribs come rolling slow towards the turn just west of Barstow. Freight train comes whistling. It's a snap decision, it's gotta be … I run the line of fence, head for where it's lowest and haul up and over. Chain link fence: feet together, legs swung, land, then grab the pack and pull it back tight to shoulders. Running. I run-run-*run*. The thing's turning, train coming in at the left tilt, from the west, probably means it came *from* Los Angeles. It looks like it's turning northwards, which at worst means it came from some place else and is going *to* Los Angeles, at best means San Fran and almost certainly means it's headed the opposite direction to Vegas. Who cares? Even if it takes me to LA, worse things have happened and I've only a matter of minutes to get away from the engine, away from the crew, out of sight and stowed on a cart. I hold the straps of my pack, I head down an escarpment of sand, desert spewing, spitting mouthfuls from under each boot as I go falling, falling as sand turns aggregate. Cubes of stone rattle underfoot. I pull alongside as the train starts grinding towards a halt, and as it does I reach, reach out and grab hand rail, hoist up, hoist quickly up one-two-three rungs of rail and then throw myself down. I smell the hot iron of the crib, I get my head down. Out of sight.

On the deck, I lie flat, maybe a few hundred metres behind the three engines that pull this thing but with another two miles of carriage behind me. Perhaps I could have chosen better, gone further back from the engines. Still, I'm aboard. I'm flat, I'm out of sight and that's all that matters. I pull my arms back out of the backpack, hurriedly undress of it. I throw the thing down beneath a bench, get myself flatter as if they were looking for me already. I try to keep my head down but my heartbeat has gone so crazy I keep bouncing up and down in the air: I must be, what, five foot off the deck at least. I relax a moment, re-gather myself, take stock and then it hits me. I just jumped a freight train! Caught it near enough on the fly, those wheels were still rolling, I tell you!

Only it doesn't work like that. Time passes. More time passes. Scenario one: junked-up on elation, my conception of time has gone haywire and this is the longest ninety seconds of my life. Scenario two: ten minutes just went by, followed by another five. Hot blue sky overhead, the shadow of a flyover taking Interstate above the rails. Undercover I wait, staring at bubbles of rust from the metal. I watch a fly scuttle over iron, red eyes the same colour as the anti-corrosion paint: the fly right next to me and dressed in the transparent, grey hexagons of its wings folded back. I see its head open and out comes a trumpet mouth. I waft at it, and there's William, loud in my ears:

Little Fly, thy summer's play,
my thoughtless hand, hath brushed away,
for are not thou a man like me,
and am not I, a fly like thee,
for I dance and drink and sing,
'til some blind hand, shall brush my wing

A quad bike comes out from Barstow depot, nears the train engine with a high, silent plume of sand behind. They saw me. I'm sure someone saw me. I get lower, I turn invisible, transform into metal deck. I peer through the train carts: of course they didn't see you, Emre, it's just the crew change. Men get from the engine to the quad bike, quad bike retreats back towards Barstow. Plume settles.

Who knows how much time goes by. Lots, is all I know. The train is empty: no freight, just empty carts and me the only cargo. The train needs filling up, that much is for sure: it needs filling up with freight which, by my guess, has to happen either at the Port of LA or the Port of Oakland on the San Francisco Bay. The train sits empty: no cargo, no drivers in the engines, only the train waiting with me on the tracks, halfway through a turn and now pointing north.

Apart from the northwards direction, I'm not sitting so pretty. The guys in Ohio told me quite clearly: 'Make sure you've got plenty of water, plenty of food, because it'll be a long time before you stop, and you don't know where that's gonna be.' Without having to look, I know the contents of my bag. I've got the bottom inches of my canteen for water, a couple of biscuits. I've not eaten anything but a pot of fruit from the Mexican boy. I've been standing sweating in the sun for more hours than I care to remember. The day, too, what day is it? Pretty sure we're Saturday, early Saturday evening: train at standstill, who knows if these things roll on Sunday. No supplies. No certainty of movement. I've got to get off.

I'm marching back to Barstow, no time to lose on what must be a clear two-mile hike in and two miles back. I'll tell you the plan as we walk: I want that train, that much I know. The fence is easy to jump, pretty much concealed and the rails seem to run my way. My bet is the hitchhike along the coast from LA to San Fran will be a lot easier than the desert roads anyway, so winding up there would be a state of affairs no worse. Soon I'll need to sleep. I'll need to sleep somewhere, and why not the deck of the train? I'll wake up to the rail guards telling me to beat it, or I'll wake up to the movement of the train, rolling out. Perhaps I'll wake up to the train, still motionless, for a Sunday morning. Either way, the only situation I want to avoid is getting back out to that junction to find my train has left without me.

As I walk away from the railroad, receding in the dusk, I see a small red light, the signal box that holds the train at standstill. Again and again, I check over my shoulder. The light gets smaller as I march back to Barstow, buy a pizza from a restaurant and strap it to my back. I buy a drum of water, refill my canteen and so too the large bottle from the Navajo reserve. I march back to the train, straining my eyes until – yes, *yes*, there it is – the red light grows larger, the black shapes of my carts still at standstill.

Perhaps another hour slips away, maybe more. I eat my pizza sitting in the darkness on a short, metal bench where I consider what will happen. Cars pass on Interstate, not so often, but enough for me to consider whether I maybe missed a willing ride while waiting at the train. A memory comes back to me: the guys in Ohio warned I should get at the tail end of a container, so as to be able to shelter in its wake from the headwind and not end up 'dirty face'. If this does start rolling, I guess there'll be nothing but dirty face for it. I imagine what speed it will travel, especially with no cargo on board. Will it feel fast, will it feel slow?

As the night goes deepening, I bed down. My hitchhiking sign gives a layer of cardboard between me and the metal of the deck, which quickly goes from hot to desert cold. My sleeping bag is pulled around me, and a sweater rolled into a pillow. On my back, lying flat

I look up at the night. Trains keep coming and going, passing me by in my stationary siding so that I keep down for the approaching engines, watch the containers move by and wonder if the drivers have seen me. After a while comes a noise, faint headlamps from Barstow and those headlamps, I just about dare to believe, moving out to my train. At the head of the carriages, at the engine, the lights stop, and then they turn, before red taillights retreat through the desert and back to the terminal. Smaller dots of light appear, bobbing along at what looks like waist height, a second dot of light – smaller still – at head height. Torches and head torches. The lights make their way beyond the engine, turn, lift, climb and then disappear inside so that the scene returns to darkness. Scrabbling up on to an elbow, pulse quickens: drivers. They must be drivers going inside the engine. I wait with the sound of a heartbeat in a desert.

Five minutes later it comes. A whip of electricity: an electromagnetic snap as a switch is flicked and one coupling pulls in to the next with a humming. Heartbeat. I wait, wait with time all absent as the train creaks, it creaks and *creeeaks*. The creaks move near to me from far away: getting closer, moving towards me, pulling out the slack in heavy links of chain, pulling at the inertia of metal discs on metal rails. The creaks get louder, I hear them moving closer, under me, passing me by, receding, receding, receding into a long groan and – *shit* – we're moving.

Orion's Belt sees me north, so that I remember that cycle south to Austin on a night in 2009, a ride that taught me that in the US late-autumn, Orion's Belt sits central in the southern sky as early night comes forth. We're rattling the opposite way, heading north in what must be the direction of San Francisco. We pass Interstate with illuminated signs and I stretch my eyes, crane my neck but can't make out names. We pass another road junction and its signs, and I stretch eyes and to a *B*, an *S* and *OP*, so that I know we're all right, we're heading the way of Bishop, California, north of Barstow and that's it. We did it, this has to be the line for the Port of Oakland.

Up to the mountains the tracks run, and as we scale passes ever gaining in altitude, the train loops back on itself through switch-backs. Three miles of carts and the train spread all around that mountain pass, both its head and its tail out of sight and only empty cribs wrapped all through the bend. Up ahead I think I see one of the four engines, while the tail of the train still crawls over the far side of the valley, the end of the thing yet to come into sight from around the opposite ridge. Stowed gloriously away, unfound, I head into the Mojave Desert, the train rattling fast, wind blowing and the stars. Oh hell, the stars. They fly back and forth, shooting, shooting countless and each one so bright and clear so that they whisper it at me, so gently they say their sooths – *'Be humble, child, be humble.'* And I lie on my back, watching the night Mojave sky with the clatter of the freight train beneath, that noise I've wanted to hear all my life, and for the first time ever, I realise I was born in the twentieth century.

*

Awake again. Stars. Gone. Stone and rock right over my head, scratching the tip of my nose. Mountain and tunnel. I'm buried inside the earth and a light is coming. I can see another train, on separate rails but the thing is so horribly bright: enormous, round, like there's a prison break going on, floodlight pointed straight my way, the noise roaring so that – ogres and trolls – hard metal is coming right for me. The second train rears up on the adjacent rails but it feels like there's no way this is going to leave me intact, the noise alone will shake me to bits, break all of my bones. My eyes close shut and then torrents of air force through and pull them open once more. The thing is furious, raging, ready to pulverise me. I keep my head down, down and out of sight. The engines rear up, up above the horn fires, they greet from one engine to the next and it bounces hard against the rock. Fingers take hold my spine, sit me up straight.

Oh Jesus. *Oh Jesus Oh Jesus Oh Jesus:* this thing's going to eat me alive, it keeps on coming, cart after cart. The noise: *crash-Maersk-crash-Maersk-crashes* right for me, whistle comes shrill through the shadow of the engine. Damn, it's huge, right over me and the train rattling, each one a crashing drum, like each sleeper is splintering to shards beneath it. The engine goes rolling by with an impossible power, crushing by in a din of *Maersk-Maersk-Maersk-Maersk*.

Sleep must have claimed me because suddenly I am awake. Eyes open and *chicker-chack-chicker-chack-chicker-chack-chicker* runs below. I wake to the sight of the bivvy bag torn out from underneath, inflated like a wind sock: high in the air and full of gale, wind rushing in to trap at the foot, ready to pick me up and off the deck. I pull it down, wrestle the material back underneath me, only for it to tear free once more. I clutch it in my grip. Light hits the bag, getting stronger to reveal the lamp of another oncoming train. Only an engine: one-two-three engines, gliding fast towards a depot and some waiting cargo as *chicker-chack-chicker-chack-chicker-chack* keeps on rattling, rattling under me: the sleepers rattling with the engine and the sky rattling with the train. Squinting, something seems to be coming down from above: I lift up to get a closer sight of it.

What is that? I see sky move anew, coming down at me. Was that a letter that shifted up there? I roll to one side as it pounds down and tears paper. Another letter comes flying, then another: sky goes rattling and metal lengths with the shape of letters fly against the *chicker-chack-chicker-chack* night. What's going on? A ringing of a bell chimes and that – *yes* – but it must be. It's a typewriter on which we sit, moving through desert. The *chicker-chack-chicker* of letters typing out the night, the letters keep on flying: falling fast, stamping, snapping page as the wind tears through and I see a K, an E, an R, a flash of torn paper tails into a circle of light and then an A and a C. He sits ahead of me: the far side of the intermodal, legs dangling towards the tracks, insides of his elbows facing my way as his palms rest backwards on the cart. He wears a vest, a shirt that doesn't blow with the wind. It's Jack. He nods at me with a sense of purpose, invites words, wants me to speak.

His mouth opens, hesitates and then asks, 'Where you going?'

'San Francisco.'

He ponders. 'I hear it's different to the way it used to be.'

'Probably.'

'Where d'you start out?' He scratches stubble on his chin and cheeks.

'New York.'

'And how d'you find it? The journey?'

'Difficult, I suppose.'

Jack nods, his boots kicking lightly at the air inside the cart, swinging playful. 'Why you going to San Fran?'

The wind steals my answer before it is ready, takes my words to him. 'I don't know, not really.'

'In my time, that used to be a good answer. The best possible reason.'

'"In your time"? You mean it's not a good reason now?'

'Back then, we still had a lot to get out of our systems. Society was more restrictive. To cast all that off, well, it was heroic. It was an act of rebellion. We needed it.'

I listen, sitting up, dead opposite Jack and my own feet hanging inside their sleeping bag into the empty cart. The rattle of *chicker-chack-chicker-chack* of the train is ongoing, the punch of typewriter letters as wind pulls at my hair and clothes, while Jack's pale form sits calm, motionless, untroubled by the wind and lit by the shade of the moonlight.

'And now, what is it now? What do you think I'm doing?'

'Way I see it, society back then didn't tolerate individuals, whereas now, now it tolerates nothing but. You kids, you are pumped full of the stuff, it's all that counts. My generation, we were born under an order, and so we had to throw it off. People always have to throw off orders.' A lone tree appears and then disappears. 'Not so long ago, to be the Individual was the act of rebellion, but now,' a smile, a hand offers the answer, 'now it's just consent. Back then, humans we were younger, more innocent, we didn't know who we were, still had to find ourselves, our souls and our spirits in a place free of religion or tradition.' Each word burns. Jack cocks his thumb at the night, a highway beside us with a couple of illuminated rigs gliding down it. 'The stars remind you of your rights, of what you were put on this earth for. That's why we had to come out here, to learn for ourselves, to show something of what a life could be. Greater act of rebellion now, way I see it, is staying put, giving a damn to start with. The orders we were running away from, they're OK with escapism these days. Have to say, seems it suits 'em just fine even.'

My throat swells, hurts as I swallow. 'Then what would you do? If you were here, if this world was yours?'

'It's pretty simple,' Jack looks at me, not accusingly, but stern, more serious than I'd expected. He gives a short, quick smile, 'Main thing, really, is just to …' A train whistle fires, the letters fly and my eyes open back to *chicker-chack-chicker-chack-chicker-chack-chack-chack*.

All night I ride the thing, some four hundred desert miles with the wind pulled right through and over me. Finally the sky makes a break for blue, lightens, and up comes a curtain on the almond trees of the San Joaquin Valley. The world turns blue to orange and the silhouetted trunks split to branches against the dawn. The mist burns off and sun warms my face as the train clatters towards Sacramento. I watch the silhouetted almond trees stand humble under an orange sky of California as the freight train rumbles. My throat gives a short choke, I rub at my face and all I can see is the orange and the dark black shapes of those almond trees. And, oh hell, sweet life, but just what have you gone and done to me this time?

Modesto, CA – December 1

In a rail yard depot, alongside my ride and all around me carts went bumping, crashing loud against one another as trains were built long. Heavy black tankers rolled whistling towards the final crash, the things black and oil-stained but with the words *Corn Products* stamped on the side of each one.

I got off. The day was up, twelve hours or more I'd been on that cart. I had to move, had to walk warmth back into myself. Without a freight container or the darkness to hide behind, I felt exposed, vulnerable. They can all see me, sitting duck. I imagine arrest, a deportation, visa problems and no more filmmaker career in the USA, not that things are looking so hot on that front anyway. But still. I get off. Besides all that, the train's going north. I saw the station names on the passenger rail line: we're well past Fresno, we've overshot SF and are headed Sacramento. Who knows if it loops back into the Port of Oakland. Kuzey's guide book says the line runs to Illinois, up to Chicago. I can't risk it. I have to get off. We're stopped, a half-hour standstill in a large, long yard. I wave goodbye to my deck, thank it for the kind passage. I scale a fence, three metres high, climb right up and precarious over the top, kick at the sky as I roll over its peak. I hear a shred, look down at my memento, denim left flapping for posterity on the barb.

I walk miles, and miles. By the time seven miles are up, there stands before me a busy junction and the lines of stationary traffic beginning to return. I walk more miles, through nothing but suburb. Dense, vast, sprawling, ugly, endless, miserable, inhuman suburb. We're in Modesto, a junction just outside the town of Modesto. Don't forget that name. I still have to walk miles and miles more to get anywhere, these things are desert towns, designed with no thought for land use or even space, misanthropic property, each building hates its neighbours, all of them as far apart as possible. I approach town: a petrol station, a busy forecourt. I ask rides. I ask metro. Where do I head for the furthest reaches of San Francisco's public transport system? A man is filling up propane canisters, he looks round. 'Pleasanton, maybe even Livermore. It's fifty miles from here, less than an hour's drive.'

The excitement builds. To consider I might be fifty miles and a metro ticket from completing New York City – San Francisco. A rude awakening waits for me, but will reveal itself only slowly. I get some rejections, rebuffs, more rejections, none of it so polite, but I've had worse. I shrug them off.

An elderly lady, a petrol station attendant, comes out. She spits the words, cranes her neck out towards me as her voice croaks. 'You can't stand here. There's no panhandling allowed.'

'Sorry, what's panhandling?'

'Begging. You're not allowed to beg here.'

'Oh, that's no problem, I'm not begging.'

I return to the man, kneeling to refill his propane canisters, ask advice for a better spot.

'Two blocks south, second intersection, towards downtown Modesto. There's a bigger junction there. Highway 32. Highway 32 is what you want.'

I set to walking two blocks, but these are big blocks, desert blocks. The sun gets higher, gets hot, I peel away layers. The heat stings at my eyes, either that or the tiredness is filling them. What have I stolen in sleep? Maybe four hours outside Vegas, perhaps two on the train. The fatigue pulls blood into my eyes, they tingle as I walk the four-lane street of this small desert town that should eventually become Modesto proper.

Across the road appears a solid sphere of a rich green: beside a house stands a tree, dark leaves with baubles of orange. I check the traffic, cross without breaking stride, slice between the passing pickups. At the foot of the tree a pile of orange rots at my feet. Orange melting black: balls falling to mounds of sludge, a few with stalks still sticking up. Up on the tree a dozen or so remain, the nearest aren't ripe, still green, tree won't relinquish them as I give a first tug. I pick up a fallen stick, I jump higher, up to those that catch most sun. I hit the branch. *Take that!* I jump again, grab one down. It falls into my hand with a soft clap. I lift it up to my nose, I sniff: smells good, ripe citrus and juice seeping through to the air around the skin. I hit the skin, still cold with a memory of the night. It's firm, a slight thud. My palm claps the thing, thud. Thud. The space between flesh and ready fruit, a soft cushion. I bite at the tip, tear a hole and open it up. Ascorbic acid in my mouth. I peel off the pith, I look down at the great pile of decomposing oranges the household have left to rot. If it doesn't cost money and has no packaging, people here are sceptical. I tear out a segment of my orange. Will it be kind to me, will it be sweet or will it be tart, bitter, sour? The sun is upon my face, I stand beside the orange tree, I chew, lick the juice from out my moustache. I smile. I smile big.

Thumb out. Two signs beside me and now I'm clutching at straws. One sign, the one in my hand is a simple: *Livermore*. Another beside me, on the top of my bag, has more emotion: *NYC – San Francisco … ALMOST THERE! … GOING WEST?* Plenty of traffic is going west, that much is plain to see. It all heads my way but putting me on board is a different question entirely. They pour past, don't even look up. A couple pull in, my heart leaps. They're driving my way. She winds down the window.

'We can't give you a ride but here's five dollars. You can give it to someone for gas money.'

She sticks out the bill as I stammer, mildly offended, 'I don't need money. Sure you can't give me a ride?' This is new: they'll give me money to give to someone else to take me. They won't take me. I brighten, joke playfully,

'Can I give it back to you – as gas money?'

'Just take it!' She straightens her arm further, impatiently. I hold the paper as they drive away, the car pulling it from her fingers and leaving it in mine.

An hour passes, nothing changes. A car driver is heading the opposite way, caught by red light, he catches my eye to leave an unavoidable human contact. Collision. I've tugged his heart, the window comes down. He's got a sharp nose, dark features, I've caught his heart but it's an American heart and those things work in dollars. A hand comes out, finger beckons, the finger turns on itself. *Click-click*: he snaps finger and thumb, finger calls me over, wags me in. The finger beckons, suggests *come here and I'll sort you out*. I show him palm, wave it with a *no need* as I shake my head, give a call.

'I don't need money, just a ride.' He wags me in again, like I'm a halfwit who can't read between lines. I shake my palm again: just need a ride. The traffic pulls away.

Beside me is a parking lot stacked with Christmas trees for sale, truck after truck pulling in. I watch them loading up festive cheer, December 25th only a matter of weeks away, as they go stowing pine-shaped spirit, love for all mankind into the back of their trucks, prices starting at seventy dollars. Pine after pine is hauled away, tail-gate slammed shut before they drive home double quick. Drive right by me and my stupid thumb.

To be honest, to say it straight, I'm hardly taking any of this so well, not at my most stoic. I just rode a freight train through Mojave and now I'm begging miles again, I'm asphalt scum, remembering how it felt to be an emperor and now only a pauper once more. This is too much like anti-climax. I don't want this any more, I'm through with it. Besides all that, I see no light at the end of this tunnel. The Barstow junction before, this one outside Modesto. Hundreds of cars have passed – bohemian, hillbilly, Mexican too, all the usual rides – hundreds have passed my inland California spots without even a sniff of possibility. Sometimes I see them joke about it, see the car turn towards me: driven by a man, axles pointing my way quite suddenly, only for the hope inside to subside as the windscreen reveals a woman who squeals horrified laughter, grabs the steering wheel back to the centre of the road, and I know that his joke went: 'Look! Let's pick up a hitchhiker.' They disappear.

Central California and finally I've stopped believing, no longer think a ride possible. It's pointless. Nobody picks you up. Central California is a hitchhiking wasteland, desert: three generations of your family could die out here before anyone got anywhere. A front of Nevada conservatism is coming in from the east, full of the right to be selfish and 'fuck you, bum'. From the west comes South California, plastic California, full of media fear and a conformity that will live for decades without need of an alternative impulse or original experience. The two meet in central Californian desert, and you, your children and your children's children will all have time to perish before anyone is given a ride. Nobody picks you up. There's only fifty miles to go, but I'm done. Albino was my last ride and since setting out into New Jersey I've aged, the people at the roadside no longer see a young person hitchhiking, only an adult who doesn't own a car and the difference is enormous. I pick up my bag, turn, and I walk. I walk, throw my signs in a bin. I'll pay money, I'll buy tickets, I'll ride buses and trains to the BART line. I don't care.

I set to walking into Modesto. At the Christmas tree lot they advise one word: Greyhound. I'm back on my way to Greyhound and just the thought of it is painful. My feet move heavily, my head heavier. I smell fumes, smell diesel: the exhausts of one driver-only vehicle after another. There are no people, only me and the cars again. I see a woman from through the open driver's side window of a pickup. I walk towards her with 'Which way to the Greyhound station?' in my mouth. She sees me, corner of her eye sees me as the words make their way on to my tongue. An electric window slides up like a slap in the face. The car accelerates, muffler fires, you see it piss petrol out the exhaust.

On I walk, I fume, meditate on this consummate absence of respect for a living, breathing human being. And yet how could they ever show me any respect, to respect people you need to form independent thoughts all of your own. Americans don't have thoughts, or emotions, Americans have only responses. Everything has been beaten out of them by Hollywood and commerce.

Walking streets, I snarl at each step: every building a ten-metre house surrounded by a hundred-metre fence enclosing empty land. A muddy pond stands at the centre of a plot for sale, with two hundred metres to the next house. It's rising in me, I'm about to start hating America all over again. I wonder if maybe there's some sort of public transport system here, then I remember this place doesn't even have a public. My feet move on and I feel concrete, feel splints, feel concrete creeping into shins. I curse. I think John Steinbeck and *Travels with Charley*, one of his last, a book for the publishers. Steinbeck is living in New York: out of touch with the America he once wrote of, he resolves to buy a camper attachment for his pickup and drive across America from behind windshield and by the power of gasoline. Nice try, John, but driving across America won't teach you nothing, scarcely more than conformity. What he needed was a thumb and a rucksack. I can feel my heart rising up my chest, hell, this time I'm getting it bad … I'm even turning on Steinbeck. I pass a driveway. A woman – European fat, American average – is unloading her pickup, a small, practical pickup. She fusses under a tarpaulin: tattooed arms, white T-shirt, jeans, hair scraped back.

'Excuse me. Which way to the Greyhound station?'

She laughs. She looks down and laughs at my feet, as if it were a stupid idea to even consider using them for an idea so absurd as walking.

'You've got quite a trek there. Give me two dollars gas money, I'll drive you.'

I think, I ask distance. I don't like her much, but I'm no fan of strolling in Modesto either. 'How far is it?'

'Maybe another five miles.'

In my pocket is the five-dollar bill the couple gave me for gas money. Good form says I can't be asking three dollars in change. The woman's getting keen, I sense it. Tiny, square teeth, pale skin in spite of California sun. Small eyes and puffy lids.

'How much money you got for gas?' she asks.

I'm honest: 'Five dollars.'

She nods, nods a *that'll do* satisfaction.

'Five dollars I'll take you there.'

I step it up, I drop human exchange and play her game, play transaction, play taxi.

'Well, really what I need is to get to Livermore, or at least Tracy. I'll give you twenty-five if you take me there.'

She tips her head, shakes it. 'I'll take you to the bus station, but I'm not leaving the city. You could be dangerous.' She looks right at me, talking so plain it's as if she's simply said my laces were undone and it's a reasonable thing to point out. 'I mean, you could be crazy.'

I turn sad, genuine sad. She doesn't even realise that, where I come from, a doubt so straight in the face like that could be considered insulting. I have no energy to pull punches now, I'm beat.

'You Americans are such nice people, but you're all so afraid and mistrusting of one another. Doesn't it get tiring?'

She laughs at my apparent joke. 'Well, I don't know who you are, what you want to do with me. There are a lot of crazies out there. How do I know you aren't one of them?'

She's right, I can't be trusted. Even now cruel thoughts are taking me, suggest I give her good reason to think me a madman. Damn, this country it breaks people, could take the most gracious and turn them insolent, the gentle and make them violent. None of this is sentimentality on my part, just basic common sense: why can't they take a bit better care of one another? Steadily, against your wishes or notice, this country brutalises people and now in Modesto I too have become Americanised, naturalised American, that name given to the state of mind where you have been worn down by your countrymen and women, to a point where you expect only repeats of the same behaviour by which your heart has already been made hard. Europeans aren't cut out for this kind of business, we haven't enough spirit to wade through it all.

Fury seeps out of the Modesto earth, this country built on mistrust, hellfire, fear and unbridled consumer satisfaction. She's too candid, she's so rude and dumb, so far from anything that ever resembled manners, she doesn't even realise it's impolite to accuse someone flat that they could be a murderer or rapist. She picks a bag from the back of her truck.

'Let me take this inside, then I'll drive you to the Greyhound for the five bucks.' She ambles away, says with a laugh, turning her back as I hear, 'That British accent of yours could be a fake for all I know.'

In spite of all the venom in my head, my face and speech have concealed it, I haven't given the first whiff of what I really think. I weigh things up. No doubting that I hate Modesto, I'm through hitchhiking and through walking too. I hate it all, but right now I hate her even more, more than anything I've ever hated. Pride: as far as I'm concerned the stuff it comes and goes, can be suspended or forgotten, compromised now and then in the name of pragmatics, eventually it grows right back. Pride is like an earthworm under the blade of a shovel, real resilient, knows how to make itself whole again. But this time though, this person is too much. I can't share a car with her, can't sit beside her and can't give her the money in my pocket. My brain, compulsive as ever, thinks comms and campaigns, considers how to be the change I want to see in the world. In terms of shifting a human heart, which, I ruminate, is the stronger: to engage, ride together, communicate and disprove, show her she was wrong? Or else is it a more effective statement to withdraw altogether: show that her suspicions are so foul as to be intolerable.

'*Shuttup, Emre*! Forget your damn equations! Yes to the latter, but who fucking cares all the same? You're not doing it.'

She walks back out, soda in hand, large soda with a big, ribbed plastic straw. Slurping.

I open my mouth. 'You know, it's a nice day, I'm just going to walk I think. I don't want to make you uncomfortable.'

A man has followed her out: beard and baseball cap, he shuffles, drinking a cigarette as her ribbed straw slurps next to him. He shuffles, puts a hand deep into the pocket of his jeans, watches.

He laughs, 'You've got a long way.'

She puts in, a slow, singing mockery, 'Oh dear, did I offend you with that British comment?'

'It's just so sad that you're all so afraid of other people.'

I'm turning on my heel, hear her voice, 'You know, I'm having a really lousy day, and I was looking forward to doing my good deed for the day, helping out a stranger, but that's fine, just fine, you walk away.'

I do as she says, walk away from this central Californian saint, loud and aggrieved in my ears, full of her good deeds for the day, five dollars apiece.

Two more hours I walk Modesto, this nowheresville, small town of nothing that still stretches ten meaningless miles. No bars, cafés or public spaces. Cars and shops and shops and cars. I'm the only human being left, an on-foot transport pervert. Drifts of leaves line the gutters of cracked concrete. Overhead are pepper trees, dropping peppercorns of bright green and pink to grind beneath the burrs of my boots, crumbling in a storm of colour, spice, scent. Blow me, but Nature created pink and green peppercorns while Mankind was creating Modesto. A man stumbles towards me, behind him the shopping trolley that contains his life, this destitution a sure sign that the Greyhound station is getting closer. Loose jeans, black duffle coat, pale skin with red blotches all over it, red cracking white. Short fair hair, blue eyes, spittle dried thick and yellow on his lips. He comes at me, his hand a-reaching:

'*Brother ... brother ... Pentrscstl chrch yiu?*'

'Excuse me?'

He repeats, words slurring: '*Brother ... brother ... you got the Pentecostal church in you? You can be saved!*'

No thanks. I'm saved already, and you ain't no brother of mine.

Eventually, finally it comes, I walk up to the Greyhound station: simultaneously the only place I want to be and the worst place on earth. I see more men with shopping-trolley lives, a woman in orange flannel hotpants and vest, reclining on a pavement and reading a book as her bloated stomach of alcohol crimson comes slipping out, and the breeze twitches at the corners of the pages. I shrug. At least she's reading a book. Beside her a proud man is finishing off an argument, the most erudite-looking creature I've seen for hours: he's clean, wearing a pressed shirt a rich blue, chinos, neat moustache and sheer sunglasses. He directs buses, seems to work here, his patience looking even thinner than mine as he tries to keep afloat in Underclass, send his daughter to college so that she can get the hell out of Modesto for good. I ask the bus to Livermore, the Livermore BART station, where I can ride a metro train to San Francisco. He gives me short shrift.

'No service.'

'What do you mean there's no service. You mean it doesn't exist?'

He looks at me, looks at me from behind sunglasses. 'Kind of wiseass question is that? What an asshole thing to say. *Jeez!*'

Exhausted, I realise sadly that the only two sane people left in the Modesto Greyhound station have now offended one another more than everyone else combined.

'Of course it exists!' he spits. 'But not until tomorrow. You'd need the bus to San Francisco. Forty-five dollars. Leaves in four hours.'

My jaw drops. Drops once at forty-five dollars for a fifty-mile bus journey, drops a second time at the idea of four more hours of life, lost forever in Modesto. I spin away, recoil like I've been shot, riddled with bad news buckshot. I'm going nowhere fast and realise suddenly that all I need is the bathroom. I shuffle priorities, that can be the new task. Taking a leak is an attainable goal. I head for the terminal, step inside, stride past human shrapnel, neoliberal carnage, shock and fucking awe. It's a living death in here: dogs curled up in jackets, shopping-trolley lives, laundry bags, cardboard *Homeless* signs staring right back at cardboard *Please Help!* signs. Jesus, and they say twentieth-century Communism was a disaster. Misery. Incandescent misery. There are no words for this disgust, this contempt ... it's burning, corrosive. If I were to spit the stuff it would scald through metal. There's no doubting it, I've had suspicions for a while but at last I'm convinced: this is the worst country in the world, largely because so many of the numbskulls around me still think it's the best. This is an abomination. Cancel the aid budgets, tell the DEC that America is the world's foremost humanitarian catastrophe. Forget the white rhinos, orang-utans and Bengal tiger, it's the bloody middle classes, the world's middle class is the fundamentally most perilously endangered species there is, the American strain in particularly close proximity to extinction, and the society around them so pitifully moribund that their reproductive rates have gone the way of the giant panda anyway. It's only once you hit Modesto, too, that you realise the scale of the problem. Having grown up British, all chipped with class-system shoulders, resentful of anything the faintest bit bourgeois, by the time you hit Modesto Greyhound station you realise that, god damn, but we need those middle classes. Because the poor fuckers outside the Greyhound station, oh my, but they won't be helping themselves any time soon.

Still, all that politics is for another time, boy. For now just get to the toilet, take a leak, then get out of here. Stop getting distracted. I stride through, I make the toilets. It's cramped in here, people everywhere and nowhere to turn. Urinal on the wall: black bag thrown over it in place of an Out of Order sign, the second urinal has fallen down and split. Hell, I've stepped into a crime scene, I've seen better toilets in the Romanian south. I make for cubicles: a toilet, shit in the bowl, door kicked off. I double out: a larger cubicle adjacent. I keep my head down, I lift head as I step to cubicle: I see feet. Two feet. There he is, bloody hell, it's Uncle Sam, American Dream himself, sitting on the shitter, door wide open, trousers around ankles, trainers full of holes, trousers full of shit, legs stained black with soot and – why can't I stop my head? – you know this won't end well. There it is, there's his cock: violet, purple, a slug crawling out of pubis, as my brain hears the calm, eminently sensible voice of Ripley: 'I say we take off and nuke the entire site from orbit.'

I beat a retreat, I'm passing out. I'm drifting into hypo, seizure. I need an espresso and don't mind admitting it either, give me a gallery and don't skimp on the annotations, not after Modesto. I need some gentrification and fast: intravenous, a hypodermic shot of taleggio, pants down and straight in the rump. This is hell and I am in it. This is not civilised. He's after me, here comes Mephistopheles, whispering at Faustus in a calm smile: 'But this is not hell, and nor are you in it.'

It's a lie! A lie! Don't listen to him. I spin, I stride back out: faces, faces everywhere, dark eyes and reaching hands: *The Horror! The Horror!* I gag. I want the subway, I want escalators and tubes that spirit you directly from a home to the safety of an office or an organised consumer recreation. I want San Francisco, I want an aubergine burrito, I want subway exit with artistic posters for a new exhibition examining gender identity, I'll even take a bank as headline sponsor. I've had enough journey, just give me a destination. Give me a destination, let it be San Francisco and get me there by metro, let it be a journey through the earth. No more of this: just give me comfort, blindness, ignorance. I want the oblivious life that the middle classes of the world create in recompense, that root, cosseted blindness by which Modesto outside is permitted to exist.

My mind sways, groggy. Here comes that time when you realise that the love and feeling you have for all this world is no match for the chaos you wish you could right. That no matter how much the suffering might hurt you, the strength of feeling it invokes inside, you cannot rectify it, your pain makes nothing better and you must do something more, something more than just to feel. It all slows, all slows away. I fall, stumble, feel myself growing thin, thinner and thinner even as a weight lets down to settle on my shoulders. I tilt, tip, feel the weight embolden, and I watch as the dark colours of my view strain off the light and gather on my vision. From out of a fog I feel it: a mist has set down all around, swirling mist turns, turns to form a black mask with only the eyes open, glowing red and evil and covering all of the world. Only the faint outline of crowds press behind the mask, descending to face me. Small in front of it I stand, and hard at my shoulders the weight it pulls, leans and I realise that it's him, at long last he's come for me, the Grand Inquisitor. The mask it speaks, speaks to me, speaks soft … so gently the mouth moves and the words come so wise and patient with all time frozen peacefully in them:

'Let all of them die. Let them be wiped from the face of this earth, for none shall miss them, and none shall weep for those who are scarcely human any longer anyway. Without them we will start anew, and none of our children shall suffer this indignity again.'

The mouth blows forth the final words in promise,

'Be sure, it is for the greater good … an act of love, of great and of final love.'

Tentatively I nod, nod at that voice so kind, so reasonable. The weight pulls down, down hard at my shoulders and at my thighs. I've never been so far away, so far away from love, from any I love or who love me back. I'm an orphan of this world, and a chill passes out of the heat and down my throat. A frost forms around the edges of my heart, with all so deathly hard and cold. Up from the chin, I stammer, my teeth chatter, the sun is packed away, the young moon dismantled. My teeth chatter, my chill bones press at my skin, and all is so cold and simple and cold. The mask, the mask in all its weight it grows too much to bear. I cannot resist these words, nor the sharp pains pressed at the blades of my shoulders, so that the black mask turns and lets out a black cloak, a cloak to wrap around me. From far away I see Nathalie dancing toe to heel at an election victory. There comes a voice, sweet and precious and caring, but so very distant: 'Do not hate. Only the unloved hate, the unloved and the unnatural.' My mouth falls open a little, and I know the words are true, but in Modesto I can feel neither love nor Nature, and so the cloak it lifts higher up my body, the thing goes draped all around my skin and yet only makes me colder still, shivering as the mask takes up a smile. I look at the eyes, burning red as they watch me: they see that I am over, spent, and that smile flickers again before giving more words so terribly perfect.

'But come now. Why do you fight? For it seems quite clear to me that you like the idea of people, so very much more than the reality.'

I stare, stare right at the simple answer waiting there. I listen. The mask nods, I begin to nod back, and then, I hear a voice, see a gleam of light on the darkness, his sunglasses removed and striding straight for me. It's the bus conductor, the ticket salesman, sunglasses off and eyes revealed: human eyes look right at me. I see his bright blue shirt from out of the black mist: a hero. The ticket inspector is talking to me, 'Say, I'm sorry for that right there, it's been a long day. I should let you know, there's a gas station round the corner. There'll be a lot of San Francisco traffic going through that way, if you're trying to hitch a ride.'

The mask unfurls, its smile hollowing as the mist lifts and smoke burns away to return the shapes of the other passengers waiting in the terminal. The blue shirt of the bus conductor, the bus conductor, the bus conductor so sweet and blessed, stands right over me as the mask recedes and then in a puff of smoke finally disappears. My mouth stutters out a word of thanks, of 'Thank you. Thank you, sir.'

He smiles, puts hand to chest as if to say not a bit of it. And together we smile the warmest smile I have ever known.

'That a British accent?'

'Yeah, yeah. I'm from Britain.'

'My daughter is there right now, studying. She's at Sussex.'

I laugh, right there, a mark of authenticity on the whole story – the evil mask, the ghosts, the lot of it – for no work of fiction would have such an absurd and avoidable coincidence.

'Sussex? That's where I studied.'

'Really? You mean, in Brighton? We hope to be visiting her at her rooms in Falmer next spring.'

'Yeah. Falmer, the University of Sussex.'

He laughs and in my mind I see the old church in the village beside the campus, with the black flint that shines in its walls, and the green hills and woods that sit above the lecture theatres.

'That's a strange thing to find here. She says it's a really nice town, says they elected a really good Member of Parliament, a woman who cares a lot about the environment.'

'Yeah,' I guffaw, stutter some more, gurgle, 'yeah, they did.'

San Joaquin Valley, CA

It was a new tactic. Desperation. I want it over with. Still hitchhiking, but now hitchhiking with commercial incentive, hitchhiking on the free market. Of the thirty characters on my piece of corrugated card, I know which one had caught Jay's eye: $. I'd used a row of the things. '$$$ *Will help pay gas.*'

Jay gets to the point: 'How much you got for gas?'

We haggle. I go in with six dollars for twenty miles, offer an unreasonably low price for the town of Tracy, far closer than I want. He knocks me back: no surprise there, but I feel he's game, biting. We'll settle for something reasonable and I was right to go in so low. Right now all I have is the imperative to get out of this dump. It will be a while before the guilt hits me: the bargaining power that Modesto's poverty rate gives me as I continue my privileged jaunt. Whatever I offer, I sense that eventually Jay will go for it. I follow up my six-dollar insult with a proper bid: twenty-five dollars for the forty miles that will take me to Livermore and the end of the San Francisco metro system. Jay pulls his hand across his mouth, the skin of his fingers a deep black against the light pink of his fingernails.

'I was gonna go to Tracy earlier today anyway. See my son.'

'Your son?' I slap his shoulder like we're old pals. Jay looks almost imposing, but slow, calm. I know that I shouldn't be so familiar but the excitement of an ending has got to me. 'Come on, let's go!'

Come on! Priorities, Jay, priorities, my good man! Family always comes first, *always!* He looks distant, rubs a hand over the corn rows neatly down his head. He's got small white eyes: dark, heavy lids that blink slow expressions as if he rarely finds himself in the territory of new thoughts.

'OK. But I gotta go home first, tell my other kids where I'm going.'

The passenger door doesn't close fully, the panelling is falling off at every joint: jump leads are snaking red-black in the footwell with empty drinks bottles gathering dust. *Buick* is proud in the centre of the dash, the speedometer runs left-right in a straight row of numbers rather than a dial. I turn to Jay, ask him:

'Your name, is that Jay, like the bird?'

He looks round: dry, curt. 'No. J like the letter.'

J drove. His legs spread wide, one hand on thigh and the other holding the wheel by its base as we accelerated through each opening of traffic. The windscreen is chipped, the split spreading all the way from north to south. The glass is smudged filthy by the marks of a driver who has rubbed frantically in failed efforts to clean himself a porthole. We head for Highway 132 west. The sun is lowering, slumps down behind the line of mountains: the Great Wall that isolates San Francisco from the horde of middle America I've stumbled through. We pull up outside the house. J heads in, tells his kids he is leaving a while. I look up at the roof of his small bungalow, see a solar panel and can't help a dry laugh: a sustainable underclass, carbon neutral, inequality forever when the socially unacceptable becomes environmentally sound. He walks back down the path, squeezes through gateposts his own width, sits down with one sigh from J and then a second from the upholstery.

'So you've got a kid in Tracy and a couple in Modesto?'

J is in his own head, or simply not listening. He turns the steering wheel lazily. He leans, chin up at the windscreen, waits long enough that I'm about to ask again.

'Got one more in Marseille too.'

'In Marseille!?'

'Fifty mile south of here.'

'Oh, not Marseille in France.'

J doesn't say anything. I'm just talking crazy again.

'Four kids?'

He nods.

'How old are you?'

'Twenty-eight.'

'Me too.'

J drives, accelerates up to speed: the engine splutters a little, but the Buick moves strong, fast. The car feels heavy, it sits low to the ground with a purpose to it, our seats slung right back. I open the window and warm air comes in. Normally I'd make conversation, but right now it seems too forced, too unwelcome. Besides, I paid for this ride: full-on transactional, hard cash. It was no goodness of heart that got me motoring into the sunset for what I hope to god is the final time. I don't have to talk and J hardly seems concerned either way. All I want is to sit here and to travel, be travelled, be moved through the particles until they've been reassembled as metropolis. A moment later my conscience pangs: makes me realise there is another human next to me and that surely we have to talk, we must have something in common. The Buick finds more speed, Modesto recedes and we pass dead vines under shrivelled leaves, then lines of orchard where short trees are regularly spaced, the fruit gone and leaves browning so that I think of Pala and his agricultural plans.

'What are these trees?'

J looks to the side. 'Don't know.'

We drive on, pass cows, first a couple and then a hundred: feeding at a trough, a line of them, hooves in the mud beneath a metal build-ing. A mound of silage is uncovered of its white, plastic sheet, steam winding up from the small tor of rotting matter. The smell of the farm comes in through the window, only it doesn't smell of shit but of squalor: squalor and industry, fear and stress, confinement, misery and then death.

'What you do in London?'

I stay vague: US-style employment, gig economy. 'I work on projects. Came over for one that didn't happen, back in New York. What you do in Modesto?'

'I'm a drug dealer.'

J's deadpan, doesn't even look at me, his mouth a little open. I see the curve of the small, white teeth, purple lips, the thin line of a thin beard. I'm getting ready not to judge, *gotta-earn-a living somehow* on my tongue.

He looks round, laughs at me. 'Not really. I been sorting myself out. Work in a warehouse, fixing remote controls to television sets.'

'How is it?'

J shrugs. 'I want to be a police officer.'

Something inside me sings a little at this news. Whatever my thoughts on the police, I'll overlook my distaste in return for the fact that J, who seems so apathetic, has an aspiration, a will to get somewhere, be some part of society.

'Really? Why?'

J keeps looking at the road, heaving ahead.

'So I can shoot people and get away with it.'

I wait for him to tell me once again that he's only joking, but he doesn't.

J drives, the exhaust of the Buick firing, snapping now and then behind us. We drive out into the San Joaquin Valley, where ponds of water lie green and stagnant with algae. The door panel starts rattling next to me. Oak trees lean over towards the road, farm country opens: metal barns and rusty old tractors are sucked like pacifiers by the dry mud that pulls them into ground. The San Joaquin River winds through with evening sun gold on its black back. Wind pulls it up into ripples, a couple pick towards the water's edge: she is pregnant, a white dress over her round stomach full of new life, while beside her he carries a garden-cane fishing rod with a wine cork hanging from it. A hand reaches out and he guides her to help her along a ledge. Long evening shadows make their way down to the river, and into the river they dive.

Up ahead are high hills, from over which the sunlight has turned the dirty windscreen pure white, trapping light inside each smear. J moves around, adjusts his visor – 'can't see shit' – he eases off the accelerator and we cruise along with the rest of San Francisco's returning traffic.

'That up there is called the Altamont Pass.'

Grassy hills loom big above us, covered in endless windmills and their stationary silhouettes.

'Altamont,' I ask, 'is that a native American name or something?'

'Don't know.'

We drive on, horses running across a field with scrap cars, the setting sun drawing a bar along the top ledge of the mountain. Starlings swarm in a cloud twisting out of the grasses, go up in smoke and then flail as a whip that beats the land.

'How's Modesto?'

'It's all right.'

'What do you do there? When you're not working. You just hang out with friends?'

'I don't have no friends.'

'How come?'

'I don't like to associate with other people. They just get me into trouble.'

'What kind of trouble?'

'Jus' trouble.'

'You from Modesto originally?'

'Nope.'

'Where you from?'

'I was born in Oakland, near San Francisco. I lived in Marseille, now in Modesto. Been all round.'

The last month has seen me travel across his United States and here is J describing three California towns as 'all round', the places that have staged the acts of his life: each within a hundred miles of one another and so too the highway on which we're talking.

'You ever go to San Francisco?'

J answers slow, 'Used to go there, every week.'

I wait for stories of when J was young, carefree: when life was good and he was hanging out in San Fran just like I'm about to.

'Yeah. Went every week, four years ago. My son was in hospital.'

'Oh. He's all right now?'

J looks into the white sunset. Flat. 'No. He passed.'

I don't say anything, simply wonder what it was: premature birth, passive smoking during pregnancy, disrupted organ development? Perhaps I'm being harsh, glib: maybe it wasn't biological, perhaps it was gang-related. I realise the ugly presumption in even a bleeding heart like mine. However crummy the luck, where people are poor you always set to figuring out how it could be their fault and how they were to blame for their misfortune. Bad luck is for the middle class and upwards. Poor people just get what they deserve.

'I shouldn't take you all the way to the train station. If a cop stops us, I'll be in trouble.' He looks round, apologetic in confession that he can't honour all of our deal. 'I'm on probation. I'm not supposed to cross the county line.'

'It's no problem.' We drive on in silence, crest the Altamont Pass. J doesn't move. Legs apart, steering wheel between them, hand still rested at its bottom spur. The traffic gets heavier: mountain bikes with purpose-made rain covers hang suspended from the backs of jeeps, trailers pass us with boats and jet skis mounted on the tail of shining cars. All around, the metropolitan return from the rural playground back to their metropolis, leaving behind the agricultural hinterland where J and others like him spend their lives. Sunset whites out the windscreen and 'can't see a thing' is all J says, over and over again.

In the end, J took me all the way to the station, decided he'd violate his probation to get me where I needed to go. He got out of the car when we arrived at the end of the BART line, came round to shake my hand as I lifted my backpack from the boot. His jeans down to his thighs, a long sweater hanging just below, he stood there: short, his eyes still slow.

He shook my hand and 'take care' travelled almost back and forth, a final trade as I turned for the train station and got my ticket. Over my shoulder I saw him standing with the long, black Buick: dust and mud and rust above the dirty wheels, rubber beading falling from around the side windows. The waist of his jeans fell to his thighs, the braids of his hair pulled back tight on his head. A last sunlight flashed a warm white on J so that he stood there, lit elegiac, illuminated like a dead man, like a saint beside the Buick and glowing. From down a tunnel I heard the subway car arrive, the electricity of it played for me, so that it snapped first once and then hummed closer like a viola, like a cello held between thighs. Over my shoulder I saw J watching me, watching as the station barricade opened its arms and let me through so that I knew, at last, the city would be waiting at the other end. The escalator went on with its eternal arrival and took me down to the tunnel. I stepped on, stopped moving, passive at last as I started sliding away. J turned. And I disappeared.

Battery, San Francisco, CA

Skyscrapers rose up dense around me, dusk breaking as I stepped out into a new land, the glass and steel of one final human forest, where people live as close as trees in Appalachia's woodland. The peaks of the towers stood overhead, clustered jealously to bedrock and sprouting, side by side, on the small patch of San Fran granite, the stuff that does not liquefy when a fault lines burps. From inside the road beside me came the rattle of a cable, the rail embedded in the asphalt and the cable coiled with its tight ringlets like a rat's tail. The cable jumped, pulled taut – *tap, crick-crack* – a rumbling whipped just beneath my shoes, pulling a tram from far away, the thing out of sight except for a single headlamp nearing from down the lengthy street. Beside me stood a man in a long white jacket, its wide belt fastened with a buckle around the front, his step the stride of a man who knew where he was going.

Disoriented, I asked for Battery Street, and with a point of the hand he answered, setting me on my way. Walking the same direction, at the same pace, awkwardly side by side we moved silently along together. The blocks are long, two of the things to pass next to one another, and so he turned to me.

'New in town?' His polished shoes stepped beside my boots.

'Yeah. Is this downtown, the skyline in all the photos?'

'Guess so. This is the edge of the financial district.' He waved upwards at red beacons flashing aircraft warnings from on top of angular frames. 'The cranes are back. They went away for a while.'

'You mean after the dotcom bubble? Is it about to crash again?'

'This time seems like genuine wealth is being created. I work on software for electronic signatures, we're about a hundred people.'

Traffic lights spanned the road ahead, marking maybe ten more seconds of conversation, a decade still to discuss and the thought of a hundred-strong office working on only the scribble of a signature.

'Sure there's problems, I mean, there is too much tech just for the problems of people who work in tech … a lot of single guys who want to hook up with girls, who can't cook or do their laundry, and who only really need technology that will help simplify paying someone else to do it for them.'

We waited together at the lights, turning towards our different directions in the city as I listened to what felt like the first elaborate thoughts to hit me in a long time.

'I hope that changes, but I think twenty years ago there was a lot of speculation and novelty, while this time it's like society itself is becoming tech, like the real world corresponds to the technology. Last time the technology was changing, but society wasn't.'

*

They take my name, it's down on a list. She's expecting me, has already signed in. They offer to take my jacket. I'd rather keep it on, underneath I must stink, and all I did was ask for the bathroom. I'm here. I've made it, it's over. America's behind me and now I stand back in a toilet with a line of disfigured, leaning orchids moving with desperate, forced elegance towards me. I should introduce H, let you know what's about to happen.

We had met a few years earlier, back in Britain, but by then she was working in San Francisco and had got in touch when she heard I might be drifting that way. We always moved in different circles, but she had an enjoyment of life that it was hard not to be charmed by. Her father had knocked her around as a child, and once that stopped, by comparison the world suddenly seemed a place really quite bright, full of optimism. The first night we met, she told me stories of the aunt she had been sent to live with, away from her father, out in the countryside. She told me proudly how it had been her job to collect the eggs the chickens laid, before the rats could eat them. Ever since then I couldn't help but have a soft spot for her. Besides all that, she's got the widest eyes in California, and twenty-five thousand Twitter followers, where Nathalie scarcely breaks two hundred. She'd be great for my career. Famous for being famous, H went on to become the radiant, archetypal example of new age enterprise and media ... Turns out people give you more face-time when they enjoy looking at your face ... like lottery balls that roll out of a hatch, down on to waiting necks to decide vast amounts of how the rest of a life unfolds. Some people get lucky, and for sure there was social mobility locked deep in that visage of hers. On our first meeting she'd thought me a communist, I thought her a plain idiot, but I suppose we grew fond of each other's company. Even if she put her own wellbeing way above that of others, the world had been too cruel to her too young, and I couldn't ask any different from her.

Above me in the bathroom is a plaque, upon the wall the words of the establishment: *Guantanamo Bay meets Victoria's Secrets with a touch of Hogwarts.* And I think of the hundreds of wrong-place, wrong-time Pakistanis and Afghans who have spent fifteen years in shackles and jumpsuits on a US military base in Cuba, so that these guys could get a risqué flourish for their private members' club. Already a part of me kicks back to the desert. This place, however different, is every bit as destitute as Modesto.

A man looks back at me from the wall as I wash a few dark smudges from his skin. It's a dark, glamorous room with a light spotted down on my face, a touch of grey on the suds that sink into the basin. My face has been flattened, two-dimensional: my nose falling to a continuous, black-grey plane that spans between my ears. I'm gaunt. I feel it. Cheekbones. The darkness sinks around the edges of my eyes, the bottom of my forehead. Bags cup my eyeballs like eggs on a spoon, the fatigue filling up each pouch. My hair curls into tight, greasy tufts and my eyes are distant, so that I suspect upstairs I'll be staring through people as if they are not even there.

Back in the bar, thick timbers are braced over where she sits, waiting in a pair of green wellington boots. I see her sitting there, dressed for countryside in downtown San Francisco and the thought hits me, suddenly so overwhelming. I wish she were Nathalie. We sit together, the two of us and three of her friends around a low table with drinks on it. Our armchairs have us laid right back, the bar sunk down a floor below us and waiters and waitresses calmly circling with drinks trays. There are a crowd of suits to one side, then others too rich to ever need to bother dressing up again. In my mind, I see the truck stop outside Vegas, that trucker shouting at me to beat it. If only he could see me now. He'd respect me this evening, be so proud of how far I've come.

A man walks in, dressed sportily with his windshell unzipped. Rosy cheeks, in his hand he carries a drone with a camera mounted to it, still 2013 and the contraption new enough that even in San Fran it turns heads. I hear as he laughs proudly to his friend: 'A few years and these things will have put every postman in the United States out of a job, and we'll be shitting ourselves that terrorists could use them as a cheap air force.'

The view of the two men is obscured as a pair of legs in tight leggings pass. I can't help but look: buttocks so perfect round, a walking statue, diva, body spilling proudly out through the synthetic fabric in each millimetre of indecent shape. I look shocked at such a candid dress, so exposed, naked but for that tight, black and shining skin. H watches the backside disappear too, leans over her arm to prolong the view, kisses her lips in approval. She smiles at my partial dismay.

'Didn't you hear? Bums are the new cleavage.'

Two rounds of drinks have already gone down at our table. The alcohol seeps in and everyone becomes themselves. H turns to me, a little of an aside, but it doesn't matter who hears, her whole life is public anyway.

'I know what you mean, about money. San Fran is so expensive now.' I nod compassion as she puts her manicured fingers to my chair arm, exclaims, 'A friend of mine had to start prostitution.'

My eyes boggle, a little.

'Well, foot prostitution.'

'Foot prostitution?'

H sips a drink through a straw, lips pursed, and she nods. 'She meets rich guys with foot fetishes, lets them play with her feet. She doesn't like it.' H's lips wrap tight at the straw. 'But she can charge six hundred bucks an hour.'

She returns her drink to the table, retrieves her phone instead, suddenly animating as she pulls me in and excitedly places her arm around the back of my neck. She looks right and meaningfully into me with those wide eyes, her lips shine in the lights, golden hair glows as she tosses the mane a little and says, 'Let's do a selfie.'

Her other arm reaches out, takes a photo with her phone. She checks it, frowns a moment, 'Oh no, my eyes are red.' Excitedly she turns in towards me, grinning wildly, shaking her head in abandon and placing a reassuring hand on my forearm, like this will all work out fine. 'It's OK, we'll sort it in post.'

To my other side is a man named Robin, sitting with Shem, a mild-mannered guy in a dinner jacket and tight waves of neat blond hair. Shem goes on talking to the other woman at the table, Chiara, with a red lace pattern across the breast of her svelte, black dress. Sharing her attention, H introduces Robin in a little more detail.

'And because it's so expensive, Robin is the only gay black man who can afford to live in San Francisco.'

'It keeps me in demand,' Robin smiles coyly, sucking at a straw and then interrupting my conversation with H, a hand delicately to my knee.

'So tell me, Emre, how long are you in San Fran?'

'Maybe two weeks.'

'Fantastic! There are lots of parties coming up, you'll have to come. Tell me, have you had any sexual encounters with a man recently?'

I laugh. 'Not recently.'

Shem looks round, 'That was pretty direct,' as Robin takes a big hand to my cheek, his razored head and polished teeth shining as he squeals, '*Whaaat*, but look at him, he's so handsome! Just look at that face!'

Chiara saves my blushes, proposes a toast: 'To how different we all are, but how we came together here!'

Shem bridles, holds his glass up, all of us waiting mid-air as he looks with curiosity. 'Really? I was just thinking how similar we all were.'

Chiara contorts, turns Houdini, 'Yes! Different – *but the same!*'

Our glasses chink, Shem and Chiara return to talking and my brain quivers at the effort of keeping up. Shem, Robin explains, is an asset manager: multimillionaire Dallas Texan, just passing through San Francisco for business. H talks love life: her millionaire dating options and which of them personally drove to her with the necessary medicine when she got the urinary tract infection, which one only offered to send it in a taxi. Chiara remembers an old conversation, turns to H and extends a hand set with jewellery.

'Tell me, did Facebook reinstate your profile after your open letter to Zuckerberg?'

'Yes.' H removes the straw from her lips and glass from in front of her head. 'Eventually, but it's ridiculous! So what if that artwork involved an image of an asshole – it was art!'

Chiara's face rises with profundity. 'I completely agree.'

My brain twists again, catching up speed.

'I mean, Facebook allow images of beheadings to be published.'

'What?!' Chiara is aghast. '*They do?* I thought they banned them?'

'They did. And then they updated their beheading policy, so now it's allowed again. And a beheading is so much worse than an asshole, and Facebook will allow images of assholes with a G-string pulled over it. And that's much more degrading of women.'

H looks at me, ever eager to include. 'What do you think, Emre? Beheadings or assholes?'

I'm sliding. I can feel trauma washing up on the shore between my ears. Slowly it comes back to break me down and once again keep me modest, humble forever. The drum in my temple is quickening. I can feel sweat in the shirt under my right armpit. I'm checking out, I'm back in the snow at Flagstaff. I can see eighteen-wheelers at dawn, can see Pala, one arm in his jacket to stop the chill air of his leaking door getting at him.

Shem starts talking again, interrupts Chiara and H as a new conversation comes in while everyone else picks up their glass. 'A friend of mine made his money in oil and gas, he's worth four billion now. *Billion!*

And I'm twenty-four again and cycling the Oregon coast.

'Billion?'

'*Billion.*' A pause for effect. 'And he keeps going to Hollywood, Tom Cruise calls him up looking for a budget.'

Everyone starts shaking their heads knowingly, H puts a concerned expression on her lips and holds her cheek as Shem goes on:

'First time he loved it. Invested sixty-five million bucks.' I see the Pittsburgh bus station at 2 a.m. 'But it's all just vanity. Hollywood's dead. I'm telling you it's the quickest way to lose money. Now my friend hates it any time Tom Cruise calls him, he just doesn't pick up.' I notice Robin and Shem closing in on each other with each drink, wonder if Shem's simply in the closet. 'Absolute vanity, but this guy, still he just can't stop because one day he wants to hook up with Cameron Diaz.' I see the pink sky, the full moon rising on Kentucky forest. I see his sleeping face with its fat, bloodied lip split in two. 'He's just desperate for Cameron Diaz. Like it has to be her, he's so obsessed.'

I see the Indianapolis prostitutes at the Punjabi café. I see one night in Paris, her dress as she cycled up Gambetta, the shadow of that rooster on her balcony. From across the table, Chiara's words come out plainly: 'Totally, I'm telling you, all any of them want is a blowjob from a B-list actress.' I see the mist opening on the Grand Canyon, I hear its echo at night, I see Chris defending unions in Kingman, Will pricking a finger on the tusk of his taxidermied javelina. I see it all, I hear everything. The sky, that enormous sky. Where am I? The steppe, the steppe. It's all collapsing and I can see the Midlands, the old quarry, sinking.

Down in the Battery a great noise is starting up, artillery rounds, the timbers are shaking overhead as I clatter up and out of my armchair, heads around me looking at all angles. A clock, its second hand fallen to rest across the face, ticks loud beside me, mocking as it makes the noise of passing seconds in time I cannot see. The San Andreas Fault judders, hits the walls – trembling – as if they were just a dusty old drum skin, shaking back to life, beaten hard by a stick. The brickwork jumps and I alone stumble to my feet. In an instant, there comes a snap, a snap in the San Andreas Fault, the Big One that was promised and I don't need telling twice. I scarper, I scram. I'm under a doorway, a wooden frame: knees up, head covered as the roof caves in. My feet carry me wild up the stairs and out into the street, as bricks turn dust and there comes the sound of entire orchestras sliding into the sea. Back in the street the night air hits me, the road torn asunder and water hydrants ruptured. A cab speeds by, misses my hail as I stumble at the night and then, from out of the corner of my eye, I see light coming from the subway while people run in panic and a beggar wheels a supermarket trolley off the kerb, the thing toppling to one side. I shield my eyes as the white glow grows above the subway, only this light looks somehow strangely out of place. Somehow it does not look artificial, does not have that cold chill of fluorescent tubes and electricity. Instead the frame of light nearing me resembles more the warmth that guards the flame of a candle. I see a sheer outline, somehow familiar. I see raven hair and a large, straight fringe across a forehead. I see dark eyes and her quick, neat steps coming towards me. Surely not. But it is. It's her.

Port of Oakland, CA – December 2

'How did you get here?'

'I flew.'

'You flew?'

She smiles a patient nodding as my head comes up to speed and she moves beside me. I feel the ball of her once-dislocated, gymnast shoulder pressed against me, my arms around her. I'm sorry, it's time I put down my *I*, my *me*. I'm not alone any more, we're together, we're 'We' . We, we, we. And I'm so damn happy.

We sit together at the Port of Oakland. The winter sun warm on our faces, the sound of reversing vehicles, forklifts, the unstevedored cranes moving over a freight liner that came from Siam with a charter from China Main Shipping. Five tug boats pull it into position and then slide off stage: seagulls trail the ship, smoke rising yellow from its chimney. The sunlight falls so bright, glows red through my blinking eyes. Everything floats up with the waves at the quay. A gentle ringing hums in my ears, turns to the bell of the railroad crossing and the horn of a freight train sounds, sounds as that old rumbling comes through. The boat carries the name of Valetta, the capital of Malta, which I know has light-touch regulations for vessels registered to it. For a moment I consider pitching an article about the low price of freight aboard such boats, because in the good years, when the world economy boomed, they built too many of the things, and now there's a surplus of capacity. And then I realise that I don't care.

From out the open door of a nearby bar spills the sound of laughter, Mexican music and pool balls, cracking in a break and barrelling across a table, maybe a couple of them dropping, with a thump, into pockets. The boat turns, it must be a quarter-mile long and two hundred metres tall. It turns, blocks the sun a moment as two more tugs come into view and pull it to the wharf. A helicopter goes overhead, chopping up the sky like a knife on a board, the sky pattering down in slices. Beside the port is a scrapyard where metal recycling is littered along the dock. A crane with a magnet the size of a bungalow goes about tidying the old metal into neat piles, scrap hanging from it. Car bumpers and door panels and tangles of steel cable sweep the deck, as if it were all only as gentle as the bristles of the brooms sold by that Brooklyn shopkeeper a month ago.

I feel sun on my face, her body rises and falls, rises and falls with her breathing. She closes her eyes, and I see the folds in the back of her lids, gentle veins like the skin of a grape. I look at the boat, think how I might one day get aboard, how I could go about getting all the way up to one of the ladders and one day be a stowaway again. The sun warms my face, and I think of the Gulf of Aden, where a young Somali man might be thinking the same thing for very different reasons. Beneath my arm, down in the nook beside my body, she turns as I realise I've drifted already back into myself, my schemes for escape. She puts a hand on my face, looks at me, stern-soft.

'You OK?'

I smile, 'Yeah, I'm OK.'

The sun sinks into my skin as I breathe, and for the first time, I think perhaps I really mean it. I feel something leaving me, and sure thing, no mistaking it. It's gone. Finally gone. It's out of my system.